Clan of the Wild Cats

Clan of the Wild Cats

A Celebration of Felines in Word and Image

Introduction by Elizabeth Marshall Thomas

Edited by Diana Landau

Original Illustrations by Paul Kratter

A WALKING STICK PRESS BOOK

THE NATURE COMPANY

The Nature Company owes its vision to the world's great naturalists: Charles Darwin, Henry David Thoreau, John Muir, David Brower, Rachel Carson, Jacques Cousteau, and many others. Through their inspiration, we are dedicated to providing products and experiences which encourage the joyous observation, understanding, and appreciation of nature. We do not advocate, and will not allow to be sold in our stores, any products that result from the killing of wild animals for trophy purposes. Seashells, butterflies, furs, and mounted animal specimens fall into this category. Our goal is to provide you with products, insights, and experiences which kindle your own sense of wonder and help you to feel good about the world in which you live.

Sources of text and illustrations and acknowledgment of permission to reprint copyrighted material appear on pages 190–191.

Original illustrations and map by Paul Kratter (represented by Barb Hauser).

Cover photo: Leopard pair *(Panthera pardus)* lying together, Masai Mara, Kenya. By Anup Shah/Anthony Bannister Photo Library.

Frontispiece photo: Bengal tiger *(Panthera tigris),* running through water. By Tim Davis/Tony Stone Images.

Prepared for publication at Walking Stick Press, San Francisco
Linda Herman, Design and Production Director
Diana Landau, Editorial Director
Miriam Lewis, typography
Cynthia Bix, text contributor
Nancy Barnes, art management
Rebecca Freedman, editorial assistance
Verne Lindner, calligraphy
Beatriz Coll, special photography

The Nature Company staff:
Ed Strobin
Priscilla Wrubel
Georganne Papac
Tracy Fortini
Steve Manning

Printed in Italy by A. Mondadori, Verona

To order this book or to learn the location of The Nature Company store nearest you, call 1-800-227-1114, or write The Nature Company, P.O. Box 188, Florence, Kentucky 41022.

First printing

CONTENTS

A pride of lionesses (Panthera leo) rests on a granite outcropping under a candelabra tree in Tanzania's Serengeti National Park. By Kennan Ward.

Wild Cats, Far and Near

by Diana Landau

My cat Jemima was a San Francisco park stray who came to live with my dog and me. Despite her undersized frame and large food bowl, she remained a mighty hunter. Gophers were her speciality; she spent (apparently) motionless hours crouched over their tunnels and in the season when they had young usually brought home several a week. She also killed mice, rats, and (though belled) the occasional mockingbird or mourning dove. I chastised her for the birds, but a significant part of me rejoiced in her skill and independence.

This, of course, is part of what people who like cats really like about them—that their domestication goes only so far. That in their eyes, relaxed and intense by turns, and in their graceful bodies gliding through a stalk, we glimpse the wild predators that are their close cousins. That, as Alan Moorehead says, they remind us of lions.

While many cat owners privately admire their pets' tooth-and-claw tendencies, at the same time we prefer that they are small and cuddly and unthreatening to us. Someone once said, on meeting a tame mountain lion face to face, that it's a good thing our pet cats aren't that big—and many a cat owner has mused on how our relationship with them might change if they were, indeed, lion-sized.

Behind such innocent musings lies the fact that if our cats were suddenly to increase twentyfold in size, they would look very much like odd-colored, longer-haired pumas (or closer still, leopards). Cats, whatever their size and wherever they live, are basically the same kind of animal. That's part of why we find domestic cats so fascinating. Compared to dogs or cattle, cats have lived with humans for a relatively short time and may still be evolving from wildness to tameness. That tame cats are still partly wild is central to their magic. Especially in today's

world, where most of us have so little opportunity to come into contact with wild nature, we appreciate our cats for the living link they form between ourselves and the world from which we sprang, but have become distanced.

But what about cats that aren't small and cuddly? What's to be the fate of the great cats, who require lots of land to hunt on and quantities of large game to kill? With one notable exception—the mountain lion of North America—big cats live today in mostly poor countries where expanding human populations are desperate to use any available land. This puts pressure on wild animals, especially those with big ranges; even protected reserves are not always safe for them.

Wherever wild cats and humans come into close contact, both suffer, but the cats more so. Big cats will inevitably kill or injure some people, or the domestic stock of those people—because they can, and because human presence impacts their natural food supplies. In response, humans kill a lot of wild cats, or simply occupy and develop their habitats to such an extent that the cats cannot hunt, breed, and raise young. In such a scenario, cat populations, races, sometimes entire species disappear—a pattern repeated throughout history. In more hopeful scenarios (of recent times), we may carve out preserves where the cats' way of life can go on unmolested, but often these are too small to sustain a well-mixed gene pool—cheetahs are seriously threatened in this way—or inadequately policed to avert destructive poaching. Smaller wild cats, though many species are considered rare, may have a better chance in the long run, as they need slightly smaller chunks of habitat to maintain a species in a healthy state.

The future of wild cats in the wild is not an issue that can be settled in a book. The solutions are

Exalted and denigrated, admired and despised, no animals have so aroused the emotions of man as have the large predators. The lion is the King of Beasts, once venerated as an animal god; the tiger is extolled for its beauty and strength.... Yet at the same time these predators have been and still are persecuted to such an extent that they have vanished from much of their former range.

GEORGE SCHALLER
Serengeti: A Kingdom of Predators

Tiger, lithograph by Edvard Munch, 1908–1909. Munch Museum, Oslo.

> The cat, being at best but half tame, forms a shadowing, or rather stands in a medium between domestic and wild animals.
>
> GEORGES LOUIS LECLERE BUFFON (1791)

> Everything about a lion in its wild state is immediately recognizable from your own domestic cat; it has the same soft delayed tread across the grass, the same quick turning of its head to lick the fur on its shoulder, the twitching tail, the same terrible indifference.
>
> ALAN MOOREHEAD
> *No Room in the Ark*

Striped tabby, *drawing by Théophile Steinlen (1859–1923).*

complex, global, and long-term; they lie in the hands of field scientists, zoological societies, local and national governments, those who enforce international trade laws, and wildlife conservation organizations. What this book can perhaps do is demonstrate the importance of keeping wild cats in our world by showing how important they have been to us—emotionally and psychically as well as ecologically—in the past. Why is it important to have wild cats as well as tame ones? Because without the wild ones, much of what we cherish in our domestic cats loses its reference, its meaning, its power. Because wild cats do not exist as isolated species but as part of a web of life that, if torn in too many places, may no longer sustain us.

Since the dawn of human memory, wild cats have evoked strong responses in us, and inevitably those responses have found their way into our art, our mythologies, our literature, our spiritual traditions, and our scientific investigations. This book attempts to show how people over the ages have responded to these animals, from all of these angles. Most of us are unlikely to meet wild cats in person, except in zoos, so the words and images collected here can, we hope, help us know them a little better. And while they reveal much about the cats themselves, they are sometimes even more revealing of the human spirit, and what it needs and values.

Photographs of cats are here juxtaposed with artwork, from the powerful pictographs of extinct cave lions at La Marche to thoughtful contemporary visions of cats. On the word side, we have sought explanations of cat biology and behavior from scientists, and well as literary selections that reflect humankind's changing views of felines.

For all their similarity, cats do come in upwards of thirty-six flavors (species), so we have provided in Part I an identification section that briefly profiles and illustrates each species. Useful reference information may also be found in a list (in Part I) of the species, their familial relationships, and their status as endangered or threatened creatures; and in the Appendix.

The world's outstanding photographers of wildlife have created dramatic, illluminating images of wild cats, and many are reproduced here. We are infinitely grateful to these gifted, persistent artists, who travel vast distances and endure considerable hardships to return with pictures of cats in their native habitats. Readers should be aware, however, that photographing big cats close-up, or capturing certain behaviors, can be risky to nearly impossible in the wild; moreover, many small wild cats are so rare and elusive that they are hardly ever seen—never mind photographed. For these reasons many of the photographs here were taken in captive situations—in zoos, in game parks or private reserves in the United States, or using animals that are privately kept chiefly for filming and photography purposes. Such enterprises are regulated with increasing stringency—which is as it should be—and wildlife photographers typically exercise strong personal ethics about the circumstances in which they work with animals. In identifying the images published here, we have provided locations where supplied by the photographers; most longer-range pictures including natural habitats are clearly shot in the wild. For close-up shots, where not otherwise identified, the reader can assume that many were taken in some kind of controlled situation.

Thanks are due to all who contributed to the creation of this book, and are found in the Acknowledgments. Beyond this, we'd like to express our gratitude to those who have written so eloquently and insightfully about cats, wild and otherwise, and the artists and photographers who have so beautifully depicted them. And further, to the animals themselves: the wild ones whose presence, though unseen, is inspiration and reassurance that the world retains its wholeness. And to the cats at home, who bring something of the wild inside by having chosen to share with us their destinies.

The Cat–Human Equation

by Elizabeth Marshall Thomas

It seems almost compulsory to start a book on the cat family with the observation that cats have always fascinated people. Indeed, I happen to believe that the frequency with which those words appear at the beginning of books on cats only emphasizes the truth of the statement. I further believe that the key word is "always." After all, the appearance of our species on the African savannah closely followed that of lions, who were there waiting for us. Surely we did not escape their notice, and they certainly didn't escape ours.

Lions must have seemed even larger to us then than they do now, as we were much smaller, and in the likely event that we occasionally became their prey, it is easy to understand our ensuing fascination. We would have had with the lions the same relationship that, say, modern zebras do. And surely, like the zebras, we expressed our deep interest in them by hanging about in groups and eyeing them from a distance whenever we got the chance. It seems reasonable to envision groups of our ancestors sitting high on rock kopjies or up in trees, all intently focused on a large cat who happens to be eating or strolling by or just lying quietly. We do the same thing today in Africa, where busloads of tourists now watch lions with the same fascination that the zebras display, if with less practical need. Meanwhile the former hunter–gatherers of

these savannahs treat lions in a way that they treat no other animal, but rather with the same awe and reverence that they reserve for the spirits of their own dangerous dead.

The big cats continued to hold our interest. Ever since our kind could pick up a paintbrush or a carving tool, the likenesses of cats have been rendered. A most dramatic example is a pair of shadowy figures in a European cave, figures which are definitely cave lions and which stare spookily at visitors to the dark sanctuaries. A painting from ancient China shows a huge and frightening although fluffy creature with stripes around its knees. When the painting was discovered by art historians, this was deemed to be a tiger, since tigers have stripes and, when the painting was made, inhabited China, but it may just as well have been a cave lion. The fascination with big cats—even if only with imagined big cats—showed itself beautifully in twelfth-century Japan, where someone who had never seen a lion or a leopard decorated an armored breastplate with elegant large cats that had round manes and rosette spots—surely a conglomerate cat drawn from a traveler's descriptions of leopards and lions. The breastplate is displayed in the National Museum in Tokyo.

Further evidence of our fascination, if more is needed, appears on all continents where big cats share or once

Above: African belt mask in the form of a leopard head, c. 16th century, Benin kingdom. Seattle Art Museum. Left: Aztec stone figure of a jaguar, c. 1440–1521 A.D. Brooklyn Museum. Wild cats, especially the great ones, have served as emblems of power, authority, and hunting expertise in every culture where humans have lived near them.

shared the land with human beings, from the heraldic lions of Europe to the jaguar images of Central and South America to the tiger images of Asia. To call the preoccupation with big cats "fascination" would be an understatement in West and Central Africa. Here secret leopard societies flourished, wherein certain people pretended to became leopards and anonymously did the work of leopards, hiding in the reeds by waterholes as leopards do and killing, in leopard style, the first person to

Japanese silk hanging scroll of a tiger licking its paw, by Itō Jakuchū (1716-1800). Tigers never lived on the Japanese islands, but many were painted there from traveler's descriptions and sketches. Los Angeles County Museum of Art

come along. At times of social discord the leopard societies would become active, and the deeds of the leopard men would so upset the local population that the discord would usually vanish in the face of the worse disaster. The leopard men were cruel and murderous, to be sure, but socially unifying nevertheless. Reminiscent of the lion skins worn by Hercules and other Greek heroes, leopard skins and other leopard parts such as teeth and claws are to this day the marks of rank and royalty throughout Africa, not merely because these items are beautiful, but because they symbolize their former owners—big, powerful, dangerous cats.

And then there are the small cats. What the big cats can do to us—namely, eat us—the small cats can do to our age-old competitors, the rodents that destroy our food supplies. Our species learned this more or less by accident about 9,000 years ago, as we began to domesticate some of the grasses (wheat, sorghum and the like) and built granaries to store the harvested seeds. In doing so, we managed to scoop up an entire little ecosystem: we got the grass seeds, we got the mice and rats who ate the grass seeds, and we got the little tabby wildcats, *Felis sylvestris lybica,* who ate the mice and rats.

Our fascination with our small feline associates seems no less than our fascination with their large cousins. As we feel about the big cats in a way that we feel about no other wild animal, so we feel about our domestic cats in a way we feel about no other domestic animal. In ancient Egypt, the obsession with domestic cats probably reached an all-time pinnacle, with a cat goddess, Bastet, and her city, Bubastis, and her minions, the hundreds of thousands of mummified cats that almost seem to personify the Middle Kingdom. That the near deification of cats might have had something to do with their role as protectors of the harvest, and thus of human life, seems plausible when considering the dependence of the ancient Egyptians on harvested grains. Furthermore, among the mummified cats are also a few other mummified animals, mainly mongooses, also known for preying on mice and rats.

A dark fascination with cats occurred in Europe and Great Britain in the Middle Ages, when they were believed to be the familiars of witches, and provoked extraordinary cruelties to cats in the name of exorcising Satan. In keeping with the superstitions of the times, cats were built into the walls of houses in the belief that rats would stay away—a dark version of the honor paid by the Egyptians for the cats' role as pest destroyers. Such crimes against cats were terrible, yes, but were certainly proof of the cat's importance. In Asia, meanwhile, the Asiatic form of the tabby wildcat, *Felis sylvestris ornata,* became the Siamese, Burmese, and other related breeds. That these cats are thought to have originated as the pets of royalty further suggest our species' high opinion of them.

Since then, images of cats have been drawn, painted, sculpted and embroidered throughout Asia. And stories have been told about them. There's the famous Chinese folktale of the boy who drew cats (in a temple one night the cats he had painted on a screen came to life and killed a giant rat that threatened him while he slept; in the morning the rat was found dead and the cats, by then back on the screen, had blood on their mouths). And there's the famous Japanese three-volume autobiography of a cat, first published in 1905 and still read widely, still much loved, still known to virtually every Japanese person—the very popular, much beloved *I Am A Cat* by Soseki Natsume.

Cats are death, or they surely were to our species for much of our time on earth. To some people in the wilds of Africa, Asia, and South America, they still are, and the rest of us haven't forgotten. Cats are also life, symbolic of fertility. They bring forth litter after litter of beguiling kittens, whose large eyes halfway down the face, small jaws, and hair standing straight up so closely resemble the features of our own infants that we cannot help but adore them. These beguiling creatures then assist us by guarding our most important food without asking for a share of it. On the contrary, their food is the very rodents that endanger our food. And we're grateful. Anyone who has lived on a farm with stored grain will have seen what a few rats can do in a single night—on our temporarily catless farm one winter in New Hampshire, we lost 15 percent of our total grain supply in just a few nights, after rats gnawed into the wooden bin from behind. They ate a lot of the grain, spilled more, and fouled with urine, hair, and feces most of what was left. If we had not been able to buy more grain to make up the deficiency, we would not have been able to feed our livestock through the winter. The cats who later took care of that problem for us were welcome indeed—lifegiving, actually.

So our fascination with cats is easy to understand. It's the human side of the equation. Not so easy to grasp is who these cats are, and why they do what they do—the things that so fascinate us. But that is what this book is about—the cat side of the equation.

Mountain lion (or puma) mother and cub (Felis concolor). The bond between mother and young is the strongest of all social ties in the cat world. By Tom Tietz/Tony Stone Images.

Depending on whose system you use, there are currently some thirty-six species of cats in existence, from the diminutive kodkod, a rare resident of the Argentine woodlands, to the great Siberian tiger. The feline family can claim some of the world's most familiar creatures—lions and tigers, surely—as well as a whole host of small wild cats that are among the least-known mammals on earth. Yet despite dramatic differences in size and habitat preferences, a cat is a cat, immediately recognizable as a cat by any observer. All cats share a similar body type and a particular arrangement of teeth. Unlike other carnivores, all are meat-eaters almost exclusively. And all, in varying degrees, practice a hunting style based

A World of Wild Cats

on stalking and ambushing prey. As Roger Caras says, the world's cats are "amazingly and pleasingly consistent." ❧ Representatives of the cat clan (the Felidae, or true cats) have inhabited landscapes around the world for nearly 25 million years. In the last 8 million years or so, felines have become the largest and most dominant carnivore in many mammal communities: tigers, lions, and cougars, for example. Wild cats live in the deserts of central Asia and southern Africa, in the jungles of Malaysia and the Amazon, on the East African savannahs and the frozen heights of the Himalaya. Clearly, the basic cat recipe is among the most adaptable and successful the animal world has ever produced. ❧ How did cats evolve into their present form, and what are the physical gifts that make them such successful animals? What are those myriad cat species, where do they live, and why are many of them so little known to us? How are wild felids related to our domestic cats, whom they so closely resemble? And why do cats so powerfully stir human emotions toward the extremes of adoration and terror? Though some cats have been much studied, many mysteries remain, so our answers thus far are incomplete. ➤

*E*verywhere the plain is dotted with animals. In every direction are herds of round-bellied zebras, bovine wildebeests, and tail-waggling Thompson's gazelles, as well as scattered groups of shiny-coated topi and elegant Grant's gazelles. Toward the river there is a concentration of sleek, reddish-brown impalas, one buck lording it over a harem of nearly a hundred does.

From the top of the nearest granite kopje we might overlook an even wider tract of country, with more game. But it would not be advisable to scramble up over the boulders, for the towering fortress has already been commandeered as a look-out post: on one of its highest battlements stands a big cat, a lioness, her amber eyes sweeping the plain below.

After a few moments she turns round and begins to descend, jumping lightly from one rocky step to the next. She is heading toward a broad bench of granite, jutting out like a platform about halfway down. As we follow her course, we suddenly realize that she is not the sole occupant of the fortress. Five lionesses lie asleep on the stony bench, and a number of cubs of various ages can be seen playing among the surrounding bushes. Two dark-maned males and two more lionesses are stretched out in the shade of an umbrella tree at the foot of the hill.

The sleepers on the platform wake up as the lioness steps into their midst. There is some rubbing of heads—the leonine version of a friendly greeting—but she does not tarry for more than a couple of minutes. Continuing on her way, she is almost immediately followed by two of the five lionesses whose rest she has disturbed....Leaving the cubs behind among the bushes and boulders, all the adults of the pride are [soon] moving away from the kopje.

The three lionesses which were the first to set out are well ahead, their eyes fixed on a herd of grazing zebras. Having at first advanced fairly briskly, they now move more and more slowly, adopting a lowslung, almost crouching, gait....The main party meanwhile has spread out, its members advancing like skirmishers. They intend to circumvent the herd from the right, but the zebras are by now fully aware of what is happening....

As the zebras move off to the left, a black-tufted tail suddenly jerks up out of the yellow grass, and a lioness from the separate party of three races forward. She misses by a few feet—but at that moment a second tawny shape flashes past and, after a short rush, catches up with a zebra. Over it goes, and for a few seconds its legs can be seen flailing above the grass. The other lions approach at an eager trot. A kill has been made, and soon the vultures will be circling overhead.

All this time, the tawny hunters' strategy has been watched by a spotted cat standing on top of an ant-hill about half a mile away—a

Tigers, panthers, jaguars, lions, etc. Whence comes the emotion that the sight of all that produces in me? From the fact that I am lifted out of the every-day thoughts that make up all my world, out of my street which is my universe. How necessary it is to rouse oneself from time to time, to stick one's head outdoors, to read something of the creation which has nothing in common with our cities or the works of men! Surely, such a view leaves us better and more at peace....

EUGÈNE DELACROIX, 1847

Above: Head of a lion, watercolor by Eugène Delacroix, c. 1843. Delacroix delighted in painting the great cats, and it was said that his own features had a feline look. Page 12: Jaguar (Panthera onca) portrait in profile, Brazil. By Erwin & Peggy Bauer. Pages 14–15: Leopard (Panthera pardus) stalking a herd of impala, Masai Mara Game Reserve, Kenya. By Mark Newman/Bruce Coleman, Inc.

female cheetah, whose half-grown cubs are playing nearby. Intent on keeping as great a distance as possible between herself and the lions, she calls the cubs with a birdlike chirp and moves off in the direction of the river. Several herds of Thompson's gazelles take flight at the cheetah family's approach, while a couple of topi, snorting and stamping, watch the passage of the cats and even follow behind for a short stretch until they see the cheetahs disappear among the reeds and bushes fringing the river.

Coming out into the open after having crossed the river-bed, the mother cheetah discovers a dozen Thompson's gazelles. She stops in mid-stride, watching them....The cheetah cubs settle down in a patch of scrub, while the mother begins to stalk forward, stiff-legged, head straight out in front. She advances slowly, step by step, and gradually the 120 yards that separated her from the gazelles shrinks to 100, then 80. Suddenly she literally shoots forward, racing at a tremendous speed, straight as an arrow. The "tommies" have seen her now—they run—but she is already among them and bowls one over. After ten minutes or so she comes back to her cubs, dragging the dead tommie along with her.

About a mile from where the cheetah crossed the river-bed, on one of the yellow-barked acacias, there lies another spotted cat, asleep, chin resting on paw, the hind legs dangling on both sides of the branch, and the long tail hanging below. It is a leopard, a big, beautifully marked male. The afternoon is now well advanced, and the rays of the setting sun have taken on a golden tinge....

The leopard opens his eyes, yawns, gets to his feet, and casts a searching look around. He stretches with luxurious elaboration and, having gone through this relaxing exercise, settles down again, but with his legs drawn up. The paws and shoulders get a few licks, there are some more yawns, and then, getting up for good, he proceeds to walk purposefully along the sloping branch, golden in the evening light. He pauses briefly at the main fork before running down part of the trunk and jumping off elegantly to the ground. Without a moment's hesitation he sets out through the grass, walking more or less parallel to the river-bed.

After covering about a quarter of a mile, the leopard stops dead and raises his head, his alert eyes fixed on a spot close to the riverbank. A solitary reed-buck has come out of cover for its evening grazing. Watching it for some time, motionless except for the nervously twitching tip of the tail, the leopard now begins to stalk through the high grass, keeping his body well down and moving slowly and with utmost deliberation....Now he is in a patch of scrub next to the buck, crouching flat, invisible even to the hammerkop sitting in a near-by tree. For most of the time, the reed-buck has been half-facing in the direction from which the leopard has made his approach, but now it turns its head away to look at a female that has just stepped out of a reed-bed. It is the last thing he will ever do....

Even as these lines are being written, similar incidents involving wild cats are taking place the world over—in northern forests and Indian jungles, on Scottish hillsides, in Arabian deserts, and on the densely wooded banks of the Amazon. The few glimpses of life and death on the African veld might as easily have been other visions: a lynx pouncing on a snowshoe rabbit, a tiger stalking a chital deer, a wildcat grabbing a vole, a sand cat chasing after a jerboa, or a jaguar bounding on the back of a tapir....The members of the cat family, or Felidae, are the most highly developed of all the present-day terrestrial carnivores.

CHARLES A. W. GUGGISBERG
Wild Cats of the World

Whence Came the Cats

Creatures we would recognize as cats have lived on earth since the Miocene period, about 25 million years ago, but these lynxlike proto-cats evolved from mammalian ancestors that had been around much longer. After the demise of the dinosaurs, the small, inocuous mammals that had survived in their shadow began to proliferate and diversify, taking advantage of the sudden vacuum in the carnivore niche and the huge supply of large, slow-moving plant-eaters (mastodons and the like) that had arisen.

The common ancestor of all modern carnivores, known as Miacis in one form, was a tree-climbing insect-eater resembling a genet. Around 40 million years ago, the miacids began to diverge into two distinct branches, sometimes referred to as the Fox tribe (ancestors of today's dogs, bears, raccoons, mustelids, and seals) and the Mongoose tribe, which eventually produced the mongooses, genets, civets, hyenas—and cats. Catlike "paleofelids" began to appear as early as 37 million years ago, followed by the so-called "true cats."

Fossil records in North America and Europe have yielded dramatic evidence of fearsome saber-toothed cats—which have since become glamorous attractions at every natural history museum lucky enough to have one. Various sabertooths appeared at different times, starting with the paleofelids, and remained on the scene as recently as 10,000 years ago. Smilodon—the one most famous through re-creations—was among the later neofelids, or true cats.

What defines a "true cat"—as distinct from a civet cat, genet, or one of the ancestral felids—is a matter of shared physical and genetic traits. Some are fairly obvious: the cats' shortened face with large, front-facing eyes; their particular number and arrangement of teeth; their retractable claws and weight-on-the-toes stance. But not all these features are unique to cats; scientists now base their definition of "catness" mostly on the specialized structure of the skull and inner ear.

More than other carnivores, cats are meat-eaters almost exclusively, and this has shaped their destiny. While cats have fewer options than, say, bears, which can survive on plants and honey, this dedication to meat-eating has kept the cat genetic formula fairly consistent over the ages. As Elizabeth Thomas notes, "…while the glaciers came and went, while the vegetarians struggled against all odds trying to digest new plants and adapt themselves to overwhelming global changes, the cats simply kept on hunting, waiting to pounce on whoever managed to survive into the next epoch." ❧

In all modern and many fossil mammalian communities, the largest species of pure carnivore is a felid. For example, the lion dominates in Africa, the tiger in Asia, and the jaguar in South America. This pattern of large cat dominance has been true in both the Old and New Worlds for about the last eight million years. Prior to that time, a variety of predators assumed the large body size roles.…

BLAIRE VAN VALKENBURG
Great Cats: Majestic Creatures of the Wild

Fossilized skeleton of the saber-toothed cat Hoplophoneus, from the early Oligocene Period (around 37–24 million years ago), found in the White River Badlands of South Dakota. The saber-toothed cats survived until only about 10,000 years ago. By T. A. Wiewandt/DRK Photo.

CATS AND OTHER CARNIVORES

The diagram at right shows the chronological development and branching off of the modern families in the mammalian order Carnivora. From a group of primitive carnivores called the miacids (see below), two large groups evolved: the catlike mammals (aeluroids) and the bearlike mammals (arctoids). The true cats (Felidae) are most closely related to the hyena, mongoose, and genet tribes. The designations "65–57 million years," etcetera, indicate that the geological period occurred 65 to 57 million years ago.

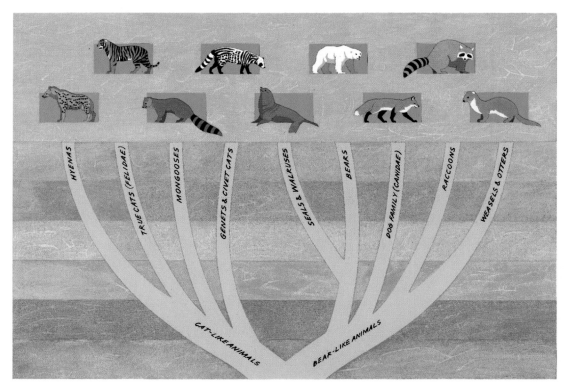

PRESENT

PLEISTOCENE
(2 million–10,000)

PLIOCENE
(5–2 million)

MIOCENE
(24–5 million)

OLIGOCENE
(37–24 million)

EOCENE
(57–37 million)

PALEOCENE
(65–57 million)

The upper illustration is a reconstruction of Miacis, one of a group of ancestral insect-eaters from which sprang all of today's carnivores. It bears a strong resemblance to the modern-day genet, Viverra genetta (above), a close relative of the true cats. Miacis illustration by John McLoughlin; genet illustration, Corbis–Bettmann.

THE CONSISTENCY OF CATS

The cat family was surely here long before we were (they used to eat us when we first began emerging from ancient ancestral loins) and we have been able to do little more than clean up a few of the rough spots around the edges to achieve the little home-body with which we are concerned here. Much of what we found is a lot of what we've got. Wildness so genetically close to hand is surely one of the most fascinating things about our pets....

Our companion cat almost certainly is descended from the North African wildcat, not to be confused with our own domestic cats that due to misadventure or our mismanagement return to the wild. Although we often hear them called wild, they are more properly called feral. The four-thousand-year-old domestication process for the cat is nothing when compared with the history of goats and dogs. Our modern domestic cats belong to a different species from their direct ancestors, but strange-

ly enough they can still breed with the truly wild ones and on occasion, at least, do....

And what are the cat's wild kin really like? People who first see wildcats (best done, by the way, in the wild), besides being excited almost beyond containment, comment on how catlike they are. That is an innocent case of careless semantics, of course. They should be catlike since they are in every sense cats, family Felidae in the Order Carnivora. But are these other cats, big as some of them are, really like our home-grown cat? A Siberian or Amur tiger can, after all, weigh between seven hundred and fifty and eight hundred pounds—outweighing a Siamese cat as much as two hundred to one.

Yes, cats are very much alike in more ways than we can possibly count. The cats of the world are amazingly and pleasingly consistent.

ROGER A. CARAS
A Cat Is Watching

Animals that can be recognized as true cats are known from the early Pliocene, and in the course of this period, the last of the Tertiary subdivisions, many of the genera which we know today must have come into existence. As far as the fossil record goes, big cats resembling lions and tigers turned up quite suddenly during the Villafranchian, as the early Pleistocene is called. There was, for instance, the Tuscany lion, which roamed through northern Italian and central European forests. It was the size of a small lion, but differed from that species in its dentition and may have been more closely related to the leopard. Two possible ancestral forms of the latter—*Panthera pardoides* and *Panthera palaeosinensis*—have come from the Villafranchian of Europe and China respectively. India at that time also had a large cat, *Panthera cristatus,* but it was fairly aberrant and not related to any modern species. Of the lynxes, a species known as *Lynx brevirostris* has been recorded from late Pliocene deposits, while two species have become known from the Villafranchian of Europe (Issoire lynx) and China (Shansi lynx). The cheetah's origin must go back a long way into the Pliocene, for it makes its appearance in the Villafranchian as the very highly specialized giant cheetah *(Acinonyx pardinensis),* which, apart from being as big as a lion, differed from the present-day species only in some minor features of skull and dentition.

During the Middle and Late Pleistocene, the Northern Hemisphere went through a series of glaciations....For most of what is popularly referred to as the "Ice Age," Europe was inhabited by cave lions and leopards, China by giant tigers, and North America by giant jaguars. The Issoire lynx held out until the Mid-Pleistocene, while the earliest records of the northern lynx have come from the last or Eemian Interglacial.

There were, of course, a lot more chances for the robust skeletal remains of big cats to be preserved than for the delicate bones of the small ones.

CHARLES A. W. GUGGISBERG
Wild Cats of the World

Painting of Smilodon fatalis, *the great saber-toothed cat of the Pleistocene, by C. R. Knight, 1906.*

SABER-TOOTH!

Once I was privileged to examine the skull of a saber-tooth. A relic of the La Brea tarpits near Los Angeles, the skull had belonged to a male *Smilodon fatalis,* one of the largest cats the world has ever seen. The skull's mass alone was impressive, but the famous eyeteeth were awesome—strong, curved, pointed, and almost six inches long. The eyes had been large and the chin small, which must have made even this great face somewhat catlike. Beyond that, though, the bones of his lower jaw were fairly narrow, and the bony processes at the corners of his jaw were tiny, just two points, really, so that nothing stopped the jaw from dropping straight down like a trap door.

Other cats have lesser gapes, the result of heavier jaws with wider hinges to anchor the muscles that clench the teeth. But the smilodon didn't need to clench his teeth. What he needed from his lower jaw was that it drop out of the way to let him deploy his sabers. A number of reconstructions suggest how he might have done this, and although these reconstructions differ on how he mounted his attack, all agree that he drove his eyeteeth home not by pushing up against them with his lower jaw as other cats do but by plunging them down into his victim, driving them home with the vicelike force of his neck and shoulders and indeed with the whole curl of his body. Considering the size and strength of that body and the length of those teeth, to be bitten by a smilodon must have been a terrible experience. If he had attacked a person, and he could have, since in those days our species shared the New World with his species, his teeth could have speared right through his victim like toothpicks through a little pork sausage. Rightly was he named *fatalis!*

ELIZABETH MARSHALL THOMAS
The Tribe of Tiger

Where Cats Live

Cats are extremely adaptable and can live virtually anywhere there is enough prey for them to hunt and enough cover in which to stalk it. By the middle of the Pleistocene Era, around a million years ago, true cats had colonized every continent except Australia. Even in that biologically isolated land, a catlike creature known as *Thylacoleo carnifex* (now extinct) evolved on its own to prey on marsupials.

Fossil records of ancestral cats, though scanty, tell a fascinating tale of how various species developed and migrated, often ending up on the opposite side of the world from where they originated. A form of cheetah first appeared in North America, for example, and the earliest jaguars in Africa. Like other cats, they made vast continental migrations across the Bering Land Bridge. Pumas, among the most widely distributed wild cats with a range from northern Canada nearly to Patagonia, got to the Americas from Asia that way.

Along with wide geographical distribution, cats can occupy a wide variety of habitats, from desert to jungle to high mountains—though the greatest number of species occurs in the tropics. Many of their physical differences evolved in response to habitat: in general, cold climates favor bigger, more heavily furred cats, and warm places smaller sizes and shorter coats. Spots and stripes provide concealment in the dappled light of forests, while solid, tawny fur blends in with grasslands. Several cat species can occupy the same patch of geography, avoiding competition by specializing in different kinds of prey, and hunting at different times or in different habitats.

Most felines once inhabited much larger ranges than they do now. Lions, for example, originated in Africa but moved north into Eurasia some 250,000 years ago, and even in historical times were found around the Mediterranean and the Near East. But the ranges of most species have contracted due to habitat destruction and other human pressures—the sole exception being the domestic cat, which has followed people into every part of the globe. 🐾

Cats are almost preternaturally adaptable. A clouded leopard, an arboreal native of tropical rain forests, escaped from a zoo into the English countryside in 1975 and was expected to die or be recaptured within days because of the drastically foreign habitat. Nine months later, the sleek, healthy cat was shot by a farmer who was missing rabbits and lambs.

CHRIS BOLGIANO
The Mountain Lion

The elegant clouded leopard (Neofelis nebulosa) is native to Malaysia and elsewhere in the forests of Southeast Asia. Yet like most cats, it can survive in quite different habitats, as long as there is prey to hunt and cover to hide in. But wild cats need large, intact areas of natural habitat to sustain viable populations of their species. By Alan & Sandy Carey.

Once, it is said, there was a famine on the island of Java. The Raja of All Tigers called his tiger ministers to meet with him to discuss the scarcity of food. They came and sat before him, and he spoke:

"Day by day our food is harder to find. We are growing thin. What can we do about this situation?"

The ministers of the tiger Raja talked anxiously, and at last they said: "There is no other way—we must conquer Borneo and make the inhabitants pay tribute to us. Otherwise we shall starve."

The Raja of All the Tigers of Java said:

"Very well. We shall send the inhabitants of Borneo an ultimatum."

He selected three of his tiger ministers to act as messengers, and he told them: "Go to the Raja of Borneo. Tell him the Raja of All the Tigers of Java commands him to send us quantities of food and gold. If he refuses, I shall send an army against him to conquer Borneo. And to convince him, and so that he may know my strength, show him this!"

The Raja of All the Tigers of Java plucked out the longest and heaviest of his whiskers and gave it to his ministers....[They crossed the Java Sea and arrived in Borneo, where they met Kantchil the mouse deer.]

They stopped and looked down on him, for they were large and ferocious and he was very small.

"Insignificant One," they said, "where is your king? We come from the Raja of All the Tigers of Java to demand surrender!"

"Ah!" said Kantchil. "Our king is hunting in the forest."

"Then say these words to your king," the tigers said. "Tell him that our Raja demands gold and food. If your king does not give it, we will come with a great army of tigers and wage war upon the inhabitants of the forests of Borneo. And when you have said all this, give him this whisker which our great ruler himself plucked out of his face, so that all men might see how large and strong he is!"

Kantchil took the royal whisker respectfully. Then he turned and went into the shadows of the forest.

"Oh, what will become of Borneo now?" he said. "When tigers say food they mean meat. I am meat. If they send an army they will destroy us, and they will remain in Borneo forever."

After Kantchil had thought for a while he went to Landak, the porcupine. "Friend," he said, "so that the tigers of Java don't come and destroy Borneo, give me one of your quills." The porcupine took a quill from his back and gave it to Kantchil. Kantchil returned to the clearing where the tigers waited.

"Oh, Dignified Ones, I have found our great king," he said. "He was resting from the hunt, and his servants were sharpening his claws by grinding them between two mountains. I sat before him and delivered the message with which you entrusted me....At last he spoke this way:

" 'Tell the arrogant nothings from Java that I am extremely annoyed with them....Tell the insolent creature who is Raja of All the Tigers of Java we do not pay tribute, we only exact it. Tell him we choose war!' "

The tiger ministers listened with amazement as Kantchil spoke. But he wasn't yet through. He said: "Our king in his anger plucked a whisker from his face and instructed me to give it to you."

The tiger ministers took the quill which the porcupine had given Kantchil. They looked at it in fear. For it was twenty times the thickness of their Raja's whisker. They returned quickly across the water to Java, and then came before the Raja of All the Tigers.

"We have delivered the ultimatum, Great One," they said. "The miserable king of Borneo sends this answer."

And they gave him the long thick quill from the porcupine's back. The Raja took it and looked at it. A dreamy look came into his eyes.

"I have decided since you went away," he said at last, "that it is better for us to levy a tax upon the elephants of Sumatra."

And it is for this reason...that there are no tigers anywhere in the jungles of Borneo.

HAROLD COURLANDER
Kantchil's Lime Pit and Other Stories of Indonesia

This folktale explanation of why there are no tigers in Borneo is rooted in zoological reality. Tigers have never been known to exist on that island, possibly because it separated from the Indonesian mainland earlier than did Java. (The Javan tiger only recently became extinct). Illustration by Robert W. Kane from Kantchil's Lime Pit.

A World of Wild Cats

This map shows the geographic distribution by continent of all the known species of felines. Specific ranges for each are listed under "The Cat Clan," pages 26-45. A few species are found on more than one continent: namely, the mountain lion, throughout much of Central and South America (where it is known as the puma) as well as North America; the leopard and a very few lions in Asia as well as Africa; the Eurasian lynx in Russia and mountainous central Asia; and the desert wildcat in the Near East. No true cats are native to Australia. The domestic cat (*Felis catus*) lives there, however, and everywhere else humans live.

NORTH AMERICA

Mountain lion *(Felis concolor)*
Florida panther *(F. c. coryi)*
North American lynx *(Lynx canadensis)*
Bobcat *(Lynx rufus)*

Mountain lion   *Lynx*   *Bobcat*

CENTRAL AND SOUTH AMERICA

Jaguar *(Panthera onca)*
Ocelot *(Felis pardalis)*
Jaguarundi *(Felis yagouroundi)*
Margay *(Felis wiedii)*
Oncilla *(Felis tigrina)*
Geoffroy's cat *(Felis geoffroyi)*
Pampas cat *(Felis colocolo)*
Kodkod *(Felis guigna)*
Andean mountain cat *(Felis jacobita)*

Jaguar   *Margay*

Jaguarundi   *Ocelot*

NORTH AMERICA

NORTH ATLANTIC OCEAN

PACIFIC OCEAN

SOUTH AMERICA

LEGEND

Polar		Grassland	
Tundra		Forest	
Mountain		Rainforest	
Steppe		Desert	

EUROPE

Spanish lynx *(Lynx pardalis)*
Eurasian lynx *(Lynx lynx)*
European wildcat *(Felis sylvestris)*
Scottish wildcat *(F. s. grampia)*

Eurasian lynx

European wildcat

Scottish wildcat

EUROPE

ASIA

ASIA

Tiger *(Panthera tigris)*
Snow leopard *(Panthera uncia)*
Clouded leopard *(Neofelis nebulosa)*
Marbled cat *(Felis marmorata)*
Jungle cat *(Felis chaus)*
Asian golden cat *(Felis temminckii)*
Rusty-spotted cat *(Felis rubiginosa)*
Fishing cat *(Felis viverrina)*
Flat-headed cat *(Felis planiceps)*
Black-footed cat *(Felis nigripes)*
Bay cat *(Felis badia)*
Sand cat *(Felis margarita)*
Pallas' cat *(Felis manul)*
Chinese desert cat *(Felis bieti)*
Iriomote cat *(Felis iriomotensis)*

AFRICA

INDIAN OCEAN

SOUTH
ATLANTIC
OCEAN

Tiger

Snow leopard

Lion

African golden cat

Indian desert cat

Leopard cat

AFRICA

Lion *(Panthera leo)*
Leopard *(Panthera pardus)*
Cheetah *(Acinonyx jubatus)*
Caracal *(Lynx caracal)*
Serval *(Felis serval)*
African golden cat *(Felis aurata)*
Desert wildcat *(Felis lybica)*

Leopard

Caracal

Jungle cat

Sand cat

The Cat Clan

A species is the realization of a unique possibility of existence.

JONATHAN KINGDON

Painting of an Eastern cougar (Felis concolor couguar) female with young, by John James Audubon, c. 1840, from his great work The Quadrupeds of America. *When Audubon was roaming the country documenting its wildlife, the Eastern cougar subspecies was already in peril. Today it is deemed extinct—though a number of recent sightings are claimed. Audubon wrote: "This animal, which has excited so much terror in the minds of the ignorant and timid, has been nearly exterminated in all our Atlantic States...."*

H umans have been observing wild cats since our species emerged on the East African plains, but only in the last few centuries have we made serious scientific attempts to study and "cat-egorize" them. Earlier descriptive literature is rife with misidentifications and bizarre assertions about cat behavior. Even today, the archetypal elusiveness of the cat family makes it difficult to study them closely. The most recently recognized species—the Iriomote cat, native to the Japanese island of Tsushima—was only discovered in the 1960s.

Scientists still disagree over exactly how many species (never mind subspecies) the cat clan consists of, how they should be grouped, and their evolutionary relationships. Our knowledge of cats comes from various sources: examination of nonliving specimens, anecdotal reports, fossil records, and long-term field studies. (Such studies exist for only a handful of species, mostly the great cats.) Very recently, biochemical tools such as analyzing DNA sequences have been used to help sort out patterns of species development.

Using such tools, experts currently group cats into two "subfamilies" and several "lineages"—a system based on molecular evidence of genetic change. All cats trace back to the lynxlike ancestor known as *Pseudaelurus,* which probably arose in the Old World and migrated to the Western Hemisphere. The first group to branch off became the small, spotted cats of South America and is called the Ocelot lineage. Next came another group of small wildcats, originating in North Africa at a time when that now-desert region was forested, and spreading through Asia and Europe. These include the ancestors of domestic cats as well as the jungle cat, sand cat and a few others—the Domestic Cat lineage. The last and largest group to emerge was the Panthera lineage, which includes the great cats as well as the lynxes, puma, serval, golden cats, and several more—all derived from the ancestral lynx type.

The "odd cat out" in most methods of classification is the cheetah. It is morphologically different enough from other cats, with its rangy build and small head, to be placed in its own genus and in uncertain relationship to the main family. However, some see close similarities between cheetahs and pumas, suggesting a common ancestry.

The section that follows provides brief portraits of the species most often recognized today—thirty-six in all. 🐾

The Family Felidae

Lineage	Subfamily and Species		U. S. Endangered Species List Status	CITES Status
PANTHERA	**Subfamily Pantherinae**			
	Lion	Panthera leo	Endangered (Asiatic subspecies)	Endangered, I (Asiatic subspecies)
	Tiger	Panthera tigris	Endangered	Endangered, I
	Leopard	Panthera pardus	Endangered (or in parts of Africa, threatened)	Endangered, I
	Jaguar	Panthera onca	Endangered	Endangered, I
	Snow leopard	Panthera uncia	Endangered	Endangered, I
	Clouded leopard	Neofelis nebulosa	Endangered	Endangered, I
	Marbled cat	Felis marmorata	Endangered	Endangered, I
	North American lynx	Lynx canadensis		
	Bobcat	Lynx rufus	Endangered (Mexican subspecies)	Endangered, II
	Eurasian lynx	Lynx lynx		
	Spanish lynx	Lynx pardinus	Endangered	Endangered, I
	Caracal	Lynx caracal		Endangered, I
	Uncertain Taxonomy			
	Cheetah	Acinonyx jubatus	Endangered	Endangered, I
	Subfamily Felinae			
	Serval	Felis serval	Endangered (Algerian subspecies)	
	African golden cat	Felis aurata		Endangered, II
	Asian golden cat	Felis temmincki	Endangered	Endangered, I
	Leopard cat	Felis bengalensis	Endangered (1 subspecies)	Endangered, II (1 subspecies, I)
	Fishing cat	Felis viverrina		Endangered, II
	Flat-headed cat	Felis planiceps	Endangered	Endangered, I
	Rusty-spotted cat	Felis rubiginosa		Endangered, I
	Bay cat	Felis badia		Endangered, II
	Iriomote cat	Felis iriomotensis	Endangered	Endangered, II
	Jaguarundi	Felis yagouaroundi	Endangered (4 subspecies)	Endangered, I (S. American populations, II)
	Mountain lion, puma, cougar	Felis concolor	Endangered (3 subspecies), threatened elsewhere	Endangered, II (3 subspecies, I)
OCELOT	Ocelot	Felis pardalis	Endangered	Endangered, I
	Margay	Felis weidii	Endangered	Endangered, I
	Oncilla	Felis tigrina	Endangered	Endangered, I
	Kodkod	Felis guigna		Endangered, II
	Geoffroy's cat	Felis geoffroyi		Endangered, I
	Andean mountain cat	Felis jacobita	Endangered	Endangered, I
	Pampas cat	Felis colocolo		Endangered, II
DOMESTIC	European wildcat	Felis sylvestris		Endangered, II
	African wildcat	Felis lybica		Endangered, II
	Pallas' cat	Felis manul		Endangered, II
	Jungle cat	Felis chaus		Endangered, II
	Black-footed cat	Felis nigripes		Endangered, I
	Sand cat	Felis margarita	Endangered	Endangered, II
	Chinese desert cat	Felis bieti	Endangered (Pakistan subspecies)	Endangered, II
	Domestic cat	Felis catus		

The above list of felid species is organized by the subfamilies and lineages to which they belong. Also provided is the animal's current status according to the U.S. Fish & Wildlife Service's Endangered Species List, and the regulations of the Convention on International Trade in Endangered Species of Wild Fauna and Flora (CITES). In the CITES listings, the designation I indicates the most gravely endangered species, governed by the strictest international trade protections; the designations II and III are slightly less restrictive. (Adapted from a similar table in *Great Cats: Majestic Creatures of the Wild*, eds. John Seidensticker and Susan Lumpkin.)

THE LION

Strange spirit with inky hair,
Tail tufted stiff in rage,
I saw with sudden stare
Leap on the printed page.

The stillness of its roar
From midnight deserts torn
Clove silence to the core
Like the blare of a great horn.

I saw the sudden sky;
Cities in crumbling sand;
The stars fall wheeling by;
The lion roaring stand:

The stars fall wheeling by,
Their silent, silver stain,
Cold on his glittering eye,
Cold on his carven mane.

The full-orbed Moon shone down,
The silence was so loud,
From jaws wide-open thrown
His voice hung like a cloud.

Earth shrank to blackest air;
That spirit stiff in rage
Into some midnight lair
Leapt from the printed page.

W. J. TURNER

Above: A lioness (Panthera leo) and her young cub, Masai Mara, Kenya. Females in a pride often bear litters around the same time and care for each other's young. By Eberhard Brunner/Photographers Aspen. Opposite: The male lion, with his imposing physique and shaggy mane, has been a powerful symbol of wild nature from time immemorial. By John Wyand/Tony Stone Images.

LION
Panthera leo
ALSO CALLED: African lion

Description: More familiar to us than any other wild cat—perhaps any other wild animal—the lion is the preeminent carnivore of the African plains. Though not the largest felid (the tiger is) or even the most skilled hunter, lions dominate their environment by living and hunting in groups (prides). Adults are solid-colored, ranging from light to medium warm brown (white individuals, though not true albinos, occur in southern Africa). Cubs are spotted; the spots fade as they mature. Males grow a shaggy mane that varies from sandy blond to almost black; the extent and color of manes is partly related to climate and other habitat factors. Females are maneless but both sexes have a tuft at the end of the tail. The face is broad with rounded ears; the body is well-muscled and well-proportioned with a fairly short neck and medium-length legs in relation to body size (compared with other cats). Average size: shoulder height 48 in., body length 67-98 in., tail 35-41 in., weight 330-550 lbs. (males); females 42 in. high, 55-69 in. long, tail 27-39 in., weight 265-400 lbs.

Homeland and habitat: Lions historically ranged northward into Greece and through the Middle East into India, as well as most parts of Africa. Now only a handful of the Indian race survives in a preserve, and in Africa their range is limited to large expanses of parkland centered on Kenya, Tanzania and south-central Africa, and pockets across the sub-Saharan region. Lions prefer grassy plains (savannahs), open woodlands, sparse bush and dry scrub habitats, and can survive in semi-desert regions. Their hunting style is best suited to open country with good cover. Not at home in trees like some cats, they can and do climb trees for safety and to escape insect pests. They swim quite well and can cross rivers but do not often hunt in water as tigers do.

Behavior: Lions are by far the most social of the cats. They typically live in prides averaging about 15 members (half a dozen lionesses, a smaller number of males, and any cubs); life for a solitary lion (male or female) is problematic. Physical strength and group hunting tactics enable lions to hunt very large prey, even giraffes, but speed is not their forte, and up to 80% of their hunts do not result in kills. Aside from hunting advantages, living in good-sized prides enables lions to defend large territories, protect cubs from other predators, and fend off bands of male lions that try to take over prides. Lionesses do most of the hunting, though males take precedence at kills; by lagging behind in the hunt, they help protect the cubs. Lions are opportunistic hunters, taking whatever prey is available, large or small, and will even eat insects and plants in desperate straits. They often, especially males on their own, scavenge from other predators; it's estimated that up to 50% of their food comes from scavenging. Lionesses in a pride often come into estrus close together, and mating takes place over several days. A lioness may mate with several pride males. Cubs, up to 7 in a litter, are born after a gestation period of 110 days; the lioness dens away from the pride to whelp and returns in about 3 weeks. Cubs are raised communally, and suckled by other lionesses; still, cub mortality is high, up to 50% in the first year. Young females may remain with their home pride—pride lionesses are usually closely related—but males are driven out at around age 2. They may remain nomads for several years, forming coalitions with other nomads; when circumstances permit, a band of young roving males will take over a pride from its resident males. Lions in the wild rarely live longer than 12 years.

Recognized subspecies: Only one species. The Barbary lion *(Panthera leo leo)*, a race that inhabited North Africa (Tunisia and Morocco), was extirpated in the wild in 1922, followed shortly by the Cape lion of South Africa *(P. l. melanochaitus)*. A few hundred individuals from the Asian race *(P. l. persica)* survive in India's Gir Forest reserve.

Lions are not animals alone; they are symbols and totems and legends; they have impressed themselves so deeply on the human mind, if not its blood, it is as though the psyche were emblazoned with their crest.

EVELYN AMES
A Glimpse of Eden

TIGER
Panthera tigris

Description: A creature of legendary power and mystery, the tiger is a consummate predator. In its forest habitat, this powerful hunter glides on noiseless feet, its striped coloration blending with the night shadows to render it nearly invisible. Working alone, the tiger remains concealed as it stalks its prey, then rushes in from close range and grasps it with sharp claws to deliver the killing bite with its large, strong canines. With its massive build—powerful legs and long, muscular body—the tiger is the world's largest feline. It's also the only one with stripes. The stripes, which run vertically over a dark orange or reddish-ochre coat, may be gray, brown, or black. Observers believe that no two tigers have exactly the same markings; in fact even the two sides of the same individual usually differ in their patterning. The tiger's undersides are white or cream-colored. In India, examples of pure white tigers, as well as those bearing stripes on a white or cream background, have been found. (The tiger's stripes probably evolved from spots that became elongated; some tigers have stripes that are open in the center.) All tigers have rounded heads and small, rounded ears. Tigers fall into two main types—the Siberian tigers and those native to Southern Asia.

Average size: shoulder height 42 in., head and body length 108 in., tail 30 in., weight 440-595 lbs. (males); females 40 in. high, 96 in. long, tail 30 in., weight 275-355 lbs. (Siberian tigers are generally larger and heavier—up to 790 lbs.)

Homeland and habitat: Once broadly distributed over most of Asia, the tiger's range has shrunk to smaller, fragmented areas in India, Nepal, Bhutan, Bangladesh, Burma, Thailand, Vietnam, Russia, and, it is thought, China. Tigers thrive in a variety of habitats, including evergreen tropical forests, mangrove swamps, dry deciduous forests, and mountain forests. They also inhabit savannahs

Mammals do not get more fearful than the tiger. The champion of all cats: the champion of all carnivores. Perhaps the most handsome beast in creation: certainly the most effective ambush predator on the planet. A size bigger than the lion and adapted to work alone: every grown-up tiger must kill for itself every time it wishes to eat. Self-reliant: independent: massive: the tiger is arguably the most spectacular killing machine that nature has come up with, at least, if we discount a certain mischievous ape.

SIMON BARNES
Tiger!

The Bengal tiger, Panthera tigris bengalensis, *remains the most numerous of the tiger races. Numbering some 40,000 in India at the turn of the century, its population had dropped below 2,000 by 1972. Heroic preservation efforts have improved that figure to around 4,500 at present, but all tiger populations are still endangered and new ways must be found to reconcile wildlife conservation with ever-expanding human needs in poor countries. By Andy Rouse/DRK Photo.*

(grasslands) and, in Siberia, snow-covered taiga—coniferous forests edging the tundra. Tigers rarely climb trees but prefer to live among them, where they can find cover to conceal them when stalking prey, as well as shade in which to escape from heat during the daylight hours. A water source is a necessity; tigers love to cool off in a stream or waterfall and are excellent swimmers.

Behavior: Unlike the highly social lion, the tiger leads a mostly solitary life. Individuals may come together briefly (and usually amicably) at the site of a kill, and of course at mating time. Mothers and cubs stay together for a year or two, and groups of youngsters may move about together for a while after leaving their mothers. But in general, tigers hunt on their own. An adult occupies a home territory but does not hold it exclusively. Perpetually on the move in search of prey, females may roam over a home range as small as 8 square miles or up to 200 square miles or more, depending on the availability of prey. Males usually occupy even larger ranges. Tigers hunt all kinds of large prey animals—deer, wild pigs, and buffalo, as well as domestic animals. Largely nocturnal, they begin the hunt at dusk. After a kill, a tiger drags its prize into cover—no small feat considering the prey may be as large as a 400-pound buffalo. In addition to eating fresh game, tigers have also been known to eat carrion. When these hunters do get together to mate, several males may fight over a female; fights are bloody but are rarely fought to the death. The mating male and female stay together for about 6 days; then the male resumes his wandering. At the end of the gestation period (from 95 to 110 days), the female gives birth to a litter of 2 or 3 cubs. Tiger cubs are born blind and helpless and depend on their mother's milk for the first 8 weeks; then they begin to feed on her kills. By the time they are about 2 years old they usually go out on their own. They are ready to mate at 3 to 4 years old. In the wild, tigers usually live to age 20 or so.

The Siberian, or Amur, tiger (Panthera tigris altaica) *is the largest of the all felids; its numbers in the wild are currently unknown but presumably shrinking. By Tom & Pat Leeson.*

Recognized subspecies: Eight subspecies once existed—the Bengal tiger *(Panthera tigris tigris)*, Indochinese tiger *(P. t. corbetti)*, Chinese tiger *(P. t. amoyensis)*, Caspian tiger *(P.t. virgata)*, Siberian tiger *(P. t. altaica)*, Sumatran tiger *(P. t. sumatrae)*, Javan tiger *(P. t. sondaicus)*, Bali tiger *(P. t. balica)*. Of these, the Caspian, Javan, and Bali tigers are now extinct. Tigers may have swum to Indonesia from the mainland, or walked there before those islands became separate. All the surviving species are considered seriously endangered.

Every inch of his richly colored body was beautifully proportioned, and its movements were liquid and graceful. His head was massive, very broad between the ears, and the ruff round his chin was evenly curved and of the palest saffron color. Across his bright hide the stripes sprawled like black flames. Perhaps the most beautiful part of him was his eyes: large and almond-shaped, set slanting in his face, like sea-polished pebbles of leaf green.

GERALD DURRELL
A Bevy of Beasts

LEOPARD
Panthera pardus
ALSO CALLED: Panther, black panther

[Leopards] seemed to me to be the most beautiful of all the animals, the most lithe and wild. Those that I saw—and you don't see very many—were very pale in colour, almost silver, and their throats were marked with a circular band of black fur patches that hung like a necklace from the base of their round cat-heads. There is a hair-trigger ferocity about the leopards. Each time one lifted one's binoculars for a closer view one was confronted with two green glaring lamps that burned directly into one's own eyes....No animal, not even the lion, has such an implacable gaze.

ALAN MOOREHEAD
No Room in the Ark

The leopard, Panthera pardus, *is among the most wide-spread and adaptable of all wild cats. Photographed in Okavango, Botswana. By Lex Hes/ABPL.*

Description: With a grace that belies its muscular power, the leopard has been called by one expert "the most perfect of the big cats." In addition to its striking beauty and its considerable skill as a predator, the leopard is highly adaptable. It can thrive in a variety of habitats and subsist on a widely varied diet. The leopard's coat is its most distinguishing physical feature. Over a background of straw-colored, gray, or reddish-brown fur is a pattern of black spots and rosettes of infinite variation. (The throat, belly, chest, and insides of the legs are white.) These beautiful markings provide the big cat with excellent camouflage as it stalks its prey. Melanistic (black-phase) leopards occur rarely. The leopard's body is lithe and muscular, with massive limbs and a long tail held in an upward curving position as it steps along on silent, padded paws. The claws are sharp and curved for grasping prey and for climbing trees, which the animal does frequently and with ease.

Average size: shoulder height 21-28 in., head and body length 35-75 in., tail 22-43 in., weight 81-198 lbs. (males); females 62-132 lbs.

Homeland and habitat: The most widespread big cat, the leopard is found throughout much of Africa, China, and Siberia, as well as in Israel, the Middle East, Pakistan, India, Sri Lanka, and Southeast Asia, including parts of Indonesia. It is equally at home in all types of forest, in savannahs, in scrub, in semidesert, and in rocky mountain areas.

Behavior: Leopards are noted for their secretive ways and their ability to "disappear" into their surroundings. This serves them well as they stalk prey, often creeping up undetected to within a few feet of an unsuspecting animal. They are opportunistic hunters and will kill almost anything, from insects and rodents to larger animals including deer, gazelles, pigs, and monkeys, as well as domestic animals. The kill is often dragged up into the fork of a tree to keep it safe from scavengers, a real test of the leopard's strength when the prey is a large, heavy animal. Leopards often spend considerable time in trees, dozing and washing themselves between bouts of feeding. A solitary creature, the leopard maintains a territory of 3 to 25 square miles; a male's territory often overlaps that of several females. Mating may occur at all times of the year in most areas. After a gestation period of about 100 days, the female gives birth to 2 or 3 cubs in a concealed den. They remain with their mother until the age of 18-24 months, when they generally become independent.

Recognized supspecies: Fourteen subspecies or races include the Javan leopard *(Panthera pardis melas),* Amur leopard *(P. p. orientalis),* Indian leopard *(P. p. fusca),* North Chinese leopard *(P. p. japonensis),* Somali leopard *(P. p. nanopardus),* Zanzibar leopard *(P. p. adersi),* Sinai leopard *(P. p. jarvisi),* Sri Lankan leopard *(P. p. kotiya),* Barbary leopard *(P. p. panthera),* Persian leop-

ard *(P. p. saxicolor)*, Arabian leopard *(P. p. nimr)*, Anatolian leopard *(P. p. tulliiana)*, Caucasus leopard *(P. p. ciscaucasica)*, Indochinese leopard *(P .p. delacouri)*. Of these, the Amur, Anatolian, and Barbary leopards are all but extinct.

JAGUAR
Panthera onca
ALSO CALLED: El tigre (tiger), onça

Description: This beautiful New World cat has been a compelling symbol of the South American jungles for centuries. Similar in size to its Old World cousin, the leopard, the jaguar has a stockier build, with short, massive limbs and a large, rounded head. Its black spots, distributed over fur that ranges from pale yellow to rusty red, can be distinguished from those of the leopard by the smaller spots which occur within each rosette. Along the back, elongated black spots may merge into a solid line. The animal's undersides are white or buff; the long tail is spotted, with a black tip. All-black jaguars are not uncommonly found. While the jaguar lacks the grace of the leopard, it is an equally formidable predator, with the power to kill prey considerably larger and heavier than itself. Jaguars from the Pantanal region of Brazil are significantly larger and heavier than average, one record male weighing 356 pounds.

Average size: shoulder height 28 in., head and body length 72-84 in., tail 21 in., weight 121.5 lbs. (males), 79.5 lbs. (females).

Homeland and habitat: Once extending as far north as the southern United States, the jaguar's range now covers southern Mexico, Central America, and areas of South America as far south as northern Argentina. Jaguars inhabit not only tropical rainforests but also swampy grasslands and drier savannah areas near rivers and streams. They require plenty of access to water; they are excellent swimmers and seem to enjoy playing in water as well.

Behavior: The jaguar hunts in the dawn and dusk hours, or on moonlit nights. Though it hunts mostly on the ground—its chief prey is an overgrown

Among the big cats, the jaguar, Panthera onca, *is the best adapted to hunting in and around water. By Frans Lanting/Minden Pictures.*

rodent known as the capybara—it is a good climber and takes prey such as birds or monkeys in the trees. In the water it catches fish, turtles, and even caimans (Amazon crocodilians). Also included in the big cat's diet are reptiles, small mammals, wild pigs, and livestock such as cattle. This accomplished hunter uses a combination of stalking and quick dashes to capture its quarry. Jaguars are solitary and territorial; each jaguar lives alone within a home range that varies between 4 and 65 square miles for females, 11 and 59 square miles for males, depending on habitat and prey availability. The animal's hoarse call, which has been compared to the ending part of lion's roar, is thought to have territory-marking significance as well as being a mating call. A female jaguar may attract as many as eight males during breeding season. After a gestation period of 93 to 105 days, a pregnant female gives birth to 1 to 4 cubs under dense cover. The cubs are about half-grown at 9 or 10 months. They will remain with their mother until the age of about 2 years and may mature fully by the age of 3 years.

The jaguar is the greatest cat of the Americas, resembling a very large, heavy-set leopard. Like the much smaller ocelot… "el tigre" was formerly an established species north to the Red River in Arkansas, and a number of debatable early records place it as far east as the Appalachians. An account of the coastal Carolinas in 17H notes that "Tygers…are more to the Westward….I once saw one that was larger than a Panther [i.e. cougar], and seemed to be a very bold Creature…."

PETER MATTHIESSEN
Wildlife in America

"Everything has a Jaguar." (Equivalent to "there's a snag to everything" or "Where's the catch?")

ARAWAK INDIAN SAYING

CHEETAH

Acinonyx jubatus
ALSO CALLED: Hunting leopard

If the lion is gregarious, demonstrative in its actions, ritual in its habits, fearful of no natural enemy, and placidly self-possessed, the cheetah is elusive, high-strung, always on the alert, and with an instinct for concealing itself.

JOY ADAMSON
The Spotted Sphinx

The cheetah, Acinonyx jubatus, *is a superbly efficient hunter and bears more young than other big cats. Yet its numbers are declining, from factors that include habitat destruction and consequent inbreeding, competition with more aggressive predators, and disturbance by safari tours. By Anup & Manoj Shah/Planet Earth Pictures.*

Description: Lean and long-legged, the cheetah is built for speed; in fact, it's the fastest-running land mammal on earth. Its light weight, flexible spine, and exposed claws that dig into the ground—all contribute to the cheetah's ability to get a fast start and to sprint flat-out at speeds up to 68 mph for short distances when chasing down prey. This elegant cat's fur is short and yellowish, marked with small, round dark spots. A black stripe runs from each eye down to the muzzle. The tail is spotted but ringed near the tip. The head is small and neat; the eyes have been described as being particularly lively and alert, as indeed they must be for spotting prey over the wide expanse of the savannahs.

Average size: shoulder height 31 in., head and body length 44-53 in., tail 26-33 in., weight 86-143 lbs.

Homeland and habitat: Once widely distributed over central India, southwestern Asia, and Arabia, as well as Africa, the cheetah is now confined to a small area in the Middle East (mostly Iran) and parts of East and South Africa. Asian cheetahs are now all but extinct; most cheetahs are found in Africa. The cheetah frequents dry, open habitats, including grasslands, acacia scrub, semideserts, and light woodlands. It requires some cover in which to hide and stalk prey, but it never frequents dense forest areas.

Behavior: The cheetah employs its running ability rather than a stalk-and-ambush strategy to capture prey. This ability is legendary; the animal can accelerate from a standing start to 45 mph in 2 seconds. Its spectacular speed prompted human hunters from ancient times to tame cheetahs and use them to hunt game. In the wild, the cheetah hunts by day, preying upon smallish animals such as gazelles, impalas, warthogs, and wildebeest and waterbuck calves, as well as on hares. It springs out of cover to run down its quarry at top speed; when it catches up it sends the animal sprawling with a paw or tackles it, then finishes it off with a neck bite. Cheetah females are solitary and are not territorial; several adults may have overlapping territories. Groups of 2 or 3 males may hold small territories together and defend them from other males. During breeding season, a female cheetah may give birth to a litter of up to 8 cubs (more usually 3 to 5) after a 95-day pregnancy. Cubs are weaned at 6 months and leave the mother by the age of 13 to 20 months. As with other large cats, the siblings may remain together for a few months.

Recognized subspecies: The Asian cheetah (*A. j. venaticus*) has been recognized as a subspecies but is now nearly extinct except for tiny populations in Iran and Baluchistan. Up to 6 African subspecies have been proposed, but these are probably not distinct. The king cheetah (*A. j. rex*), distinguished by a longer, blotched coat, is a South African population created through a genetic mutation rather than a true subspecies.

MOUNTAIN LION

Felis concolor

ALSO CALLED: Puma, cougar, panther

Description: Wide variation—in habitat, size, coloration, even its name—characterizes this shy and secretive American cat. It has been called everything from a Mexican lion to a mountain screamer to a red tiger. Depending on where found, the puma may have fur that is reddish, gray, buff, various shades of brown, or even bluish or silvery gray. Whatever its color, the animal's coat is unmarked; it's the only big cat save the lion that has a plain-colored coat. The tail is dark toward the tip. The puma's body is long and lithe, with powerful limbs, especially the much longer hind legs. The head is small, with small, rounded ears.

Average size: shoulder height 27 in., head and body length 59 in., tail 28 in., weight 148-227 lbs. (males); shoulder height 27 in., head and body length 47 in., tail 26 in., weight 79-132 lbs. (females).

Homeland and habitat: The most widely distributed of the American cats, the puma is found from Canada through North America (west of the Great Plains), southern Florida, Mexico, Central America, and down to the southern tip of South America. It can survive in a broad range of habitats, from tropical forest and swampland to coniferous forest, grassland, brush country, and semidesert. It also adapts to many different elevations, from sea level to 14,765 feet.

Behavior: Largely nocturnal, the puma stalks its prey under cover, often leaping onto the animal to kill it. Its powerful hindquarters enable it to leap distances up to 40 feet. Deer form the majority of its diet; other prey, depending on the location, may include hare, opossum, raccoons, porcupines, beavers, rodents, monkeys, wild pigs, elk, and domestic animals such as sheep and cattle. Pumas are largely solitary, holding a home territory that ranges from 12 to 36 square miles. This cat is famous for its scream—a long, loud cry often uttered in connection with mating. Pumas may mate at any time of the year. After a 90 to 95-day gestation period the female gives birth to 2 or 3 cubs. They are born with spots which fade as they reach adulthood. Young pumas are usually independent at 2 years old.

Recognized subspecies: Of two races—the Eastern panther (*F. c. cougar*) and the Florida panther (*F. c. coryi*)—the former may be extinct, though recent sightings are claimed, and the latter is dwindling.

Above: The mountain lion, Felis concolor ("cat of one color"), can occupy varied habitats throughout the Western Hemisphere; this one walks on an ice-covered river. By Charles G. Summers, Jr. Below: The name "ounce" (onza in Spanish) has been confusingly used to refer to several different cats. As used in Europe it refers to the snow leopard, probably shown here. Some Spanish speakers use onza to refer to the jaguar. But for years a mysterious cat called the onza, resembling the puma but spotted, was rumored to exist in the Southwest; though lightly spotted specimens have been found, they are genetically identical to Felis concolor.

SNOW LEOPARD
Panthera uncia
ALSO CALLED: Ounce

The typical snow leopard has pale frosty eyes and a coat of pale misty gray, with black rosettes that are clouded by the depth of the rich fur. An adult rarely weighs more than a hundred pounds or exceeds six feet in length, including the remarkable long tail, thick to the tip, used presumably for balance and for warmth, but it kills creatures three times its own size without much difficulty. It has enormous paws and a short-faced heraldic head, like a leopard of myth; it is bold and agile in the hunt, and capable of terrific leaps....

PETER MATTHIESSEN
The Snow Leopard

Little-studied until recently, the snow leopard (Panthera uncia) has been a creature of mystery and legend. Long sought for its exquisite pelt, this species is now protected by international law but still gravely threatened by illegal hunting and lack of available prey; remaining populations are widely scattered and isolated. By Alan & Sandy Carey.

Description: The snow leopard's long, dense coat—with its unique smoke-gray color and striking light-centered rosettes—protects its wearer well in the harsh mountain climates where it makes its home. Even the snow leopard's thick tail, almost as long as its body, can be wrapped around it when at rest for extra warmth. Everything about this magnificent creature is distinctive—especially its eyes, of an unusual grayish green. The snow leopard is built for negotiating rocky outcroppings and steep terrain; its hind legs are slightly longer than its front legs to facilitate jumping, and its paws are broad and powerful. Agile and strong, the cat can leap as far as 49 feet.

Average size: shoulder height 23 in., head and body length 39-51 in., tail 31-39 in., weight 55-165 lbs.

Homeland and habitat: The snow leopard's range extends discontinuously over much of the mountainous area of Central Asia, in parts of Russia, Mongolia, India, Pakistan, China, Afghanistan, Nepal, and Bhutan. The big cats live above the tree line, at altitudes between 9,000 and 19,700 feet; during the winter months they may follow their prey to lower elevations.

Behavior: Little-studied in the past due to the remoteness of its habitat, the snow leopard has since been carefully tracked as it ranges over the mountains. A powerful predator, the creature uses the stalk-and-ambush method of hunting to capture blue sheep—its main prey—as well as musk deer, ibex, markhor, and marmots. Competing for game with human hunters, the snow leopard has often been forced to kill domestic animals as well. The big cat frequents rocky ridges where it can spot prey from above. Most of its hunting is done during the early morning or late afternoon. Snow leopards are largely solitary and roam continuously over vast home ranges. Mating time is fixed, so that cubs are born in April to June and have a chance to mature before winter sets in. After a gestation period of 90-103 days, a female gives birth to 2 or 3 cubs. After about a month they begin to follow their mother to the hunt; by the age of about 2 they are on their own.

CLOUDED LEOPARD
Neofelis nebulosa

Description: This handsome cat gets its name from the unusual cloud-shaped markings on its coat—large, irregular dark patches on grayish to brownish fur. The legs, which are short and powerful, are covered with smaller dark spots. Dark stripes run over the cheeks and sides of the head, which is large in proportion to the body. The clouded leopard has been described as having a big cat's head on a small cat's body, and has the longest canine teeth of any living cat, relative to its size. Its long body and tail, as well as its broad paws, help it to maneuver in the trees, where it spends much of its time. Average size: head and body length 36 in., tail 30 in., weight 48 lbs.

Homeland and habitat: Found from Nepal through southeastern China, Taiwan, Malaysia, Sumatra, and Borneo. Its habitat is largely tropical evergreen forest, although it may sometimes frequent drier forests where prey is available.

Behavior: A secretive creature, the clouded leopard has been difficult to observe in the wild. It is thought to be largely arboreal, resting on tree branches and hunting in the trees for birds and monkeys. In fact, its Malaysian name, *rimau-dahan,* means "tree tiger." Yet it also seems to spend time on the ground, where its prey includes pigs as well as deer and other larger

animals, which it can dispatch with its large canines. It is probably nocturnal; not much else is known about its habits. Females are thought to have a gestation period of 86-93 days, after which they bear as many as 5 young, although usually the litter is smaller.

Recognized subspecies: Four subspecies include *Neofelis nebulosa nebulosa* (in south China and southeastern Asia), *N. n. brachyura* (on Taiwan—probably extinct), *N. n. diardi* (Borneo), and *N. n. macrosceloides* (Nepal to Burma).

LEOPARD CAT
Felis bengalensis

Description: Among the most common of the wild cats, with a diverse range of habitats, this beautiful small creature is about the size of domestic cat. The various subspecies display an almost endless variety of coat markings and colors. Fur may be yellowish to reddish to gray; the numerous black spots may merge and overlap to form blotches or bands. In China, the leopard cat is known as *chin-ch'ien mao,* or "money cat," because of the resemblance of its spots to Chinese coins. Usually there are 4 dark bands running from the forehead to the back of the neck. The undersides are white. Longer of leg than the average domestic cat, the leopard cat has a small head and long, rounded ears. The Philippine race is the small-

est; the largest subspecies is found in Manchuria. Average size: head and body length 17-42 in., tail 9-17 in., weight 6-15 lbs.

Homeland and habitat: The leopard cat is distributed through Pakistan, India, Nepal, Bangladesh, Vietnam, Thailand, Burma, Malaysia, Indonesia, parts of China, and the Philippines. It has adapted to many habitats, including tropical forests, pine forests, scrub, and even agricultural areas. It requires a water source and so is not found in very dry areas.

Behavior: Mostly a nocturnal hunter, although it has also been seen in the daylight hours. Its prey includes rodents and other small mammals, as well as birds. It is a good swimmer and often catches reptiles and fish. Near human habitation, this little cat also helps itself to domestic poultry. It is solitary except during the breeding period, which may vary, except in Siberia, where harsh winters demand that kittens be born in early summer. Gestation takes 65-72 days, after which 2 or 3 kittens are born in a den—a hollow tree or small cave. The kittens reach maturity at about 18 months.

Recognized subspecies: Up to 10 subspecies have been identified, including the Indian/Indochinese *(Felis bengalensis bengalensis),* Sumatran *(F. b. sumatranus),* Javan *(F. b. javanensis),* Bornean *(F. b.borneoensis),* Pakistani *(F. b.trevelyani),* Manchurian *(F. b. euptilura),* and Philippine *(F. b. minuta).*

[I]t was the leopard's Lilliputian edition, the leopard cat….a perfect spotted leopard the size of a domestic cat. The tawny hide was soft as silk, like close-cropped plush; the big yellow eyes those of a typical leopard. The cat moved with noiseless, inconspicuous gait; the lithe body was flexible as a bamboo pole. Even the characteristic white spots that tigers and leopards have on the back of their ears were there….The way this cat set down its velvety paws as it padded softly toward us; the way it lifted its finely chiseled little head and gazed at each of us in turn with knowing, intelligent eyes…all that was the very essence of poetic, ethereal, feline grace.

LUDWIG KOCH-ISENBURG
The Realm of the Green Buddha

Above: Clouded leopard, Neofelis nebulosa. By Russ Kinne/Comstock. Below: Leopard cat, Felis bengalensis. By Art Wolfe.

The North American lynx (Lynx canadensis) hunts mainly on the ground, but like most cats uses trees as lookout posts, escape routes, and safe resting places. By Joseph Van Os/Image Bank.

The Spanish lynx (Lynx pardinus) is smaller and more strongly spotted than the other two lynx species.

LYNX

North American or Canadian lynx   *Lynx canadensis*
Spanish lynx   *Lynx pardinus*
Eurasian lynx   *Lynx lynx*

Description: Within the genus Lynx are the three distinct species named above. Closely related are the bobcat and caracal (pp. 36-37). All lynxes have in common their distinctive ears, which are triangular and topped by tufts of black hairs. They also have a ruff of fur around their necks. Their coats may be gray or tawny in color and are patterned with dark spots, the Spanish lynx being the most heavily spotted of the three. The Eurasian and North American lynxes have heavily furred paws which, in the latter, may measure as wide as 4 inches across. These act like snowshoes to enable the cats to move easily over winter terrain, thus giving them an advantage over prey animals whose feet sink into the snow. All three cats have long legs and short tails. They vary in size, with the Eurasian lynx being the largest and heaviest.

Average size: head and body length 38 in., tail 5 in., weight 27 lbs. (Spanish lynx); head and body length 34 in., tail 5 in., weight 22 lbs. (North American lynx); head and body length 31-51 in., tail 5 in., weight 44 lbs. (Eurasian lynx).

Homeland and habitat: The Spanish lynx is found only in southwestern Spain and parts of Portugal; the North American lynx in Canada and Alaska, and in parts of the Rocky Mountains in the U.S. The Eurasian lynx is widely distributed over western Europe, Russia, Scandinavia, Asia Minor, Iran, Iraq, Mongolia, Manchuria, and Central Asia. All three animals frequent forested areas, although they may also live in scrub or more open areas.

Behavior: Lynxes are solitary, although in the North American lynx, adult females with kittens have been observed hunting in cooperation with each other. The size of the home range varies; Eurasian lynxes may hold a range of up to 116 square miles. Lynxes are good swimmers and will even cross rivers in their quest for prey. The lynx hunts during dawn and dusk hours, relying on its keen sight and hearing to locate prey, then stalking it silently and dashing in for the kill. Although the mainstay of most lynx diets is rabbit or rodents, lynxes will take almost any available prey, including birds, deer, and sometimes livestock. Female lynxes usually give birth to litters of 2 to 4 kittens after a gestation period of 63 to 70 days. Kittens remain with their mother until the next breeding season; after that siblings may stay together for a time.

BOBCAT

Lynx rufus
ALSO CALLED: Bay lynx, wildcat

Description: A close relative of the North American, Eurasian, and Spanish lynxes, the bobcat is thought by some experts to have evolved separately from those species. The bobcat is generally smaller than the other lynxes, with short legs and smaller feet. Its short, soft fur may be colored various shades of brown or gray, marked with dark spots and streaks. The ears are less conspicuously tufted than those of its relatives, with white spots on the backs. Average size: head and body length 65-72 in., tail 5-6 in., weight 15-22 lbs.

Homeland and habitat: Once common over the entire United States, the bobcat is now found from southern Canada to Central Mexico but has all but disappeared in parts of the East and Midwest. An adaptable animal, the bobcat inhabits many types of forest, brush, semidesert regions, and even deserts.

Behavior: Shy and secretive, the bobcat does much of its hunting at night. Its diet mainly consists of rabbits, but it also preys upon rodents, birds, and snakes; in winter, large adults may hunt deer. In turn, this small-sized cat is sometimes preyed upon by the larger puma. Bobcats are solitary; the

The bobcat, Lynx rufus, *lives in warmer, drier North American habitats than the lynx does. By Thomas Kitchin/First Light.*

adult females occupy exclusive home ranges, while males' ranges may overlap those of other males. Females give birth to litters of 2 to 4 kittens after a 62-day gestation period; the young become independent the following spring. Bobcats are said by observers to have a more aggressive, fierce character than their cousin lynxes.

CARACAL
Lynx caracal
ALSO CALLED: Desert lynx

Description: Known for its remarkable leaping ability, the caracal is possibly the fastest feline of its size. This handsome animal is very similar to the true lynx but is smaller and has a longer tail. The caracal is sometimes classified in its own genus and called *Caracal caracal.* Its legs are long and slender, with the hind legs being longer than the forelegs. The body is also slender, with reddish brown fur on every area except the chin, throat, and belly, which are white. The eyes are ringed in white, with a distinctive black line running from the eye to the nose. The ears are typically lynxlike—narrow and pointed, tipped with a long tuft of black hair; in fact, the animal's name comes from the Turkish word *karakal,* meaning "black-eared." There are reports of all-black caracals seen in parts of Africa.

Average size: shoulder height 17 in., head and body length 28 in., tail 9 in., weight 37 lb.

Homeland and habitat: The caracal is found in dry areas scattered throughout Africa, the Middle East, the Arabian Peninsula, Russia, Afghanistan, Pakistan, and India. But their numbers have greatly declined in Asia; most caracals are now found in Africa. It ranges over dry woodlands, acacia scrub, savannah, steppes, and mountain areas.

Behavior: Caracals are largely nocturnal, hunting by night for prey such as rodents, hyraxes, klipspringers, dik-diks, and fawns of impalas and various antelopes. They also prey upon birds, which they have been known to take from the air, leaping up several feet to knock them down. Easily tamed, caracals have been trained to hunt for birds and hares in India and Iran. The phrase "to put the cat among the pigeons" comes from a practice in India, where tame caracals were put in an arena with pigeons and wagers made on how many the cat could down before the rest flew off. With a gait somewhat like that of the cheetah, caracals are fast runners. They are also good climbers and will sometimes drag their kills up into trees to eat them. In the wild, caracals are solitary animals. When they mate, the female produces a litter of 2 to 3 kittens after a gestation period of about 70 days. The kittens remain with their mother for a year or so before adopting the solitary lifestyle of adults. Their lifespan in the wild is estimated at 16 or 17 years.

I had seen the lynx [caracal] already and knew him well. We had a couple breeding happily as pets on our farm but even more, in a remote complex of the hills which cut across the centre of it…several families still lived unthreatened in their natural state.…There, repeatedly, I had seen how bright with flame and quick with light and colour the lynx was, so that his movement was like the flicker and flame of a vestal lamp. It explained why no pioneer ever spoke of him by any other name than red-cat.

LAURENS VAN DER POST
Testament to the Bushmen

The caracal, Lynx caracal, *is Africa's member of the lynx clan; its long, dramatically tufted ears are its trademark. Photographed in Namibia. By Jim Brandenburg/Minden Pictures.*

The ocelot, Felis pardinus (above), and the margay, Felis weidii (below left) are among the most beautifully marked of the Western Hemisphere's wild cats. Ocelot, by Frans Lanting/Minden Pictures. Margay, by Art Wolfe.

The most magnificent thing about an ocelot are its markings. The ground colour on the head and shoulders is a rich orange or yellow and this becomes lighter towards the tail. Down the sides of the body it is usually grey, and the belly is white. The length of the back from withers to rump is marked by a regular, closely connected chain of spots, and gives the impression of the animal being striped. This striped effect is then further accentuated by the elongated rosettes down the sides of the body, parallel to the spine. The rosettes are quite unlike those of the jaguar, being very long and thin.

STANLEY BROCK
Leemo

OCELOT
Felis pardalis

The strikingly beautiful ocelot comes in a remarkable variety of colors and markings, resulting in many erroneous subspecies designations. Its coat color ranges from whitish to yellow to reddish gray or gray. The markings tend to be elongated spots that run into streaks and blotches—no two patterns are alike. This handsome coat has cost many ocelots their lives, as it has been taken by hunters for the fur trade. Often mistaken for the margay, the ocelot is larger and has a shorter tail. Once found throughout the southern U.S., ocelots are now restricted to a few in Texas. The rest range through parts of Mexico and Central America and into South America as far as Argentina. They inhabit a broad range of habitats, including tropical rainforests, mountain forests, and all types of thick bush, as well as marshy areas and riverbanks. These cats lead largely solitary lives, occupying non-overlapping home ranges of .3 to 5.8 square miles. They hunt mainly on the ground, at night or during dawn and dusk. Their diet consists of small mammals and rodents, as well as birds, fish, snakes, and lizards. Females bear litters of 1 or 2 kittens after a 80-day gestation period. The offspring go out on their own at about 2 years old. Average size: head and body length 33-39 in., tail 11-16 in., weight 19-28 lbs. (males); head and body length 26-32 in., tail 10-15 in., weight 15-22 lbs. (females).

MARGAY
Felis wiedii
ALSO CALLED: Long-tailed spotted cat

Although very similar to the ocelot in appearance, the margay is quite different in habits and behavior. It shares the ocelot's coloration and markings, the yellowish brown coat being marked with dark, pale-centered spots and blotches. The margay is smaller than the ocelot and larger than the similar oncilla; it has the longest tail of the three. Its eyes are especially large, possibly an adaptation to a nocturnal and arboreal life style. It is found from Mexico, where it is rare, through Central America and into South America. Its preferred habitat is forest; it is almost exclusively arboreal. This agile cat is an expert climber and does most of its hunting in the trees by night. Sometimes engaging in remarkable displays of running and jumping among the branches, it preys on birds, rodents, reptiles, and insects. The margay is a solitary creature; little is known of its reproductive habits in the wild. Average size: head and body length 18-31 in., tail 13-19 in., weight 5-8 lbs.

ONCILLA
Felis tigrina
ALSO CALLED: Little spotted cat, tiger cat

Among the smallest of the South American cats, the oncilla is often mistaken for the margay, which it closely resembles. Its soft fur is ochre-colored, marked with dark spots and blotches. The tail is black at the tip and has 10 or 11 rings. Oncillas are much smaller than either margays or ocelots—usually no heavier than 6 pounds. This little cat is becoming increasingly rare in its native areas—

Central and South America. It makes its home exclusively in the forest, particularly in the cloud forest and humid lowland forests, up to 3,280 feet. Oncillas have even been seen among the trees on coffee or cocoa plantations. An agile climber, this cat is nocturnal and is thought to prey upon rodents and birds. Little is known about its diet and its habits in the wild, however. Average size: head and body length 15-21 in., tail 9-15 in., weight 3-6 lbs.

JAGUARUNDI
Felis yagouaroundi

Likened by many observers to an otter or a weasel, the odd-looking jaguarundi is built low to the ground, with short legs and a long, flexible body. Its head is small and flat, with short, rounded ears. This is one of the few cats that is not spotted; its coat ranges in color from reddish-brown to gray. Distributed widely in the New World from southern Texas through Mexico, Central America, and South America, it lives in a variety of lowland habitats, from forest to bush, and from dry areas to swampy grasslands. It is often found near rivers and is a good swimmer. Unlike many cats, the jaguarundi goes abroad during the day. Able to prowl easily through dense undergrowth with its low-slung build, the cat hunts for rodents, birds, opossums, rabbits, monkeys, and armadillos; it has also been known to steal farmers' chickens and ducks. Jaguarundis have been tamed with moderate success and kept as pets to control rodent populations. Largely solitary except at mating times, the jaguarundi is thought to produce litters of 2 kittens on average, after about 72 days' gestation. The kittens have spots when born, but these fade. Average size: head and body length 20-30 in., tail 11-20 in., weight 6-13 lbs.

SERVAL
Felis serval

This medium-sized African cat has a highly distinctive appearance. Very long-legged and daintily built, it has large, oval ears on a small, slim head. Its coat, which is yellowish buff, is marked with a pattern of round black dots. The tail is quite short, black-tipped and ringed near the end. All-black servals have been reported. This most graceful of the small African cats ranges over most of the continent. One subspecies, *F.s. constantina,* was once found in the Atlas region of North Africa but has almost disappeared. Servals frequent grasslands where there is plenty of cover and a reliable water source. Its long legs help it move easily through the high grass, hunting for the rodents that make up most of its diet. With its large, sensitive ears, the cat listens intently for the small, rustling sounds of its prey and, after pinpointing its exact location, pounces with great accuracy for the kill. Swift and agile, it has been observed to bound high above the grass when hunting, which is often during daylight hours. Adults are solitary, females occupying exclusive territories of at least 3.5 square miles, the male's territory overlapping that of females. Females give birth to litters of 1 to 3 kittens after a 74-day gestation period. The young leave when they are about a year old. Average size: shoulder height 23 in., head and body length 26-39 in., tail 9-17 in., weight 17-39 lbs.

Left: Oncilla, Felis tigrina. *By Art Wolfe. Above: The jaguarundi,* Felis yagouaroundi, *resembles some members of the mustelid family, but its biology and behavior are those of a cat. Photographed in Belize. By Alan & Sandy Carey*

The serval, Felis serval, *is a rangy, athletic cat of the African savannahs. Its specialty is hunting rodents in the tall grass, and it is often found near water. By Alan Briere/Superstock.*

African golden cat, Felis aurata. By Art Wolfe.

He could whip his weight in wildcats.

Proverb, coined by Eugene Field

This animal [the Scottish wildcat] may be called the British Tiger...

THOMAS PENNANT
Tour of Scotland and Voyage to the Hebrides

Asian golden cat, Felis temmincki. By Art Wolfe.

AFRICAN GOLDEN CAT
Felis aurata

Prized as a talisman by local people, the fur of the beautiful African golden cat displays the most varied coloration of any cat's coat, ranging from chestnut to reddish, from fawn to gray-brown or dark gray. It may be plain or spotted, either all over or in parts. All-black individuals have been documented. This species is about twice the size of domestic cat—sturdy and long-tailed, with a dark line running down the tail. Distributed through West and Central Africa, as well as some parts of Uganda and the Ivory Coast, this species lives in high mountain forests and other moist forest areas or along waterways in drier areas; it requires a well-watered habitat. Sometimes called "the leopard's brother," it frequents similar country as its larger relative. Little is known about the species' habits. It is thought to be solitary, hunting at dawn and dusk for prey that includes rodents, monkeys, duikers, and probably birds. It is also known to raid villages for domestic poultry. Females are thought to give birth to litters of only 1 or 2 kittens. Average size: head and body length 24-39 in., tail 6-14 in., weight 11-26 lbs.

ASIAN GOLDEN CAT
Felis temmincki
ALSO CALLED: Temminck's cat, Temminck's golden cat

Though found thousands of miles from the African golden cat's home, the Asian golden cat shares some of its cousin's traits. Variable coloration is one similarity; this cat's coat ranges from golden to dark brown to reddish or gray, and may be plain or spotted and striped. One subspecies, Fontanier's cat *(F. f.tristis)*, is especially heavily marked—for a time it was even thought to be a subspecies of the leopard cat (p. 35). The face is marked with white lines, and the tail has a white patch on the underside. Found throughout Southeast Asia, from Nepal east to Burma, China, Thailand, Malaysia, and Sumatra, it lives, like its African cousin, in forest habitats, including deciduous and tropical evergreen forests. In parts of China it is known as the *shilului,* or rock cat, because it frequents wooded areas interspersed with rocky outcrops. It is a good climber and sometimes captures birds in the trees. But it hunts mainly on the ground, taking prey such as hares, small deer, and lizards, as well as some domestic animals. Little is known about its habits in the wild. Females give birth to litters of 1 or 2 kittens after a 75-day gestation period. Average size: head and body length 19-23 in., tail 13-15 in., weight 26-33 lbs.

Marbled cat, Felis marmorata. By Art Wolfe.

MARBLED CAT
Felis marmorata

This lovely little cat has been described as a "miniature clouded leopard" (p. 34). Its coat is very similar—brownish gray to yellow or reddish brown, marked with large, irregular dark blotches, spots, and stripes. Significantly smaller, the marbled cat also has thicker, softer fur and a longer tail—in fact, the longest tail of any felid in proportion to its body. It is found in parts of India, Nepal, Burma, Thailand, Malaysia, Sumatra, and Borneo, in forested areas where it hunts in the trees for birds and squirrels. It also preys upon rodents and frogs on the ground. We know little about this mysterious cat, which is becoming increasingly rare within its range. It is thought to be solitary; nothing is known of its reproductive habits in the wild. Average size: head and body length 17-24 in., tail 13-21 in., weight 4-11 lbs.

FISHING CAT
Felis viverrina

Powerfully built and strong for its relatively small size, the fishing cat is a good swimmer; it will even dive to pursue prey in the water. This cat has a large, broad head, rather short legs, and a thick, short tail. Its short, coarse gray fur is marked by rows of elongated dark brown spots and lines running along the head and back. It uses its forefeet, with their partially webbed toes and slightly protruding claws, to scoop fish out of the water, and to grasp other favorite prey—birds, snakes, frogs, snails, and small mammals. These water-loving cats are found scattered throughout Asia, in southwest India, Sri Lanka, Bangladesh, Vietnam, Thailand, Burma, China, and Sumatra and Java. They require a wetland habitat: marshes, coastal creeks, or mangrove swamps. Little studied in the wild, they are believed to lead largely solitary lives. Kittens are born in litters of 2 or 3 after a 63-day gestation period; they are full-grown at about 8½ months. Average size: shoulder height 15 in., head and body length 32 in., tail 12 in., weight 25 lb.

JUNGLE CAT
Felis chaus

Its ancestors are portrayed in the art of ancient Egypt, and the modern jungle cat still prowls among the Egyptian reed beds, as well as through woodlands, swamps, and agricultural areas across the Middle East and southeast Asia to southwestern China and Indonesia. In Central Asia they tend to be larger (up to 36 lbs.) than their southern counterparts. This cat's ears are distinctive—tall and rounded, topped with tufts of black hair. Its coat shows wide variation in color, from sandy or yellowish gray to brown to reddish. The long legs may retain traces of the black stripes the species displays while a kitten. The jungle cat is solitary; it hunts mainly hares, as well as other small mammals, birds, reptiles, and fish. It can jump to a remarkable height, straight into the air, to capture birds. Females give birth to 1 to 4 kittens—sometimes in another animal's abandoned burrow—after a 63-day gestation period. The young can hunt on their own after about 6 months. Average size: head and body length 24 in., tail 9 in., weight 8-18 lbs.

Above: Jungle cat, Felis chaus. *By Erwin & Peggy Bauer. Left: Fishing cat,* Felis viverrina. *By Kenneth W. Fink/ Bruce Coleman, Inc.*

WILDCAT
African or desert wildcat   *Felis lybica*
European wildcat   *Felis sylvestris*

This broad group of wild cats, widely distributed over Europe, Asia, and Africa, bears many similarities to the domestic cat, which is thought to be descended from *Felis libyca*. The wildcat's appearance is as varied as its habitat range. Its coat may be more or less spotted and/or tabby-striped, varying among shades of gray and brown. In colder northern Europe, the coat tends to be long and thick, while that of the African and Asian cats is short and close. Once common over most of Europe and Britain, the European wildcat's distribution has narrowed. The African wildcat is found over most of Africa. A subspecies, the Indian desert cat (*F. s. ornata*) is found in parts of Central Asia. In Europe the wildcat lives in forest habitats; in Africa and Asia its habitats include open rocky areas and brush. Wildcats are solitary and territorial. Rodents form the bulk of their diet, but they will hunt birds, various small mammals, and even insects. Litters usually consist of 2 or 3 kittens, born after a 65-day gestation period. Average size: head and body length 19-29 in., tail 8-14 in., weight 6-17 lbs.

The desert wildcat, Felis lybica, *above, is generally smaller and more lightly furred than the European wildcat,* Felis sylvestris. *By Art Wolfe. Shown below is the Scottish subspecies,* F. s. grampia *, among the largest and darkest in color of the true wildcats. By Erwin & Peggy Bauer.*

Above: *Flat-headed cat,* Felis planiceps. *Right: Pallas'
cat,* Felis manul. *By Gary Milburn/Tom Stack
and Associates*

**I had a [rusty-spotted] kitten brought to
me when very young in 1846, and it became quite tame, and was the delight
and admiration of all who saw it. Its activity was quite marvellous and it was
very playful and elegant in its motions.**

T. C. JERDON
The Mammals of India

Below: *Rusty-spotted cat,* Felis rubiginosa.
Right: Sand cat, Felis margarita. *By
Alain Dragesco/Planet Earth Pictures.*

FLAT-HEADED CAT
Felis planiceps

This unusual-looking small cat takes its name from its
broad, flat head and long, sloping forehead. Its ears
are very small and set low on the head. The soft, thick
fur is reddish brown tinged with silver. Two distinctive
white stripes run up the sides of its nose to its forehead; the cat's underside is white with brown spots.
The teeth are all pointed—thought to be adapted
for fishing. This little feline is found in Thailand,
Malaysia, Indonesia, Sumatra, and Borneo; up to
2,300 feet in the mountains. It frequents river banks,
where it hunts for the frogs and fish that make up
most of its diet. Little is known about the species, as it
is nocturnal and secretive. Average size: head and body
length 16.25-19.75 in., tail 5-6 in., weight 3.5-4.5 lbs.

RUSTY-SPOTTED CAT
Felis rubiginosa

One of the world's smallest cats (about half the size
of a domestic cat), this species resembles a paler version of the leopard cat (page 35). Its coat ranges from
brownish-gray tinged with red to russet-colored and
is marked with rusty-brown elongated blotches and
spots. The subspecies *F. r. rubiginosa* inhabits open dry
grassland and scrub, mostly in southern India. *F. r.
phillipsi,* the more brightly colored Sri Lankan subspecies, lives in humid tropical rainforests. Next to
nothing is known about this tiny creature's habits
in the wild. It is thought to be solitary and nocturnal, and to spend time in trees, as it is an agile
climber. Its prey probably includes birds, small
mammals, reptiles, and frogs. Average size: head
and body length 13-19 in., tail 6-10 in., weight 2 lbs.

PALLAS' CAT
Felis manul

With longer, denser fur than that of any other wild
cat, this small cat is built for the cold. Its coat, ranging from grayish to reddish, is tipped with white on
each hair. Two dark stripes run across each cheek;
small, rounded ears are set very low on the sides of
the head. This fluffy fur provides warmth in the
harsh steppes and mountainsides of Central Asia. It
is found from the Caspian Sea and Iran to southeast-

ern Siberia and China, up
to 13,120 feet. Pallas' cat is an
adept climber, using their
short legs to scale nearly
vertical rock walls. It preys
on marmots, pikas, squirrels,
hares, and birds. A secretive creature, it is probably
solitary, but little is known
of its habits. Females give
birth to litters of 3 to 4 kit-
tens after a 66-day gestation. Average size: head and
body length 19-25 in.,tail 8-12 in., weight 5-8 lbs.

SAND CAT
Felis margarita

This cat is well-suited for life in the arid desert regions it inhabits. Its feet have dense fur covering the
pads, allowing the cat to walk over scorching-hot
sand. The powerful short legs dig a burrow in the
sand, into which it retreats during the day. The soft,
dense fur is a light sandy or gray color; reddish
streaks run across the cheeks. The very large ears
are set wide apart, low on the sides of the head.
Found in parts of the Sahara, through the Middle
East to Turkestan, it hunts by night for birds, small
mammals, hares, reptiles, and locusts. It gets its
moisture primarily from its prey. Almost nothing
is known about the habits of this rare creature.
Females give birth to litters of 2 to 4 kittens, after a
66-day gestation. Four subspecies are recognized.
Average size: head and body length 17-22 in., tail
11-13 in., weight 4-6.5 lbs.

BAY CAT
Felis badia
ALSO CALLED: Bornean red cat

One of the least-studied cats, the bay cat has been described as a miniature version of the Asian golden cat (page 40). Its coat is bright chestnut, with faint spots on the legs and underparts. The face is marked with white streaks, and the tail is white at the tip, marked with a black spot. Found only on the island of Borneo, this cat is thought to live

in dense forest and in rocky limestone areas at the jungle's edge. Nothing is known of its habits; it probably hunts small mammals, birds, and monkeys, and is said to feed on carrion as well. Average size: head and body length 19-23 in., tail 13-15 in.

BLACK-FOOTED CAT
Felis nigripes

This little creature is another of the smallest cats. Its name derives from the distinctive black on its underparts and foot pads. Its fur is dark to light yellowish brown, marked all over with black spots that may merge into bands. This tiny cat is found in southern

Africa—Botswana, Namibia, and South Africa—in dry, open areas where there is some scrubby brush or grass. It gets all its moisture from its prey—rodents and insects. They hunt at night; during the day they take cover in abandoned springhare burrows or termite mound holes. Solitary for the most part, they have a short mating season, after which females give birth to 2 kittens, following a long gestation period. There are two recognized subspecies. Average size: head and body length 14-18 in. tail 7-9 in., weight 3-5.5 lbs.

CHINESE DESERT CAT
Felis bieti

This little-studied cat has yellowish-gray fur, sometimes marked with brownish bands on the cheeks, haunches, and legs. The ear tips have short pencils of hair, and the tail is tipped black. The feet have pads of hair on the bottoms. The Chinese desert cat inhabits not the desert but steppes and forest areas in a very restricted part of north-central China and Mongolia. Nothing is known of these cats' habits in the wild. Average size: head and body length 26-33 in., tail 11-13 in.

IRIOMOTE CAT
Felis iriomotensis

This handsome small cat is found only on the island of Iriomote, Japan, where it inhabits wooded areas, mangrove forests, cultivated areas, and beaches. About the size of a housecat, it has a dark brown coat marked with rows of dark spots along its body. The bushy tail is striped; the backs of its ears have a white spot. Its low-slung build enables it to stalk through dense undergrowth. Solitary, but establishes a territory of .8-1.2 square miles which it prowls in search of prey. Its diet includes birds, rodents, bats, reptiles, crabs, and amphibians. Little is known about its reproductive habits. Identified only in 1967, the Iriomote cat has dwindled to fewer than 100 individuals; it is now protected. Average size: head and body length 19.75-23.5 in., tail 8-11.75 in., weight 6.5-10 lbs.

Above: Chinese desert cat, Felis bieti.
Left: Bay cat, Felis badia.

A most interesting but locally rather rare small wild feline is the Sebulabulakwana or black-footed cat. This is the smallest of the African wild cats; but what it lacks in size is fully compensated for by its extreme ferocity. Though its weight is only about a quarter of that of a small sheep, this little feline readily attacks those animals.

E. CRONJE WILMOT
Always Tread Lightly

Below: Iriomote cat, Felis iriomotensis.
Left: Black-footed cat, Felis nigripes.
By Art Wolfe.

PAMPAS CAT
Felis colocolo

With its broad face and pointed ears, the pampas cat closely resembles the European wildcat (page 41). Its coat, usually silvery gray, may have reddish brown stripes—more pronounced on the legs—or many red-gray spots, or any number of variations on these patterns. The long fur may form a mane running along the back; this may stand erect when the cat is frightened. This small South American cat inhabits open grasslands in Argentina; elsewhere in its range it favors humid forests and relatively high altitudes. It is terrestrial and nocturnal, preying on rodents and ground-nesting birds. Little is known of its reproductive habits. Average size: head and body length 23-27 in., tail 11 in., weight 7-14 lbs.

GEOFFROY'S CAT
Felis geoffroyi

This little cat was once thought to be related to the kodkod but is now considered a separate species. Geoffroy's cat is small and lightly built, with a coat that may vary widely in color (brilliant ochre to silvery gray) and pattern (more or less distinctly spotted). It lives in a variety of habitats, including open bush and scrubby woodland, through parts of the Bolivian Andes, Argentina, Uruguay, Paraguay, Brazil and Chile. It is solitary and hunts mostly at night, when it preys upon rodents and other small mammals as well as birds, which it can climb to capture. Four recognized subspecies include: *Felis geoffroyi geoffroyi, F. g. salinarum, F. g. paraguae,* and *F. g. euxantha.* Average size: head and body length 17-25 in., tail 9-14 in., weight 4-13 lbs.

ANDEAN MOUNTAIN CAT
Felis jacobita

This cat has long, soft fur that is silvery-gray and marked with dark brown stripes and spots; its long, bushy tail has 7 dark rings. It is found at high elevations—from 9,480 feet up to 16,730 feet—in cold, rocky areas above timberline. Its restricted range includes parts of the high Andes in Peru, Bolivia, Chile, and Argentina. Rare and little-studied, it is thought to

prey upon small mammals, lizards, and birds. Nothing is known of its reproductive habits. Average size: head and body length 22-25 in., tail 16-19 in., weight 8.75 lbs.

KODKOD
Felis guigna

Smallest of the New World cats, the kodkod is about the size of a small domestic cat. Its gray-brown to buff coat is marked with round black spots which sometimes form streaks on the shoulders; the tail is ringed with black. All-black individuals are common. Found in restricted areas of Chile and Argentina, the kodkod frequents both forests and relatively open countryside. Little is known about this creature; it is rare in the wild. Two subspecies—the brightly colored *F. g. guigna* and the larger, paler *F. g. tigrillo*—are known. The kodkod is thought to prey on small mammals and birds. Average size: head and body length 15-20 in., tail 7-9.7 in., weight 4.5-5.5 lbs.

Above: Pampas cat, Felis colocolo. By Art Wolfe.
Right: Andean mountain cat, Felis jacobita. By Gunther Ziesler/Peter Arnold, Inc.

Below: Geoffroy's cat, Felis geoffroyi. By Art Wolfe.
Right: Kodkod, Felis guigna.

DOMESTIC CAT
Felis catus

Generally acknowledged to have been domesticated first in ancient Egypt, today's domestic cat is thought to be descended from the African wildcat (page 41). Many experts also argue that the European wildcat shares its heritage—these wild species can breed with *Felis catus*. The Asian breeds—Siamese, Burmese, and others—probably were developed from a subspecies of the African wildcat, the Indian desert cat (*Felis lybica ornata*). The domestic cat shares with its wild relatives general body features—keen vision and hearing, sharp canine teeth, retractable claws, flexible body, and padded feet—as well as the instincts of a predator.

Within the last century, about 30 breeds of domestic cats have been introduced worldwide. These fall roughly into two main categories: longhair and shorthair. Within these categories occur a wide variety of coat colors (red, brown, black, gray, white, or a combination), and patterns (including the stripes and bars of the tabby cat's coat, and the patches of red, cream and black on the calico). Eye color also varies from blue to yellow or gold to orange to hazel. Two breeds—the Manx and Cymrix—are tailless; one, the Scottish Fold, is in appearance nearly earless.

Domestic cats are found in every part of the world, living either with humans or as feral cats. Both tame and feral cats hunt almost any small animal, including rodents, birds, and reptiles. Female feral cats may be solitary or form small groups with other females. Males generally lead a more solitary existence. Females may be in estrus 3 or 4 times annually; after a 9-week gestation period they may give birth to litters of 3 to at most 6 kittens. The kittens are weaned after about 4 weeks.

Average size: head and body length 15-13 in., tail 9-13 in., weight 6-9 lbs.

Above: Domestic cat, Felis catus. *By Nicholas Devore III/ Photographers Aspen. Below:* L'hiver: chat sur un coussin, *1909. Color lithograph by Théophile Steinlen. British Museum.*

The Embodied Cat

The skulls of a tiger and a bobcat are shown side by side. There is relatively little variation in skull shape throughout the cat family, because hunting and feeding styles vary little among species. Compared to other carnivores, cats have fairly short skulls, large eye openings, and a reduced number of teeth, which are specialized in function. The long, strong canines have sensitive tips that apparently probe between the vertebrae of prey to locate a fatal bite.

Looking at cats, we respond instinctively to qualities that we find beautiful: the cat's round, glowing eyes in its short-muzzled face; its compact, well-proportioned frame; the smooth, richly colored pelt sliding over muscles as it walks or leaps with consummate grace. That cats please the human eye is a happy accident, however. How they look and move has little to do with our sense of aesthetics and everything to do with their ability to survive and thrive as predators.

To begin with, cats are immensely strong relative to their size, whether the size of a Siberian tiger or a housecat. Anyone who has seen a leopard haul an antelope thirty feet up a tree, or struggled to bathe or medicate an unwilling pet cat can attest to this, and studies prove it. Cats have more than 500 voluntary muscles and great density of muscle mass, accounting in part for their ability to leap long, grip hard, deal potent blows, and drag heavy weights.

Their bones, on the other hand, are proportionately light, contributing to their agility and speed. The basic feline frame is remarkably similar in all species. Its notable features include a highly flexible spine, which helps cats cover ground and enhances the potential power of shoulder and neck muscles, and a "digitigrade" stance. Cats are literally light on their feet, standing mainly on the toes, so they can move silently and leave few tracks. This stance also effectively lengthens the limbs for a longer stride. Leg length varies considerably: cats that are mainly arboreal have shorter limbs, while the coursing cheetah, which runs down its prey, has the longest in proportion to its body.

Those superb muscles and strong bones are coordinated by an exquisitely calibrated nervous system, whose reflexes are among the fastest in the animal world. Most cats can seize an object out of the air faster than our eyes can follow. Minutes of nearly perfect stillness can be followed instantaneously by a full-speed rush or a well-judged leap. In motion or in repose, few animals convey grace and physical assurance as completely as cats do.

Because cats are almost exclusively meat-eaters, their digestive systems are simpler than those of other carnivores (all of which are simpler than those needed by plant eaters). Their reproductive systems are much like other carnivore's: the male's penis has a small bone and backward-facing spines that may help sustain the mating tie. Females have up to six pairs of mammary glands, and are "induced ovulators"—they do not ovulate until after mating has occured.

The cat's crowning glory—and often its fatal liability—is its elegantly furred skin, protection from the teeth and claws of competitors and prey, and from unfriendly elements. The skin with its glands helps regulate body temperature and forms an interface with the world and other animals. Since most cats don't bathe in water, they groom this coat most efficiently with a tongue covered in spiny papillae. The cat's killing equipment—its teeth, jaws and claws—are discussed in "The Way of the Hunter." 🐾

HOW THE CHEETAH GOT HIS SPEED

Once upon a time the Creator decided to find out which of His animals could run the fastest—and so He entered the cheetah in a race with the tsessebe, which is the swiftest of all the antelopes. The cheetah had soft paws then, and he realized that they were not suited for real speed. So he borrowed a set of paws from an obliging wild dog.

The race started from a high baobab tree. The Creator Himself was in charge, and the two contestants were told to run right across the plains to a hill on the far side. The animals lined up, and then—go! They leapt away.

The tsessebe soon took the lead, and by halfway, he was so far ahead he seemed sure to win. But suddenly—disaster! Tsessebe stumbled on a stone and crashed to the ground; he had broken his leg.

The good-natured cheetah, instead of running past and winning the race, stopped to help his opponent.

The Creator, seeing this, was so pleased by the cheetah's unselfish act that He bestowed upon the cheetah a gift; He made him the fastest animal in the land; and what's more, allowed him to keep the paws of the wild dog.

Bushman Tale

There are certain things in Nature in which beauty and utility, artistic and technical perfection, combine in some incomprehensible way, the web of a spider, the wing of a dragon-fly, the superbly streamlined body of the porpoise, and the movements of a cat.

KONRAD LORENZ

The lightly built cheetah (Acinonyx jubatus) is perfectly designed to be the fastest land animal known. Very long legs, an ultra-flexible spine, and mobile shoulder blades give its stride both length and quickness. The pads of its feet are harder than those of most cats and slightly ridged for traction; the strong claws dig in to aid acceleration. By Stan Osolinski/FPG.

Coats of Many Colors

As seen in this leopard pair, individuals of the same species can vary considerably in coat color and pattern. Field biologists studying leopards and jaguars can positively identify their subject cats by the spot patterns on their faces. By Anup Shah/ABPL.

Why wild cats are colored and patterned in certain ways seems fairly straightforward at first glance. Concealment is vital to the hunting strategy of most cats, so camouflage is the general rule. Lions are the solid tawny shade of the (usually) dry grasslands where they live and hunt; even when the grass is green, its tonal intensity is similar to the lion's, so other animals may not perceive a difference. The leopard's coat (and that of other tropical spotted cats) mimics the sun-dappled shadows of the deep forest. The tiger's stripes blend well with both the sparse shrubbery of open woodlands and the reedy banks of rivers—their favored hunting grounds.

The tabby markings of small Old World wildcats also evolved for a woodland environment, and remained even after some forested places (like northern Africa) became deserts. Cats of northern climes—snow leopards and lynxes—have grayish tones in their fur, helping them

move unseen through changing seasons and habitats that feature rock and snow. And the phenomenon of melanism—the occasional nearly black leopard, jaguar, or smaller cat—is seen most often in the tropics, where it may work to the cat's advantage.

But there are interesting exceptions to this commonsense order of coloration. The spotted cheetah hunts on the same golden savannahs as lions do, but with its great speed is less dependent on staying hidden. Did cheetahs perhaps originate in more forested climes? Pumas are born spotted and grow up tawny, but they inhabit so many different environments that any single color scheme might be irrelevant. (Some suggest they are colored to match their favorite prey, deer.) The prominent mane of male lions—especially when black—makes them much more visible. In the lion's social system, however, this potent advertisement of a male's size and condition has taken precedence over camouflage, and the king of beasts lets his harem do most of the hunting.

Some details of cat coloration don't relate to camouflage but to caring for the young: the bright white spot on the leopard's tail makes a flag for cubs to follow through dense vegetation, and the bobcat's black-marked ears can flash a clear warning to her kits. 🐾

A melanistic (black-phase) leopard. By Andy Rouse/DRK Photo.

HOW THE LEOPARD GOT ITS SPOTS

In this African tale, a tortoise appeals to a hyena for help shaking fruit from a tree, but the mean hyena sticks the tortoise high in the tree instead. Help comes unexpectedly from a leopard.

Afraid to move, clinging to the branch, the tortoise stayed up there for hours, while the sun slowly dipped over to the west, lengthening the shadow of the tree. Every time he looked down at the ground far below, he felt dizzy and terrified, but he had to keep his eyes open for he knew that help wouldn't come from the skies. At last, with darkness falling and despair growing, the tortoise saw a leopard padding past the tree and cried for help. The leopard leaped gracefully into the tree and brought the frightened tortoise back to the ground. At his request the leopard shook the branches so that the fruit fell to the ground for the tortoise to eat.

A young leopard investigates a tortoise. By Jonathan Scott/Planet Earth Pictures.

The leopard didn't wait to be thanked and was gliding into the gathering darkness when the tortoise called him back. "Leopard, listen to me before you go. You have been very good to me, and I would like to do something for you in return. If you let me paint black spots all over your tawny coat, you will be admired throughout the jungle. Come in the morning when the sun gives us light."

The leopard's dull coat was completely transformed by the black spots that the tortoise painted in with care and artistic skill. And just as the artist had predicted, when the leopard swaggered through the jungle he was followed by the admiring glances of the other animals.

Retold by FORBES STUART
The Magic Horns: Folk Tales from Africa

Above: The rosettes on the jaguar's coat (bottom) are usually larger and farther apart than those of the leopard (top), and often enclose one or more smaller spots, which the leopard's do not. Right: A cheetah cub with its distinctive mantle. By Alan & Sandy Carey.

BLACK CATS

The so-called "black panther" does not exist. Cats thus named may be either a leopard or (less often) a jaguar, with melanistic pigmentation. This author disposes of another "black cat" myth.

A number of writers, of both fact and fiction, have kept alive the tradition that the melanistic or black Leopard is more savage or potentially ferocious than the normally coloured creature. This is patent rubbish, and is nothing more than the human mind creating comfortably remote bogies for itself, associated with the supposedly sinister colour of black. It has been put that a black Leopard finds its colouring to be a disadvantage, and that this makes it bolder and less reliant on colouring to enable it to steal away from disturbance. In the first place it is very doubtful if the black specimen knows that it is black, and if it finds its stalks are being detected, it will simply do as any other Leopard would, and take more care over them.

PETER TURNBULL-KEMP
The Leopard

HALO OF FUR

Unlike their mother [the cheetah cub's] fur was almost black with faint dark spots, and a mantle of silky blue-gray hair covered them from crown to rump. When the sun touched this mantle, it radiated like a silver halo, turning the cub into a shining ikon of exquisite beauty. No other cat has such a distinctive natal coat. For years I have pondered about the possible selective advantage that such a coat may have, but I remain perplexed. It makes the cubs conspicuous and hence vulnerable to predation. Someone suggested that the coat resembles that of the ratel, or honey badger, and this is true. The ratel is strong and short-tempered—one attacked the tires of my car when I halted near it—and predators would supposedly shy away from such an irascible beast. When the cubs are hidden in a thicket, the coat would seem to be of little advantage, and, afterwards, when they follow their mother, no predator would be fooled. And by the age of three months, the mantle begins to fall out. Perhaps the prominent light and dark pattern helps a mother to keep her cubs in view when they are still small and slow on their feet.

GEORGE SCHALLER
Golden Shadows, Flying Hooves

Deux léopards du Pérou, watercolor by Antoine-Louis Barye (1796–1875). The French painter made the common error of confusing jaguars with leopards.

Mighty Sun,
You who made woman,
You who made man,
You who made all the animals—

We remember how you painted Jaguar—
Dipping your hands into coal,
You painted the spots on his coat;
But Jaguar, in a hurry as always,
Dashed away to show off his coat
   in the forest,
And so the spots became blurred.

We remember how you painted Puma—
Seeing Jaguar, Puma came to you and said,
"Paint me, too, so I might be as
   handsome as Jaguar."
You took two red stones, ground them
   together,
And with the dust, you painted Puma.
"More colors," said Puma, "more colors."
But you told him this was to be his
   color forevermore....

Retold by MICHAEL ROSEN

He's a winsome creature
   most wondrous fair,
Of varied hues. As holy men tell
How Joseph's coat was coloured
   with dyes
Of every shading,
   each shining more fair,
More excellent than the others
   to the eyes of men,
So the coat of this beast
   is wondrous bright,
Glowing in beauty and
   gleaming with hues
Each than the others more rich
   and more rare...

Anglo-Saxon poet,
Cynewulf school, 8th century

A magnificent mane adorns this male lion, photographed in Serengeti National Park, Tanzania. By Joseph Van Os/ Image Bank.

THE MANE IDEA

[The male lion's] mane seems to be an important asset. As a sexual characteristic, it functions in two ways: as a signal to females the lion is courting and as a warning to rival males who try to invade his territory. When a male courts a female, he literally struts sideways in front of her, giving her the best view of his hair style. The very distinct outline of a maned lion enables other lions to distinguish males from females at a great distance and thus to avoid unwanted encounters. If males should fight, the mane helps to protect them from scratches and bites.

However, one disadvantage of having a mane is its conspicuousness; as Schaller pointed out, males look like haystacks moving through the grass. A male trying to stalk prey is much more likely to be detected than the sleek, golden female. When the females set off to hunt, the males usually follow behind along with the younger cubs, and in this way, whether consciously or not, the males protect the cubs from other predators. One can only assume that the advantages of the mane to the male patrolling the territory, for example, far outweigh any disadvantage, or else the lion's mane would have disappeared long ago in the course of natural selection.

CYNTHIA MOSS
Portraits in the Wild

The Sensing Cat

The leopard's extraordinarily long tail may help the cat with balance in pursuit on the ground, and when climbing. By Telegraph Colour Library/FPG.

CAT TAILS

Experts disagree on exactly what functions are served by the feline tail, since several species do fine without one. It may aid balance when a cat is running fast, and the fact that many cat tails have contrasting color on the underside or tip suggests another purpose.

On one of the tributaries of the Seronera, we one morning came upon a big, golden brown male walking parallel to the bank without paying the slightest attention to our car. From time to time he sat down to scratch his chin with a hind paw. He had a beautiful tail, which he carried curved upward in the way leopards always do, and when he was walking through scrub, he lifted it so high that we could follow his march simply by watching the white spot on the underside of the tip gliding along above the bushes. We thus had an excellent demonstration of what a useful guiding star this white spot must be for any leopard—young or adult—following another.

CHARLES A. W. GUGGISBERG
Wild Cats of the World

The sensory responses of wild mammals are generally more finely honed than those of humans or domestic animals. Those of the cats are especially well developed for locating prey; for silent stalking and quick, accurate attacks; for concealing themselves and their kills from competitors; and for communicating with others of their kind.

Cats are most dependent on sight to identify potential prey, evaluate its distance and condition, and calculate pursuit and capture. Their large eyes, set frontally for accurate binocular vision, have pupils that can adjust for an exceptional range of available light. The stimulus provided by the sight of prey—especially when it moves—is primary in motivating cats, more so than smell or hearing. The strong response of housecats to birds on the other side of a window and to "cat videos" demonstrates this; as does one account of a tame puma leaping at a deer in a museum diorama.

Cats have less acute hearing than dogs, although their ability to recognize sounds is excellent. This helps them judge the size, nature and nearness of prey or danger. Part of the intricate structure of their inner ear is responsible for the cats' legendary sense of balance and body orientation. Smell likewise plays a lesser role in hunting than with the canines—big cats have been known to hunt from upwind of their prey, for example—but a major role in communication. Cats rub against other cats and objects to release scent from glands on their faces in a gesture of possession and bonding. Wild cats scent-mark territorial boundaries, while domestic cats on first meeting each other try to sniff the other's anus, the more dominant animal usually succeeding.

As with most mammals, the taste organs reside mainly in the tongue papillae. Little more is scientifically known about how and what cats actually taste—as long as it's flesh, wild cats seem to relish it. A sixth sense, related to both smell and taste, is the more subtle ability to detect minute amounts of airborne chemicals with a "vomeronasal" organ in the mouth palate. When exercising this sense, they pull back the lips and open the mouth slightly; it's called "doing flehmen" and is how cats detect a female in estrus, for example.

The tactile sense is extremely important. A cat's entire skin and coat is a finely nerved organ for receiving external stimuli, and the face area is particularly sensitive, with the whiskers (vibrissae), the fine hairs in the ears, and even the teeth coming into play. Cats aim their whiskers forward to help detect and "read" whatever is up close, or seems dangerous, and lay them back at rest when feeling secure. The whiskers also come forward to enfold prey the cat is carrying—possibly to evaluate it for remaining signs of life.

Not uncommonly, cats are credited with a distinct homing sense, possibly a neurochemical response to the sun's seasonal angle in their native geographic location. Both this, and the psychic powers sometimes ascribed to them, await further investigation. 🐾

…I stepped closer and put my face within six inches of the lion's. He promptly spat on me. I had to steel my nerve to keep so close. But I wanted to see a wild lion's eyes at close range. They were exquisitely beautiful, their physical properties as wonderful as their expression. Great half globes of tawny amber, streaked with delicate wavy lines of black, surrounding pupils of intense purple fire. Pictures shone and faded in the amber light—the shaggy tipped plateau, the dark pines and smoky canyons, the great dotted downward slopes, the yellow cliffs and crags. Deep in those live pupils, changing, quickening with a thousand vibrations, quivered the soul of this savage beast, the wildest of all wild nature…

ZANE GREY
Roping Lions in the Grand Canyon

REFLECTIONS

A cat's primary sense is sight, and it has very efficient eyes designed to facilitate the work and survival of a night hunter. First, its eyes are large when compared with the size of its head. If our eyes were as large in comparison to our heads, we would have something midway between a softball and a bowling ball looming over each cheek. That is unpleasant to contemplate, but the cat, because its eyes look forward, has somewhat the look of a baby primate and we find that appealing. The cat's eyes are mysterious to us. More has been written about them than about the eyes of any other animal. When was the last time you heard of a semi-precious mineral named for a rhinoceros's eye or a poem written about the orbs of a wombat? We have looked back at cats, into their eyes, and we have wondered about secrets and other special things.

ROGER A. CARAS
A Cat Is Watching

WILDCAT EYES

The eyes are distinctively large, with yellow-gold irises which seem to grow paler with age, and no British animal's eyes are so expressive of mood— from rage and ferocity to peaceful relaxation and pleasure when basking in the sun. I noticed wildcats' pupils stay rounder longer than those of domestic cats in similar light conditions. They also expand to full roundness in bright daylight when they sense danger, are afraid or are hunting. This tendency to greater roundness may link wildcats more closely than domestics with the big "cats" like lions and tigers whose pupils do not contract to vertical slits.

MIKE TOMKIES
My Wilderness Wildcats

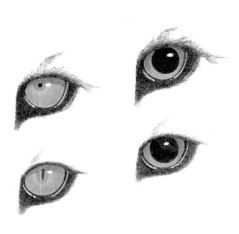

Above: Smaller cats typically have vertical slit pupils, which can exclude more light than the round pupils of most big cats, possibly reflecting the small cats' greater need to hunt at night. Both pupil shapes can enlarge dramatically in low light. Top left: The eyes of a male puma in Belize. By Frans Lanting/Minden Pictures.

...her eyes were her most extraordinary feature. Pale, with a frosty glitter softened only by a tinge of amber, they were the eyes of a creature used to immense solitudes and snowy wastes.

GEORGE SCHALLER
National Geographic

Top: This snow leopard's eyes show some of the "night-shine" effect shared by all cats and most other carnivores. It is produced by a specialized layer of reflective cells called the tapetum lucidum, *which enhances the eye's response to light by reflecting light back through the sensory rods and cones a second time. This allows cats to function well in nearly complete (to us) darkness. By Erwin & Peggy Bauer. Above: Head of a serval, by Todd Sherman. The serval's oversized ears can detect the slightest rustlings by a rodent in the tall grass where it hunts.*

To watch an alert leopard is to realise that not only the sight is in constant play, but also the hearing. One gains the impression that every sound is carefully sifted. The chattering alarm-calls of the minor inhabitants of the forest, jungle or bush are each noted; but additionally there is the feeling that the most insignificant trifles of sounds are being registered and analysed. In sound range the hearing of a normal human is confined to frequencies of 15 cycles per second to 20,000 cycles per second. The hearing of a leopard ranges from about the same low limit to approximately 45,000 cycles per second. An additional feature of such fine hearing is the ability of the leopard to detect the precise origin of a sound.

PETER TURNBULL-KEMP
The Leopard

I have sometimes seen it stated that lions have no power of scent and hunt entirely by sight. I am sure nothing could be farther from the truth. Putting aside the fact that, for instance, in parts of the Kruger Park, visibility is limited to a few paces, and that a lion, like all other wild animals, except the primates, is unable to distinguish a perfectly stationary object even at a comparatively short distance, I have again and again seen them testing the wind and following up a tainted breeze, while less experienced ones always get to the leeward of a strange object, such as a motor car, and sniff the scent quite audibly. I have seen a single lion who thought itself unobserved, working out a spoor methodically like a hound.

J. STEVENSON-HAMILTON
"Lion and Leopard"

KEEPING IN TOUCH

The most complex part of a cat's pelt are the greatly enlarged, enormously stiffened hairs we call whiskers. Vibrissae is their proper name, and they grow on the upper lip, to some extent over the eyes, far back on the cheeks, and even on the backs of the forelegs. The odd placement of the leg vibrissae probably has something to do with the fact that cats frequently hug or grasp their prey....

The whiskers on the upper lip are arranged in four rows that extend well beyond the width of a cat's head. They can be fanned out on command and are verifiers, particularly when light is low. They supplement sight. They judge which openings a cat's body will clear, they feel around for food that is too close for the eyes or nose to focus on....

The whiskers or vibrissae are at least twice as thick as ordinary cat hairs and are imbedded at least three times as deeply in the skin. At their bulbous ends deep down inside the dermal layers, there are masses of nerve endings that can receive and transmit information about touch and even information about changes in air pressure, which is touch in the final analysis. There are, on the average in a normally configured cat, twenty-four whiskers. The top two rows can move independently of the bottom two. Apparently rows two and three are the most sensitive and useful rows of all.

ROGER A. CARAS
A Cat Is Watching

The entire face of this caracal has great tactile sensitivity. Its long whiskers transmit detailed information about its physical environment and other animals within touching range (especially prey). The hairs inside its ears help to channel sound and analyze air currents. Its distinctive black ear tips function more as a signaling device, emphasizing any aggressive or defensive gesture of the ears. By Erwin & Peggy Bauer.

Tigers do not live in flocks.
HINDU PROVERB

How cats live in the wild remains largely mysterious to human observers, even in our age of field studies, radiotelemetry, and wildlife preserves. The lives and purposes of domestic cats, our companions for thousands of years, are sometimes only slightly less mysterious. Cats, with their talent for moving silently and disappearing at will, have not made it easy for us to know them, but we have begun to fill in some details. ❧ The solitariness of cats is celebrated in lore and literature, but "the cat that walked by himself" is only part of the story. While most cats don't live lives as obviously group-centered as those of wolves, say, feline society can take many forms. Lions, in their matriarchal prides, have the most communal lifestyle of all felines, but it appears that even the famously solitary leopard main-

Feline Families

tains contact with other, related leopards. And anyone who has shared a home with multiple housecats has surely witnessed some of their social interactions. ❧ The essential unit of cat society is the female with young. Mother cats attend to their young with great diligence and for a long time. When they are too young to travel, she confines her hunting to the region of their den. If she feels they are threatened, she may move the den site, sometimes many times. She defends them ferociously against other creatures (if she is nearby), and demonstrates by example how to survive. If she is a lion, she may spend the rest of her life with her female offspring; male lions and the young of other species leave home but often establish ranges nearby. ❧ Male cats, whose main jobs are reproduction and protection, live alone for more of their lives. Even so, they remain in touch with other cats through complex systems of vocal, visual and scent-based communication, especially along the territorial boundaries they vigilantly maintain. They also join together in small bands to get through hard times, or when trying to carve out new territories. ❧ So if we don't relate to feline families as easily as we perceive kinship with a wolf pack, we can at least begin to appreciate them on their own terms. ⚹

THE BOBCAT NURSERY

The sun struck the western face of the cliff and warmed the rocks. The female bobcat moved to the entrance of her den and basked in its radiation. Her two kittens burrowed under her body. Their eyes, blue slits, admitted a blurry vision of the world now. The babies were developing rapidly. In two weeks' time their weight had doubled, and on this day their ear canals were opening; pulses of sound were registering in their brains. Until now the kittens had lived exclusively in a world of scent.

Their blindness and deafness had not, however, prevented the young kittens from exploring their surroundings. Their noses were exquisitely sensitive, and they navigated about their nest by following their own bodies' scent trails. Had they been removed from their den, deprived of their own odor traces, and placed in fresh surroundings, the babies' disorientation would have become obvious, their distress audible. Only amid familiar smells could they negotiate space and feel safe.

Two ducts situated in their upper gums and leading to a special sensor, the Jacobson's organ, enhanced the bobcats' ability to "read" with their noses, enabled them to plot routes across the stony floor. This nose adjunct even permitted them to locate a preferred nipple on their mother's body. So discriminating was their sense of smell, the babies would return to the same teats each time they nursed.

But today the kittens' world was opening wider. Light bombarded their eyes and sound vibrated in their unfolding ears. Distressed by so many new sensations, they wriggled under their mother's protective body and began kneading her scratched belly with their tiny forepaws. Milk, familiar milk, comforted them.

Although nursing could be accomplished quickly, the female bobcat spent much time tending her two kittens. She groomed them with care. With her rough tongue, coated with minute, hook-shaped papillae, she rasped away dust and debris that clung

Alert bobcat (Lynx rufus) *in a tree, southern Montana. Once common throughout North America, bobcats now are found mostly west of the Mississippi. By R. E. Barber.*

to their spotted coats. She attended to their bodily functions, licking their anal regions until the kittens defecated. Then she consumed the waste. In so doing, she kept her home free of flies and odors which otherwise might attract the attention of an enemy.

As for her own waste, that material she put to another use. Since moving to the cliff den, the female had not buried her stools, but repeatedly defecated on one or another of three conspicuous rocks. Eventually, these piles of scat became visible features along the cliff rim, like stones stacked by a surveyor. And like a surveyor's markers, her scat piles notified others of her claim, discouraging them from settling in the same area. Thus, inadvertently, the female reserved for her own use what cottontails bred in the immediate vicinity. While her kittens were young, it was important that she be able to hunt close to home.

In the days immediately following the traumatic birth of her litter, the mother cat had felt no impulse to hunt. The three placentas she had consumed had answered her nutritional needs. When the kittens were four days old, however, she suddenly experienced an urge to stalk prey, and she left her babies, ascended to the top of the cliff, and ambushed a young rabbit.

Uncharacteristically, she ate the kill where she felled it. Normally, she would have dragged the cottontail to some less conspicuous feeding site, but on this occasion, her impatience to return to her young did not permit her to indulge her passion for privacy. Nevertheless, after dining, she did take time to clean her forefeet and scrub her face thoroughly with a wet paw. Her fastidious nature was uncompromising, a behavioral trait that no doubt served the species by protecting her kittens and herself from bacterial infection.

The hunting foray could be counted a success inasmuch as the nourishment she obtained far exceeded what calories she had to expend to catch the rabbit. Her survival always depended on just such a cost-benefit balance. Especially now that nursing kittens were sapping her body's reserves, she could ill afford hunting failure. When she returned to the den, her kittens smelled traces of rabbit on her breath and registered the impression. But, as yet,

the infant carnivores had no appetite for flesh, no inkling of their top-of-the-food-chain destiny. Only their mother's milk, now flowing copiously, excited them, and, like every infant mammal, they found their way to her full teats with amazing ease....

Not only did her young evoke [the bobcat's] profoundest interest, they aroused in her states which, when observed in human beings, are ordinarily described as affectionate or protective, even altruistic. The mother cat met any perceived threat to her offspring with selfless combativeness, the intensity of which far exceeded what her slight stature suggested possible. The proverbial "mother tiger," it would appear, could come in any size, and the female bobcat was a twenty-pound mother tiger.

HOPE RYDEN
Bobcat Year

The distinguished naturalist and author Hope Ryden studied bobcats in the wild and in captivity for several years. In Bobcat Year, *she "fictionalizes" this experience and knowledge into the enthralling tale of several bobcats in the western United States, following their fates and interactions from birth to death.*

Above: Young lynx kittens (Lynx canadensis) begin to explore their environment. By D. Robert Franz/The Wildlife Collection. Page 56: A mother lynx and her young, nose to nose, southern Montana. Facial contact is an important means of communication among cats. By R. E. Barber.

Considering the affection that cats in groups show for one another, one might almost consider it the tragedy of the cat family that whether they want to or not, most young cats sooner or later move away from their group.

ELIZABETH MARSHALL THOMAS
The Tribe of Tiger

The Social Spectrum

*Below: Lions in a pride engaging in rough play, Serengeti
National Park, Tanzania. This lioness is probably reacting
aggressively to a younger male, and her cub joins in. By
Konrad Wothe/Image Bank. Facing page: A pride rests
under a tree in southern Africa. By Gerald Hinde/ABPL.*

Cats can be highly social or solitary in their habits. Where on this spectrum a cat falls depends on its age (the young are communal by necessity), its species, gender, prey needs, and habitat resources. Many animals live in groups for protection from predators, or, as with pack hunters, to catch prey more efficiently. But except for lions, which favor large, strong prey like zebras, most cats hunt just as successfully on their own. So they must find other reasons to come together.

Economic needs—that is, food—dictate that only so many cats of any kind can live and hunt in the same place. Large cats need larger places to provide them with enough food, especially in areas where the game has been thinned by human influence. A cougar, for example, might roam its range for days without seeing another of its kind—yet it knows they are around, by evidence of scent and past experience. Indeed it depends on their presence, as potential mates if the opposite sex, and perhaps for some kind of emotional reassurance that we do not comprehend but that doesn't require physical proximity. The cougar's range may also support a few bobcats and a handful of feral housecats, living on different kinds of prey. The same holds true in other places where large and smaller cat species share habitats. Small cats cover somewhat less ground, so although their ranges are smaller, they may meet no more often than large cats.

Male and female roles also determine cat sociability. Females typically have smaller ranges and tend to stay in one place (knowing the ground is important in protecting their young). Their ranges may lie adjacent to those of a related female—a mother, sister or aunt. The dominant male of the neighborhood may have a territory that encompasses those of several females.

Lions are the only big cats that live in groups, relying on cooperation as well as strength and stealth to kill prey—ideally, a large enough meal for several lions. Males and females live together, and females share in caring for cubs. The lions' system can be seen as a compressed version of how other cats live: the related females together instead of spread out, males winning and losing their thrones on a regular basis.

Male lions temporarily without a pride often team up in pairs or small bands, as do male cheetahs. Tigers are usually lone hunters, but may meet amicably over kills and at other times. The most solitary of the great cats is probably the jaguar. 🐾

THE MALE LION'S ROLE

With time, as I began to better understand lions, the males provided me with some of the finest moments of revelation.

When a pride sets off on a hunt, the lionesses walking tensely in front, the cubs bounding playfully in the middle, and the males in the rear, their heavy heads nodding with each step as if they are bored with the whole matter, it is easy to castigate them for slothfulness. But males are bulky and adorned with such a voluminous mane that they look like wandering haystacks, in contrast to the sleek, lithe lionesses. In a business which for success places a premium on being cryptic, agile, and fast, it is of advantage to the pride that males remain mainly spectators. In addition, by bringing up the rear the males act as inadvertent guards for the cubs, which when small are vulnerable to marauding hyenas and other dangers. This is not to imply that males are incapable of hunting well: they can support themselves and indeed must do so when as nomads they may have no lionesses handy to provide them with a meal.

Frequently the cubs do not go with the pride during a hunt but stay patiently somewhere waiting for their mother to return and lead them to a kill. They may have a long wait. If the kill is small, the mother usually eats it up; if it is large she first gorges herself and then thinks of her cubs. By the time she has walked perhaps a mile or more to retrieve her offspring little or no meat may be left for them. Here the males come to the rescue. As I described earlier, males may drive the lionesses off and appropriate the remnants of a kill. Lionesses are not allowed back to the carcass, although one may try to inch closer on her belly in hopes of snatching a bite, behavior which the male discourages with heavy clouts. But small cubs are permitted to eat. The male's actions, no matter what their basis, are of subtle evolutionary benefit to the pride. At first, I had reproved males for their selfishness, and it was with total pleasure that I discarded that opinion and accepted a new truth.

GEORGE SCHALLER

Golden Shadows, Flying Hooves

Tigers live an intense social life, but at one remove, like hermits who spend their lives on the telephone. They know all about their neighbors and what they are up to. They know who they are, their age and their sex and, if with active cubs, how many. They know where their neighbors have been. Tigers will know as individuals all the tigers whose territories abut onto their own. The complex territorial patterns of males and females are all conveyed through smell. Information is constantly exchanged throughout the jungle by the silent gossip of scent. Tigers are everlastingly curious about each other, yet they seldom meet.

SIMON BARNES
Tiger!

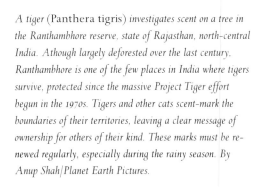

A tiger (Panthera tigris) investigates scent on a tree in the Ranthambhore reserve, state of Rajasthan, north-central India. Athough largely deforested over the last century, Ranthambhore is one of the few places in India where tigers survive, protected since the massive Project Tiger effort begun in the 1970s. Tigers and other cats scent-mark the boundaries of their territories, leaving a clear message of ownership for others of their kind. These marks must be renewed regularly, especially during the rainy season. By Anup Shah/Planet Earth Pictures.

LIFE IN THE PRIDE

There are few sights more pleasant to watch than a pride of sleek, well-fed, golden lions stretched out under an acacia tree—the females sleeping peacefully, the young cubs playing or suckling, the big males, a bit off to the side, looking regal and indolent. The life of young cubs growing up in a pride seems very congenial: they spend their time resting, eating, and playing. When they are playing, lion cubs are very appealing indeed, with their huge paws, chubby, ungainly bodies, and mischievous, slightly crossed eyes. They stalk, pounce upon and wrestle each other; attack, shake, and "kill" sticks and stones; ambush their mother and chew on her tail with impunity. Play seems to be an important element in the development of the young, and it also appears to have some importance in the social life of the adults, for lions never totally lose their playful natures.

CYNTHIA MOSS
Portraits in the Wild

It is not known why cheetahs have not evolved a social life. They might be more successful if they did cooperate in hunting and raising young, but perhaps the niche they fill can only accommodate a solitary hunter. Whatever the case, they have obviously not evolved many interactions that would create strong social bonds. What strikes one most about cheetahs is their amazing aloofness. Most of the time they seem totally detached from their companions. Cheetahs groom each other, but usually only after a meal, when their faces have blood on them, or after a rainstorm, when their coats are wet. They also greet each other, but most often just by sniffing each other's faces or briefly touching cheeks. They do not rub against each other sensuously as lions do. As Schaller expressed it, "Their contacts seemed constrained; they lacked the intense and uninhibited desire to touch one another that is found in lions."

CYNTHIA MOSS
Portraits in the Wild

The Territorial Cat

Cats are territorial: they seek out areas that fill their needs and are not already occupied by others of their species, and mark the boundaries of this territory to indicate possession. These boundaries are not as inviolate as those some animals—certain birds and canines—try to enforce. Felids may share ranges, while also sharing information that allows them to keep out of each other's way. But it's to a cat's advantage to be more or less the sole owner of its hunting grounds.

Territories vary widely in size, according to the cat's size, gender, species density, and availability of prey. In general, larger cats have larger territories, and those of males are larger than those of females. A lion pride may defend a territory of several hundred square miles. Male pumas have home ranges of 16 to 85 square miles; bobcats hold territories of about .5 to 16 square miles; and ocelots may live at densities of 100 to 200 per 100 square miles. Cheetahs reverse the usual gender pattern: females don't protect turf but follow their prey through home ranges of up to 300 square miles, while males do defend smaller territories.

Food, water and shelter are what any cat's home range must provide. Territory has different meanings for males and females, though. Females need access to safe den sites to raise their young, and a food supply fairly nearby. For a male, territory means not just feeding but exclusive breeding rights within his range.

The usual methods cats use to stake out territories are scent-marking with urine; scraping the ground or scratching trees, which releases scent from glands between the toes; and depositing feces, which also contain scent. Usually only big cats leave feces as signposts; smaller cats tend to bury them. 🐾

One hill cannot shelter two tigers.

Indian Proverb

A female leopard carries her young, possibly moving it to a new den for safety. Both females and males establish territories, but the males' are usually larger, typically overlapping the ranges of several females. By Norbert Rosing/Animals Animals.

We had assumed that the territorial systems in male and female leopards were similar and that any offspring would be pushed out of their natal area into neighbouring terrain by the mother and the territorial male. There they would come into contact with other territorial leopards which would force them off once again, until the young leopards would eventually establish themselves in vacant areas or defeat existing territorial leopards.

But the dispersal of the young female and now the Sand River female and the Tugwaan female suggested otherwise, as all these leopards had established territories immediately adjacent to the mother's. However, we lost track of the males shortly after they became independent, suggesting that the male dispersal patterns differed from those of the females.…Studies carried out on some of the other large African carnivores such as lion, spotted hyaena and brown hyaena show that they all live in social groups comprised mainly of closely related females with males dispersing from their natal area soon after reaching maturity. It is interesting to observe that, although the leopard is a solitary animal, this pattern of closely related females in one area still seems to exist, albeit in a more dispersed form than in the other more social carnivores.

LEX HES
The Leopards of Londolozi

The nature of this beast is, to love the place of her breeding, neither will she tarry in any strange place, although carryed far, being never willing to forsake the house, for the love of any man....

EDWARD TOPSELL
Historie of Foure-Footed Beastes

A puma (Felis concolor) scratching a tree trunk, Rocky Mountains. Cats perform this ritual not only to sharpen their claws (it helps shed the old sheaths), but to release scent from glands between their toes, thus marking territory. By Tom & Pat Leeson.

THE PULL OF HOME

Why is the pull of home so powerful? Again, the answer lies in meat. Every cat must live amid a population of prey animals, whether mice or bison, in a place where there is suitable feed to keep the prey from wandering away. Every cat also needs water, and every cat needs shade or shelter, particularly if she is female, since she will need several hidden nests in case she must move her kittens. To meet these requirements, each cat tries to establish and hold a territory which, of course, varies in size according to the species of the cat and the habitat of the prey animals. The size of a territory also varies by the sex of its owner. Female cats of most species tend to own adjacent or almost adjacent territories of relatively modest size. These fan out through a jungle or drape down a mountainside, sometimes overlapping very slightly, sometimes touching at the corners like the petals of a wild rose. A male cat tends to own a larger territory that may partly overlap the territories of several females or may encompass the territories of these females. If their territories are the petals, his is the rose....

Cat properties are like ranches. The space enclosed by the cat's boundaries is actually the grazing land for livestock, whether deer or deer mice, which belong to the owner and to no one else, and which the owner does not disturb except to harvest.

When new land is difficult to find, mother cats often share with their children, keeping their sons with them until they are full grown and keeping their daughters or some of their daughters even longer, sometimes even dividing the ranch with one or more daughters. Lions and housecats carry the practice to an extreme, so that the members of a pride—really a group of females who are related to each other, grandmothers, mothers, daughters, sisters, nieces, and grandchildren—own one enormous ranch together. The area owned by a pride of lionesses can be hundreds of square miles, particularly in southern Africa, where game is sparse, while the area owned by a group of housecats is usually someone's farm, particularly the barn and its surroundings, where most of the mice are. Female cats share nests with their sisters and help to birth, groom, feed, protect, and teach one another's children.

ELIZABETH MARSHALL THOMAS
The Tribe of Tiger

COUGAR CROSSINGS

Wandering lions of both sexes appear to know when they are in another lion's home ground. The resident scrapes together leaves, twigs, or pine needles into mounds from four to six inches high, then urinates on them, to make sight and scent markers delineating its territory. We found such "scrapes" under trees, on ridges, and at lion crossings, where the markers act as traffic lights on regularly traveled paths. Whenever we traced a newcomer to one of the scrapes, the trail showed that the lion had abruptly changed its course, knowing that another lion or family was in the vicinity, and retraced its route for two or three miles before trying a different area.

MAURICE HORNOCKER
National Geographic

Young tiger making a "flehmen" face, the action cats perform when detecting a scent with the vomeronasal, or Jacobsen's, organ. Humans lack this organ, with which other mammals identify airborne molecules too heavy to inhale. By Rita Summers.

THE SUN COMPASS

A cat probably has a built-in direction finder based on the sun. If you move a cat two hundred miles away from its familiar zone, you throw the angle of the sun off by a significant degree. A cat sensitive to that change would almost certainly move in the one direction that tended to correct the change, i.e., toward familiar home ground. That sun compass may be what puts homing pigeons on the tack for home, and why should we accept that ability in a bird brain and not in a cat?

ROGER A. CARAS
A Cat Is Watching

One day, when hunting on the banks of the Uruguay, I was shown certain trees, to which [jaguars] constantly recur for the purpose, as it is said, of sharpening their claws. I saw three well known trees… on each side there were sharp scratches, or rather grooves, extending in an oblique line, nearly a yard in length….A common method of ascertaining whether a jaguar is in the neighbourhood is to examine these trees.

CHARLES DARWIN

A cat and a tiger once went out together for a walk. After they had strolled on through the wild jungle for some time the tiger began to feel hungry, and to think of the desirability of making a pounce on the cat. His sidelong looks soon aroused the suspicions of the cat, who, knowing not how else to elude the tiger's purpose, proposed that they should climb up and rest awhile in a tree, and then return home.

To this the tiger readily agreed, only asking the cat to show the way, when, while the cat was well within reach, the tiger made a sudden grab for him. But the cat was too quick for the tiger, and instantly sprang forward on to a light branch of the tree where the tiger could not follow. Then the cruel beast crouched down at the root of the tree in watch until the cat would be obliged to descend.

Long waiting, however, exhausted the tiger's patience and at last he roused himself to depart, growling out as he slunk homeward. "I cannot wait for you now, but as you cats always drop your dung in the same place, I shall be sure to catch you before long."

Then the cat cautiously descended from his perch of safety, and went round and told the whole of the cat world of what the tiger had said, and ever since then the cats have made it their custom to seek out every day a different place of egestion, and there dig a hole and drop their dung therein, and carefully cover it over with earth, so that the tigers may never know where they have been or where to find them again.

Canarese legend from the Malabar Coast

Tropical Storm with Tiger—Surprise, by Henri Rousseau (1855–1910). Rousseau's painting well illustrates how the tiger's striped camouflage works. National Gallery, London.

FIGHT OR FLIGHT?

The German animal ethologist Paul Leyhausen studied cat behavior intensively in the 1950s, making long-term observations of a group of domestic cats, as well as small wild felines such as servals and ocelots. His book Cat Behavior *is a classic, describing many aspects of feline social, territorial, and predatory behavior in almost "frame by frame" detail. His experiments, along with observations in the wild, suggest that serious fights among even large cats are rare, as these well-armed animals can do each other major harm. While fights do occur—over possession of prey or territory, and in defense of young—most feline combat displays a combination of aggressive and defensive impulses.*

…[S]ince attack can be the best form of defense, elements of both attacking and defensive behavior are superimposed on one another to form an attitude which permits the cat at any time to launch a surprise attack or to run away.…Many other carnivores or rodents behave like this. It very often amounts to no more than feigned blows not intended to hit the opponent, for there is always a danger that, once in close combat, the animal might miss the best opportunity of escape by being unable to disentangle itself again quickly enough.…Intensive territorial fights proceed similarly: Without warning the territory owner shoots toward the intruder from any direction and rains blows on it. In most cases the strange cat immediately turns and runs away…

A cat does not stand up to a really powerful attack from an enemy if there is a possibility of escape left. However, a cat does not avoid every fight as a matter of course. The very conflict between its inclinations to defense and flight often constrain it to stay on the spot even if it sights the enemy soon enough to be able to escape.…

Attack develops out of the arched posture.…Head and body stretch forward, the tail drops back into a hook and the ears are slightly raised. The pupils remain dilated and the hair continues to bristle.…Shortly before the attack, the defensive hissing changes into growling, a sign that the inclinations to defense and attack are now approximately equal. At the moment of the attack itself, the cat spits with jaws wide open. In a mock attack, it does shoot forward with one paw spread wide and raised, ready to strike. But even in an "earnest" defensive attack the animal usually contents itself with only a few blows, and recoils at once to adopt its former defensive posture or runs a short distance away.

PAUL LEYHAUSEN
Cat Behavior

A hostile encounter between jaguars (Panthera onca), *Para State, Brazil. By Luiz C. Marigo/Peter Arnold, Inc.*

THE NOMADS TAKE OVER

David Jenkins of the Nature Conservancy and I were watching fifteen members of the Magadi pride including Silver Mane and Scar Nose, two of the three males that had been with the pride for at least two years. All lounged along the edge of a small marsh, keeping their eyes on a solitary bull buffalo who stood there belly-deep in mud and water. The bloody wounds on his shoulders showed that he had been attacked and mauled but had shaken off his assailants and retreated into the marsh. We waited for the inevitable action. It arrived from unexpected quarters. Suddenly, at 9: 25 a.m., the five Moru males came at a trot, radiating power as they roared. Seeing this invincible phalanx, the pride scattered and fled. Only one lioness asserted herself by chasing a surprised male one hundred feet before retreating like the others through a thicket of whistling thorn toward the rocky slopes bordering the Mbalageti River.

Forty-five minutes later the victorious Moru males returned. They sat by the marsh, hesitating to get their paws wet, while the buffalo faced his tormentors with lowered head. Then, inexplicably, he plodded toward them, committing suicide with such serenity it was as if his end had long ago been pre-ordained. One lion grabbed his rump; another placed his paws over the bull's back, bit him there and pulled. With intolerable weariness the bull sank to his knees. There were no violent actions, no frantic tussles, as the buffalo was rolled on his back with impersonal force. Another lion joined and held the bull's throat, a fourth his muzzle. He died after a few minutes of suffocation.

At 7:00 p.m. a lion roared in the distance. Though victorious in battle, the Moru males still had the mentality of nomads and

the solitary challenge made them nervous. Two of them fled for three hundred feet, but then their thundering communal reply restored their confidence and they lumbered off in the direction from which the roar had come. Later that night, after they had returned to the buffalo, an old and emaciated nomadic male joined them on the kill. Not yet accustomed to possessing their new territory, the Moru males permitted the newcomer to eat, something no self-respecting pride owner would do. Nevertheless, from that day on the Magadi pride had new overlords. Two of the former pride males I never saw again, but a few months after being evicted, Scar Nose was on the plains, alone, now a harried-looking nomad who along with his territory had lost his friends, his security, and his quiet dignity.

GEORGE SCHALLER
Golden Shadows, Flying Hooves

Male lions, possibly nomads judging from their leanness, with Cape buffalo in the background, Ngorongoro Crater, Tanzania. By Kennan Ward.

LION

Regal, sanguine, generous me.
My bounty extends across the savannah
in little red piles—provender for hyenas,
dogs, vultures and crocodiles.

Day and night I oversee
a life and death struggle for territory
and energy to breed.

Tribal love, protection of the young, courage in senility,
daring and speed are rendered in saliva:
wildebeest, zebra, gazelle, impala.

For in my court reigns Fate,
crowned by ritual slaughter,
which neither I nor my vassals dare
tergiversate.

RICHARD GROSSMAN
The Animals

Cats Communicating

The elaborate systems of communication used by the cats confirm that they are social animals, even if their societies are foreign to us. The pioneering animal ethologist Konrad Lorenz thought that few creatures were as good as cats at conveying their moods—and they have many means to do so. The most important ones (that we know of) are sound, body language, and scent, often used in combination.

Cats produce an extraordinary range of vocalizations, from subaudible to earthshaking in volume. Two of the best-known sounds—roaring and purring—are often said to distinguish large and small cats. The big Panthera cats have a cartilage in the hyoid bone of the throat that allows them to roar, while the smaller felids can't, and purring is usually heard only in smaller cats. But some observers have reported purring from big cats, so this theory may need revision. All cats utter versions of the familiar "meow" call, though these vary greatly in pitch and duration. And all spit, hiss, and growl in agonistic situations. The lion's famous roar is used to affirm bonds within a pride, warn other prides away from its territory, and keep in touch with distant members.

Cats are "honest communicators," it's sometimes said, employing a large vocabulary of body language to convey their intentions clearly. This is critical among creatures with the potential to do each other lethal harm. Among cats, body stance, tail movements, and mouth and ear positions are among the most important signals of friendliness or aggression.

The silent language of scent may be the cats' most important means of communication—certainly with regard to territory. Scent marking may not deter a cat from entering another's territory, but does provide a wealth of information about the owner and how recently he/she was there, allowing the second cat to proceed in confidence or risk a confrontation. Scent is also important in close-up contact: by rubbing their faces against objects, fellow cats, or even humans, cats are releasing scent from facial glands to indicate possession or affirm bonds. 🐾

Perhaps the most dramatic evidence of cat sociability is their vocalizations—a logical means for animals whose economic needs drive them apart even as their emotional needs draw them together.

ELIZABETH MARSHALL THOMAS
The Tribe of Tiger

Lioness growls at a cub, not her own (though she might do the same if it were), Masai Mara, Kenya. Mother cats use a wide range of sounds to communicate with their young: to comfort and reassure, to call them to her, to warn of danger, and to say, "I've had it with you!" By Gunther Ziesler/Peter Arnold, Inc.

WHY DOES THE LION ROAR?

After the coming of man into the world, Lion became the most feared of the predators.…In these early days, Lion still had a gentle voice, not very loud at all, and so he was able to catch and eat the other animals without much trouble

This, of course, greatly worried the other animals, since they never knew when Lion was on the hunt. They decided to hold a meeting to find a way of somehow making Lion less dangerous.

They talked for a long time, but none of them could think of anything. Hare, always the imaginative one, then had a bright idea.

"I know a way that would make Lion's voice like the terrible thunder of a summer's storm,' he said, "and then we would always know when he was coming."

The other animals all agreed that this was a marvelous idea. But how was Hare going to manage such a thing? Hare just winked and set off on his difficult task.

Eventually Hare found Lion resting beneath a shady umbrella tree, and approaching him carefully, saying, "O Great One, I am truly most unhappy to bring you bad news, but your brother is very ill, and requests to see you at once." Lion was dreadfully upset to hear this news and told Hare to lead him to his brother as fast as possible.

Hare took Lion for miles and miles around the Bushveld and after several hours Lion (who, after all, had been disturbed during his morning sleep) was so weary he could go no further. He lay down in a shady spot and slept.

Now, with the help of a honeyguide bird, the crafty Hare found a wild bees' nest in a tree not too far away. After following the required custom of leaving a good piece of the honeycomb as a

"thank-you" for the little bird, Hare took some of the honey and dribbled it all over the paws and head of the sleeping lion. Hare then ran off to some thick bushes nearby and hid.

When the bees returned home and saw that someone had raided their hive, they were terribly angry. They soon found Lion sleeping nearby, with honey all over his paws. In a raging swarm, the bees attacked him, and Lion was stung so many times and was in such pain that his soft cries soon swelled to a thunderous roar that could be heard for miles around!

That is the story of how Lion's voice was changed forever. The animals were very grateful to Hare because, from then on, they could hear Lion's roar from a long way away, and be warned that the King of Beasts was on the hunt.

A Batonka story

A Lion in a Jungle Landscape, *by William Huggins (1820–1884). Christie's, London/Superstock.*

SPEECH WITHOUT SOUND

Merely to watch the constantly changing facial expressions of lions when they interact or respond to their surroundings is a fascinating way to spend the hours. The face of a lion is a marvelously subtle yet clear conveyor of emotions. Kipling's observation that "The beasts are very wise / Their mouths are clean of lies" applies particularly to cats, for they express themselves so unambiguously, their features and sounds mirror their minds so precisely, that only the most insensitive of persons could grossly misinterpret them. It is no coincidence that a lion has black lips and a black patch on the back of each ear. These markings enhance the vividness of those parts of the face that are among the most important in communication. When a lion notices something of more than passing interest, its bland eyes seem to harden, a delicate change due more to a tensing of the skin around the eyes than to a difference in the eyes themselves. The most conspicuous expressions are those of aggressive threat and defensive threat, as Paul Leyhausen calls them. An angry and purely aggressive lion lowers its neck obliquely and stares fixedly with eyes wide open at its opponent; its ears are erect and its lips are brought so far forward that they are almost in a straight line, hiding the teeth from view. Growls or coughs may accompany the expression. When a lion looks like that it is time to retreat and quickly, for attack is imminent and may not be limited to a bluff charge. The lion intends to convey emphatically, "Leave me alone; go away or I will see to it that you do." In a defensive threat, the animal retracts its ears, bares its teeth, snarling or miaowing while doing so. This expression, like most others, has many gradations. At a low intensity, a male may lift only one corner of his lip to expose a huge canine at a bothersome cub. But when highly upset, the animal opens its mouth wide, exposing all teeth in a massive display of weapons, and this gesture may be reinforced with snarls and a slap or two. The head is often turned to one side, and, if the lion becomes even more frightened, it may

turn more and more, until it rolls onto its back, facing its tormentor with exposed teeth and claws. Lions that bare their teeth are somewhat fearful and in effect they mean, 'I hesitate to attack you, but if you persist in annoying me I will do so in desperation." Emotions are seldom pure and static. A lion's conflicting impulses for flight or fight shift constantly in intensity and these changes are clearly expressed in the movements of the face, in the sounds, and finally in actions. Shifts in mood during an interaction occur so often and are so sudden and uninhibited, ranging in a second from violent passion to serenity, that it is difficult for a human observer not only to keep track of all the nuances but also to comprehend behavior that is so much a product of those emotions we tend to suppress in ourselves.

GEORGE SCHALLER
Golden Shadows, Flying Hooves

TIGER TALK

Another thing that endeared Jum and his mate to me was the curious little chats they would have with each other, employing a most unusual method of conversation. This was so far removed from the range of sounds they produced when growling or snarling that it could be classified as a separate language. It consisted entirely of sniffs, and prodigious, bubbling, nose-quivering sniffs they were, too. It was quite incredible, the variation they could achieve and the different meaning they could impart (or that I imagined they could impart) by means of this simple noise.

GERALD DURRELL
A Bevy of Beasts

Male lion yawning, relaxed

Lioness alert, watching prey, mouth closed, ears forward

Lioness in defensive threat, teeth bared, ears rotated so backs face forward; may attack

Lioness relaxed, roaring or calling

These lions display some of the typical "facial language" employed by cats to convey emotions and intent. Adapted from The Serengeti Lion, *by George Schaller.*

SOUNDS TIGERS MAKE

PURRING
Though the great cats are supposed to be unable to purr, George Schaller and other observers have heard mothers make purring sounds to their young.

PRUSTEN
A German word that describes the gentle puffing sound tigers make by rapidly expelling air through their nostrils. Indicates friendly feelings, used among mothers and cubs, mated pairs, and by sometimes by captive tigers to their keepers.

POOKING
Described by Schaller as a loud, clear "pok," this puzzling noise resembles the alarm call of the sambar deer, the tiger's chief prey. Some think it's an alarm call or an advertisement of the tiger's presence.

GRUNTING
Soft or rasping grunts often used by mothers to communicate with their cubs.

MIAOWING
The distress call of cubs; courting tigers may also miaow to each other.

WOOFING
A startled tiger emits a "woof," as when one cub slapped another at a kill.

MOANING AND ROARING
Variations in intensity of the same basic vocalization, a two-toned sound like *a-a-u-u-u* or *a-o-o-o-nh,* produced by forcing air through the open mouth while closing the jaws.

GROWLING, SNARLING AND HISSING
Expressions of annoyance, made when tigers are threatening each other or reacting to humans. These sounds often occur in sequence and blend into each other.

COUGHING ROAR
A short, loud, explosive roar that apparently indicates anger.

A Bengal tiger displays its canines in a snarl. Tigers have an exceptional repertoire of vocalizations. By John Giustina/The Wildlife Collection.

ALBERT THE VENTRILOQUIST

Many writers assert that a lion can throw his roar, so to speak, so that it appears to come from two or three different directions at once. This is not quite as impossible as it sounds, for many species of birds and insects have the most astonishing ventriloquial powers. In some cases you can actually watch the creature making the sound and yet the sound itself appears to come from several feet, or even yards, away. Obviously, if the lion possessed this power it would be immensely useful to him; he would be able to panic herds of game at night so that, in their terror, they might run toward their hunter instead of away from him....Some people refuse to believe that a lion can throw his voice deliberately. They maintain that all he does is hold his mouth close to the ground when roaring, so that the sound is blurred and it is impossible to tell from which direction it is coming. Now, in order to find out if this was true I tried very hard to be present when Albert was roaring, but with little success. Time after time I would walk hopefully past his cage thinking that he might roar while I was there to see, but every time he remained stubbornly silent. Sometimes, when I heard him start up, I would treat the visitors to the sight of a keeper running madly along the path through the trees as though some escaped beast were at my heels. But every time, when I arrived panting at the barrier rail, I would find that Albert had either finished or else had thought better of it and had relapsed into silence after two or three coughs. However, I was more than compensated for this by the magnificent sounds he would produce when I could hear but not see him.

He would start, quite suddenly, with two or three preliminary *"Aroom"* noises, with long pauses in between, as if he were making sure of the right note. Then he would launch into the full song: the *"Arooms"* would become throaty and rich and the pause between them shorter and shorter, until they ran together in a terrific crescendo of sound....It is difficult to describe the frightening possibilities that were snarled at you when the sound reached its zenith.

GERALD DURRELL
A Bevy of Beasts

VOICE OF THE WILDCAT

More varied and complicated than realized. The kits make a loud piercing note *meeoo* when alarmed and handled at only two days old, which changes to an even louder *maow* at four or five days old. At five to six weeks they can emit the latter sound and also a still more piercing whistling note *wheeoo* when really frightened. This sound is probably given in the wild if straggling kits are picked up by a fox, or eagle. From four days they give a high trilling note when seeking their mother's teats and her warm body. At less than a week old they try to hiss and spit at outside disturbance but neither are audible until the eighth or ninth day. Later they make a special suckling noise by smacking their lips when already at their mother's body but, waking up suddenly, want some milk. This lip smacking noise can continue until five months old and it is often made near the mother head. When the kits get caught up in a thicket of brambles or in fencing they warn their mother with a loud squawking *mauuw* which is louder but similar to that of a duck grabbed by fox, dog

or man. The "turtle dove"- like *brrrooo* trill is not made until about eight months. It is used for greeting, affection, and to call the kits back when they are not far, but from further away the normal loud *mau* is used. When the kits are running wild with the mother a high metallic ventriloquistic *awroori* is used, to help all keep in touch yet not give away exact position to possible predators on the kits. Wildcats can and do purr, just as do cougars and lynxes, a sudden breathy, clattering sound, which often ends suddenly. This purr is slower and louder than that of the domestic cat, but is rarely used. The ability to growl, like whining high pitched dynamos, develops at about a month. As the cats grow older this growl deepens in volume until in an old tom it sounds like the prelude to a minor earthquake. It is used to display anger and as a warning before the ferocious spits and stamps. The female can emit loud tormented screeches during her oestrus, possibly to help find the male. It is an unearthly chilling sound....

MIKE TOMKIES
My Wilderness Wildcats

If male,
A cat is apt to sing on a major scale.
This concert is for everybody,
This is wholesale.
For a baton he wields a tail.

He is also found
When happy, to resound
With an enclosed and private sound.

ROSALIE MOORE
from "Catalog"

Feb. 23, 1904. Heard panthers crying about nine o'clock last night. There were probably two of them, as the calls were sounded at short intervals, sometimes only about a minute apart, and one seemed a little farther away....The cry is a long drawn out, shrill trill, weird and startling. It commences low on the scale, gradually ascends, increasing in volume, and then lowers at the end.

N. HOLLIS (IN LOUISIANA)

This serval (Felis serval) is displaying defensive behavior in the extreme, with its ears flattened to the side and most of its teeth exposed. This cat growls ferociously when disturbed in its feeding; it also purrs like a cat and is said to utter a shrill cry that sounds like "meoa, meoa!" repeated seven or eight times. By Joseph Van Os/Image Bank

Courting Cats

I was awakened near midnight by an interrupted series of ferocious hisses, shrill screams, harsh squalls, and deep-toned yowls. No alley strays could ever have half-equaled this cat concert of the desert wilds. Luckily, it was moonlight, and I was able to see the animals almost perfectly. The female [bobcat] most of the time lay crouched upon the ground, while the big male, which must have weighed twenty pounds, walked menacingly about her. Sometimes they both sat upright, facing each other. The loud and ludicrous serenade was kept up for almost half an hour, and it ended with a dual climax of discordant, frightening squalls as mating took place.

E. C. JAEGER
Desert Wildlife

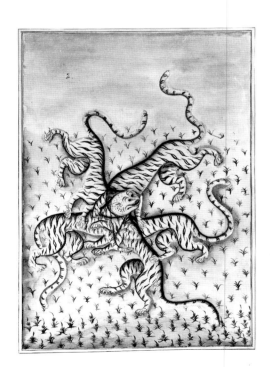

Five tigers with a single head, *watercolor from an album made in Madras, 1785. Victoria & Albert Museum.*

Unless they belong to a pride or a band of domestic cats, felines come together most often to mate. The biology of the event is fairly consistent throughout the cat family—and fairly dramatic. But the social implications of male–female roles are even more interesting.

Among many animals, ritualized conflicts between males in the same pack or herd decide which male will mate with the female or females in season. For felines, however, breeding rights come with a territory, and the male (or he and his cohorts, among lions) must first win the territory. The career of a male cat resembles a parabola that may peak fairly briefly: his youth is usually spent roaming in futile attempts to take over turf from an older, established male, and in old age he is doomed to be ousted by a younger, stronger one. Having won his place, he will try to kill any young sired by another male, so that only his own genes survive. This continual striving among males to control land and females ensures the strength of the species.

Female cats first come into estrus at different ages: often less than a year of age for small cats, and two or three years for big ones. Estrus releases distinctive pheromones, which the male of the species can detect from some distance. The courtship behavior of cats large and small is remarkably similar: the male follows the female for several days, waiting for her to become receptive, slowly drawing nearer to rub against her with cheeks and neck. At first she reacts with hisses and slaps, but eventually assumes an encouraging position called "lordosis" and allows him to mount. The male often seizes his mate by the nape of the neck and may hold on through the entire mount. The mating sequence lasts 1 to 5 minutes and may be repeated very often. Smaller cats mate less frequently, possibly because they'd be vulnerable to other predators.

After mating, males and females go their separate ways (again, lions excepted). But the male remains a protective, if invisible, presence in the lives of his wives and their young for as long as he holds his place.

During the heat of the day Muffin lay as near to her as he could, watching her every move. If she sought out better shade, he strutted so close beside her that their bodies rubbed together. Sometimes he would initiate copulation by standing at her rear. More often, however, she would walk back and forth in front of him, her tail flicking and hindquarters swaying, or she would brush her body along his before crouching in front of him. When he stood over her to copulate, he nibbled at her neck and she growled and flattened her ears. As soon as Muffin had finished, he would step back quickly to avoid getting clouted by Happy's paw, for invariably she would whirl around, snarling fiercely, and swat at him. Then, lying on her back, her legs extended, she would roll over and over in the grass, her eyes closed in apparent ecstasy.

They mated in this stereotypic fashion every twenty to thirty minutes for part of two days and all of two nights. Small wonder that Muffin did not object when Moffet took over the courtship at sunset on the third day.

MARK AND DELIA OWENS
Cry of the Kalahari

Because courting couples remain intent on their own business, other pride members usually drift away, leaving them alone. Pairs usually do not hunt except when a good opportunity presents itself. Once a male interrupted his courtship to capture a gazelle that had imprudently gone to a waterhole nearby. He carried his prize to the lioness and permitted her to eat it all, a touching and striking token considering the fact that he was hungry. For one adult lion to give meat to another is the ultimate gesture,

a negation of one of its basic tenets. On another occasion, a lioness suddenly became aware of several gazelle in high grass near her. She crouched immediately. Her consort, misinterpreting her intention, eagerly mounted her, only to have her shoot out from under him in a futile rush at the prey. He stood there with such a bewildered expression at her sudden departure that I burst into laughter.

GEORGE SCHALLER
Golden Shadows, Flying Hooves

Lions mating, Kruger National Park, South Africa. While often interrupted by violent blows, hisses, and snarls from the female, courtship and mating among lions is a prolonged affair, with mating occurring up to 100 times a day for several days. Often a lioness mates successively with several males in the pride: it may be a case of "let the best genes win." By Rita Summers.

of the bushes. It seemed to me, waiting uncomfortably among the nettles, that she would never yield, and I marveled at Jum's patience. Maurena seemed to relish this mastery over her mate, for another half hour's pacing was indulged in and Jum's movements were getting more and more jerkily impatient with every minute.

Then, as I watched, Maurena's walk become slower and more flaccid, her back curved until her pale honey-colored belly almost brushed the ground. She swayed more from side to side, and the expression in her eyes changed from one of weary preoccupation to the dreamy, mysterious expression that tigers assume when they drowse and muse after their food.

GERALD DURRELL
A Bevy of Beasts

...These Lionesses are very letcherous, and this is the cause that the Lions are so fell and cruell.

PLINY (IST CENTURY A.D.)
Natural History

Tigers greet each other by head rubbing, a gesture of bonding. Male and female tigers stay together for several days while mating; during courtship, aggressive behavior alternates with tender affection. Otherwise they lead mostly separate lives, though they often meet amicably or share a kill when their paths cross. In some places, male tigers have even been observed in company with a mother and (presumably) their cubs, occasionally playing with the cubs. One tiger expert also believes that the sibling bond between tiger littermates persists into adulthood, so they recognize each other in friendly fashion upon meeting. By Mark Newman/West Stock.

INTERLUDE WITH TIGERS

From early morning Jum had been following his mate around like a tawny shadow, belly-crawling, abject, heavy with passion....He kept his distance, for early in the day he had approached too close and she had resented it. His muzzle bore three deep red grooves as proof of her reticence. She seemed to have changed overnight from the timid, servile creature she was normally, to a slinking, dangerous animal that dealt with his premature advances speedily and ferociously.

They paced up and down among the elder trunks, and presently Jum's love overwhelmed him again and he moved closer to Maurena, giving a purring moan in his throat, his eyes frosty with desire. Maurena did not cease her leisured pacing at his approach but merely lifted her lip over pink gums and chalk-white teeth. The moan died quickly in Jum's throat and he returned to his former position. They continued to pace back and forth, their tawny coats glowing in the shadowy twilight

I listened one night to the most remarkable serenade of tigers I ever heard. A peculiar long wail, like the drawn-out mew of a huge cat, first rose from a river course a few hundred yards below my tent. Presently from a mile or so higher up the river came a deep tremendous roar, which had scarcely died away ere it was answered from behind the camp by another, pitched in a yet deeper tone startling us from its suddenness and proximity. All three were repeated at short intervals, as the three tigers approached each other along the bottom of the deep, dry watercourses....As they drew together the noises ceased for about a quarter of an hour; and I was dozing off to sleep again, when suddenly arose the most fearful din near to where the tigress had first sounded the love note to her rival lovers, a din like the caterwauling of midnight cats magnified a hundredfold. Intervals of silence, broken by outbursts of this infernal shrieking and moaning, disturbed our rest for the next hour, dying away gradually as the tigers retired along the bed of the river.

J. FORSYTHE
The Highlands of Central India

LEOPARD LOVE

Suddenly a low growling was heard from within the thicket. Dave and his tracker froze in their tracks and then backed slowly in the direction of the Land Rover, the growling all the while increasing in intensity. Everyone in the party expected a leopard to burst out of the bush at any second, but nothing appeared. Instead, the growling increased steadily, reaching a climax with a sudden loud burst of sound....

By this time it was growing dark, so the spotlights were taken out as Dave tried to manouvre the Land Rover towards the source of the sound. Then suddenly Neil saw two sets of eyes glowing in the dark and immediately signalled Dave to stop. In a little clearing in the thicket there was a pair of leopards, one much larger than the other—obviously a male and a female. Neil, who had a video camera with him, began to film them when suddenly, through his viewing screen, he saw the smaller leopard get up, brush past the male twice and then settle down immediately in front of him in a crouching position, giving the low growl that we had heard earlier. Then the male stood up and mounted her and, as the mating progressed, the growling of both leopards intensified. Then the male bit the female gently on the neck; suddenly there was the loud burst of sound that had been heard earlier and the male leapt off the female to avoid being cuffed by her....

This was the first occasion, as far as we knew, that anyone had ever witnessed the mating of leopards in the wild.

LEX HES
The Leopards of Londolozi

Leopards (Panthera pardus) *in pre-mating behavior, Motopo National Park, Zimbabwe. Leopards, among the most solitary and territorial of the big cats, are very rarely seen together except during mating (and hardly ever then, as they are so elusive). However, cases have been reported of a male sharing a den with a female and her nearly grown cubs. Females have been known to mate again as soon as a month after bearing cubs, possibly because a new male has become dominant in her range. By Anthony Bannister/ABPL.*

Growing Up Feline

No bond in the cat world is stronger than the tie between a mother and her young. Cats are assiduous mothers, and care for their children well. Yet the lives of young felines in the wild is far from easy. Like the young of any animal, they are most vulnerable to predation, disease and famine: mortality rates are high, and even adults of their own species can pose a threat.

Mothers carry their young for gestation periods ranging from about 66 days for the smallest cats to 110 days for lions. When it's time to give birth, she seeks out a den—this may be a dense thicket, a cave in a rocky hillside, or a burrow among tree roots, the chief needs being safety from predation and weather, and nearby hunting resources. The young are born blind and completely dependent; their eyes open in about two weeks (sooner for big cats). Even before then, they have established "teat ownership," which aids their nourishment by reducing conflicts. Frequent nursing and grooming in the first few days solidify the bond between mother and young.

After these few days, the mother leaves the den to hunt, which she must do with increasing frequency as her young grow larger and eventually start eating meat themselves. Leaving her offspring thus unguarded is a real risk and the mother knows it: she may move them to a new den if she feels they are in danger—often several times, especially cheetahs. The father's involvement is minimal, though males of a lion pride do protect cubs and allow youngsters to play with them, as do some male domestic cats that live in groups. On the other hand, if a new male takes over a territory, the mother must guard from him any kittens she has by a previous mate.

After a few weeks, the young emerge from the den and start exploring their environment around it. Play quickly becomes important practice in developing social and hunting skills: first wrestling and play-fighting, then stalking, rushing and pouncing on "prey" (sticks, feathers, an adult's tail). Once they are weaned (at around 3 to 4 months old), the mother starts bringing dead prey home for them, then live prey as their skills improve. When older, they will follow her on the hunt; some mothers seem to deliberately capture and release prey for the young to practice on. Young cats become independent of their mothers at varying ages—as young as 9 months for smallest cats, at least 2 years for the largest ones. Females may establish home ranges very close to their mother's, while the males are likely to strike out farther. 🐾

Cleo seemed to be positively teaching the kits to hunt with her tail. Wherever she moved, she switched it about so the kits dived, jumped, rolled, and grabbed at it with their claws or teeth, or pinned it to the ground with both paws and bit at it as though they were holding a mouse down. The jet black blunt tip made a fine target and hunting Cleo's tail now seemed a regular feature of their daily play. Perhaps this is why wildcats have black tips to their tails.

MIKE TOMKIES
My Wilderness Wildcats

WILDCATS ENTER THEIR WORLD

There were two kits, both exceptionally large, with big feet and claws. They were fully furred with beautiful chestnut brown and brown-gray stripes and elongated spots on a light buff and tawny background, big broad heads with ears set low down and eyes tightly closed. One was suckling away for all it was worth, making little squeaky noises. When I went a little too close, Cleo only growled warningly but she still didn't move. There was no way I was going to go any closer or try to touch them right then.

The whole area round Wildernesse seemed to be smiling now. The sun had shone continuously for thirteen days and the woods were a patchwork quilt of differing greens—the feathery larches covered in the light green fuzz of new needles, the tiny oak leaves now khaki before turning dark green, the beeches thrusting out brilliant green fans on

their long horizontal plate-like branches, and flicks of varying hues of jade adorned the twigs of hazel bushes, the birches, rowans, and ash trees. Around the cottage the ground was carpeted with creeping buttercups....Almost everywhere bluebells raised a foot-high canopy of blue like a background canvas to the magnificent riot of huge pink, crimson and lilac flowers that filled the rhododendron bushes. As I looked, thinking of the kittens, I thought, what a wonderful world in which to be born.

MIKE TOMKIES
My Wilderness Wildcats

Scottish wildcat (Felis sylvestris grampia) kitten, Scotland. This small cat, native to the British isles, is famed for its fierce spirit; some call it "the British tiger." Even very young kittens growl and spit ferociously when approached by humans. By William S. Paton/Bruce Coleman, Inc.

Cats sleep fat,
And walk thin.
Cats, when they sleep, slump,
When they wake, pull in—
And where the plump's been
There's skin.
Cats walk thin.

Cats sleep in a lump,
Jump in a streak.
Cats when they jump are sleek
As a grape slipping its skin
They have a technique
Oh, cats don't creak,
They sneak….

ROSALIE MOORE
from "Catalog"

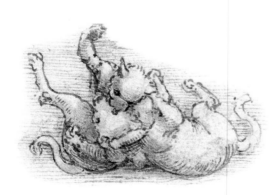

Detail from a sheet of sketches of cats in motion, by Leonardo da Vinci (1452–1519). Art historian Kenneth Clark writes: "…Leonardo's cartoon was the ancestor of all those works of romantic painting, from Rubens to Delacroix, in which artists have celebrated the heroic energy of animals." The Royal Collection © Her Majesty Queen Elizabeth II.

Cats at Play

Kittens and cubs are playfulness personified; the engaging play of kittens is one of the most endearing aspects of our pet cats. Play is vital to development for the young, but cats seem to need some kind of play all their lives. Mothers play with their offspring, courting males and females engage in play, and so do members of a lion pride or domestic cat society.

Scientists recognize different kinds of play as social, object, or locomotor play. In social play, cubs and kittens wrestle, stalk, chase and tackle each other. Particular moves prefigure their eventual hunting styles: young cheetahs bowl each other over with slaps, as they will their fleeing prey, while lions may grab each other's hindquarters. Similar, more subdued play can be seen in adults.

Cats readily play with objects—especially moving ones. Objects, of course, represent prey, and cats are notorious for playing with their prey. Much speculation surrounds this habit, which humans often find "cruel"; some think that play with prey is the cautious cat's way of testing how dangerous an animal might be. A cat tossing or pouncing on dead prey may be indulging its relief that any danger is past. The term "overflow play" describes a complex behavior in which cats appear to torment live prey without much interest in killing it (though that is the usual result). When this occurs, cats may simply be demonstrating their need for play— with the prey substituting for other cats, which may be unavailable or too threatening.

In locomotor play, cats entertain or exercise themselves by leaping, rolling, chasing their tails, or making sudden unmotivated dashes through the house. This kind of play may also express relief or blow off steam during or after a stressful situation. 🐾

MODES OF PLAY

If you have ever watched kittens play, you will probably recognize most of these postures and movements, which [researcher] Meredith West called the "building blocks" of cat social play.

In the *belly-up* position, a kitten lies on its back and makes treading movements with its back legs and pawing motions with its front legs. Usually another kitten stands over it, in the *stand-up* position. It may play-bite the kitten below, or paw at it. In play two kittens frequently change roles, from stand-up to belly-up, then to stand-up again, and so on….

In the *face-off*, one kitten sitting near another hunches its body forward and looks intently toward it. The first kitten also flicks its tail back and forth and lifts a paw in the direction of the other kitten. Sometimes two kittens face-off simultaneously.

Kittens also lift both front paws off the ground and rear up into a *vertical stance*, striking out with their front paws. They make *horizontal leaps*, which begin when a kitten turns its side toward another kitten, arches its back, then leaps off the ground. This pattern is similar to the *side step*, in which a kitten arches its back, curls its tail upward, and then walks sideways toward or around another kitten.

In its *pounce* pattern, a kitten crouches with its head low, its back legs tucked under its body and its tail straight out behind. Its tail may flick back and forth. It wriggles its hindquarters from side to side, then dashes forward. Often this leads to the eighth pattern, the *chase*, in which one kitten runs after or from another.

LAURENCE PRINGLE
Animals at Play

CUBS IN ACTION

Cubs most often played at dusk and dawn, and I eagerly looked forward to their antics. Their capacity to have fun, happy in their youthful strength and lust for life, was so infectious that it always gave me unalloyed pleasure.... One cub was now a vigorous one with a cocky expression and a slight unkempt ruff, the first intimation of his mane. These were his actions during ten minutes of play.

He pawed a twig, then chewed on it. When another cub passed by, he lunged and bit it in the lower back. The assaulted cub whirled around, slapped our hero in the face and walked off. He sat as if planning some new devilment. Suddenly he crouched and slowly, very slowly, stalked toward an unsuspecting cub. Finally he rushed. The two tumbled over and grappled before separating amicably, our cub now biting a tuft of grass instead. Tiring of this, he flopped first on his side, then rolled on his back and waved his paws in the air. Several cubs played near him and these he watched intently. When one cub ambled closer, our cub hugged the ground behind a tuft of grass and waited. Bounding out of hiding with exaggerated jumps, his mouth open and lips drawn back in a smile, he swatted at one cub and after that turned on another and nipped it in the flank, a form of greeting which led to his being clouted on the head. Two cubs wrestled gently nearby and he entered the fray enthusiastically, only to be slapped in the face, rebuffed again. A cub trotted by, intent on some errand. He lunged and tried to grab it with his

forepaws, but missed. Both cubs then reared up on their hindlegs, and, leaning into each other, cuffed clumsily until the other one fell on his back, our cub on top trying to bite its throat with mock severity. Then they sat side by side, looking for new worlds to conquer, unaware that they were being stalked until our cub was hit on the head from behind. Failing to see the humor of the situation, he turned with a snarl and swiped the air in futile fury as the silent intruder vanished in the grass. He then reclined, his playful mood seemingly dampened, but suddenly he grasped a twig with both paws and bit it, shaking his head from side to side. The twig at least would not hit back.

GEORGE SCHALLER
Golden Shadows, Flying Hooves

Lions at play, Masai Mara, Kenya. Play among young cats in a litter or a pride continues well through their adolescence, and in a pride situation may persist into adulthood. Play among cats can be specific to habitat: young margays make acrobatic leaps in trees, while tigers may frolic in water. By Galen Rowell/Mountain Light.

A serval (Felis serval) *leaps into the air in pursuit of an insect or bird. The line between hunting and play among cats is a fine one. By Gérard Lacz/Peter Arnold, Inc.*

RETRIEVER CHEETAH

When she got bored she found an old football— a toy from the filming days at Naro Meru. It had never been used since we came here, and its pressure was low but ideal for Pippa to grip it between her teeth. Proudly carrying the ball around, she asked for a game. So Local, the cook, and I tossed the ball between us and kept Pippa busy trying to catch it until it rolled into the stream. She dashed after it but, anxious not to wet her paws, waited until the current moved it near the bank and she could catch it with her teeth. She then brought it back, placed it before my feet, and asked me to continue the game. I was rather startled to see Pippa act as such a perfect retriever and, wanting to know whether she would repeat this action, threw the ball back into the water. Instantly she went after it and this time poked it carefully with her feet into position until she could grip it, then she ran back and placed it again at my feet. For the next few weeks the game became almost a ritual. On a rainy morning she would even drop the wet ball onto my bed in her effort to get me up and make me play with her. Soon she discovered a new method of getting the ball out of the water more easily. This was by letting it float downstream until it reached a little bridge we had built near the kitchen; here she could pick it up easily. Sometimes she trembled so much with excitement that the ball, as she held it between her teeth, shook with the vibrations. It was fascinating that Pippa, classified as a cat, should have such a strong retrieving instinct, yet another characteristic held in common with the dog.

JOY ADAMSON
The Spotted Sphinx

MEDICINE DANCE

The old cat knew perfectly well how to catch a fish. She had taught herself how to do it. When her instinctive rabbit-stalking movements had proved useless in an aquatic element, she had tried other strategies. Whenever one met with success, she incorporated it into her modus operandi. She had discovered, for example, that a light tap on the water would sometimes bring one of the insect-feeding species to the surface. From then on she "fished" in the true sense of the word, luring victims to her lethal claws in the same way sportsmen use their casting rods. When a victim was deceived by her ruse, she would bat it onto the bank and dispatch it quickly with a series of hard bites before it could flop its way back to a watery domain. She learned the hard way that hooking a fish twice was as difficult a feat as bringing down a bird once it had taken wing.

But on this night the old cat was not serious about capturing the sinuous forms with which she toyed. More than food, she was seeking "relief play." For several days, while mourning her kittens, she had remained quiet. Now her central nervous system craved exhilaration. And like the untimely burst of laughter that sometimes follows shock in human beings, the cat's mood altered abruptly. Suddenly she began jumping about like a fawn.

What fantasies played across her brain as she capered about in the fabulous light could hardly have been more surrealistic than the effect her performance would have created on a casual observer. Leaping from boulder to boulder like some giddy phantasma, she might well have been performing a magical rite. And in a way, she was, for this spontaneous activity was stimulating her endocrine system, helping to restore to it a more normal homeostasis. Self-excitation was therapeutic, a medicine dance, a tonic.

HOPE RYDEN
Bobcat Year

Bobcat (Lynx rufus) in mid-leap, Sand Sage Prairie, Colorado. By W. Perry Conway/Corbis.

It is as if Gaia has said to the cats: Here, my beauties—the information you need in order to hunt, mate, fight, yowl, be cautious, raise children, is safely packed in the back of your brains. Save your forebrains for whatever creative inventions may strike you; use your wits to amuse yourselves and me.

ELIZABETH MARSHALL THOMAS
The Tribe of Tiger

When we look again at the forest, we may see cats looking back.

CANDACE SAVAGE

If cats have a true homing sense, as some claim, it surely evolved because home is so important to cats, whether it be a city apartment or hundreds of square miles of African savannah. Home is where a cat can be reasonably sure of finding enough food to sustain it, shelter for raising young, high ground or trees to hunt from and escape to—and, ideally, no or few others of its species with whom to compete for these resources. ❧ The places cats call home encompass most of the world's terrestrial biomes: grassland, steppe, scrub habitats, desert, woodlands at every latitude, rainforests, and high mountains. The greatest concentration of both cat species and individuals is found in tropical regions around the globe, where there are ecological niches for cats of all sizes, ample cover to suit their stealthy

The Web of Home

hunting style, and a vast array of available prey. Some cats favor hunting in or around water; some prefer the wide-open plains; still others find their prey almost exclusively in the trees. Large or subtle variations in size, body shape, coloration, and facial structure support these adaptations. ❧ Almost everywhere in the world cats live, the largest of their kind are the dominant carnivores, operating at the peak of the food chain. Lions, tigers, leopards, jaguars, and pumas are the chief predators (apart from wolves, in some places) on large herbivores such as deer, antelope, and buffalo. And the remains of their kills become provender for a whole host of smaller carnivores, from jackals, coyotes, and foxes to eagles, vultures, and ravens to, eventually, beetles and worms. Predation aside, their relations with fellow creatures can range from wary tolerance (lions in relation to elephants, for example) to active dislike (pumas versus dogs of all kinds). Cats are also, to their distress, hosts to insect and biological parasites, all playing a role in controlling populations and resource use. ❧ The big cats' role as provider stretches far back into prehistory. Undoubtedly among the weaker carnivores to benefit from scavenging the kills of lions and saber-toothed cats were our own ancestors, the early hominids. ➤

THE LEOPARD TREE

Couched in the fork of a monumental fig tree, a leopard slept, waiting for darkness. She lay as limp as a rug, her body draped along a branch, all four legs dangling. From time to time her eyes opened, pale discs of glazed green, the pupils contracting to black pinpoints as the breeze laid back the leaves and splashed her face in sunlight. Even when her eyes were closed, the small round ears twitched and turned, sifting the sounds of the hot afternoon; the keening kites, the bubbling cries of coucals, the tremulous twittering of mousebirds in the leafy canopy. Hers was the semi-sleep of cats, in which the senses rarely fall below a level of subconscious awareness.

The tree she had chosen was the oldest of all the wild figs in Leopard Gorge: massive and wide-spreading, grotesquely gnarled. A century ago, at about the time the first Europeans set foot in the Maasai country, the sweet fruit of its parent tree had been eaten by a baboon. The hard sticky seeds had passed unharmed through the animal's gut and had lodged in the crotch of a wild olive. There one seed had germinated. Roots sprang from the seedling fig, feeling their way down the trunk of the host tree until they reached the ground. The fig grew fast, and the olive supported its growth. Greedily the parasite wrapped itself around until, in time, the olive tree was choked and the fig took its place on the rim of the gorge. Since then it had sheltered many generations of leopards, and its silver-smooth bark was deeply scarred from the rake of their claws....

In the tree she felt secure. Here she could rest, high beyond the reach of the Gorge pride lions. Leopards and lions feel a mutual antipathy. They are competitors, fellow carnivores sharing the same hunting grounds, but with little else in common. Lions are social cats, animals of the wide savannas, and their coats are the colour of Africa itself. Leopards are solitary, and shun the plains. In the Mara they live wherever there is cover; in the rocks of kopjes, in lairs of thorns, in the riverine forests and shady luggas, and on the overgrown slopes of the Siria escarpment. They are the

Left: A leopard (Panthera pardus) *stretches on a tree limb, Kenya. By Ken Cole/ Animals Animals.*

From the snows of Vladivostok
To the Mountains of the Cape,
Through your monkey-haunted forests
Where the long lianas drape:
From the fringe of Himalaya
To the skirts of seven seas,
You are all alone and catlike—
With your shadow, in the trees.

PETER TURNBULL-KEMP
The Leopard

Lions are animals of the sun, leopards seem to be of the moon. Though both hunt by night, the lion has always been associated with myths of the sun; he is shining and radiant; his mane frames him like the sun's rays. The leopard's coat is like the dapple of firelight and dark on the forest floor, his eyes are the pale gold of the hunter's moon.

EVELYN AMES
A Glimpse of Eden

Right: Rio Balsas, painting by Alfredo Arreguin, 1990. Page 88: Lionesses rest in a tree. Popularly supposed to dislike climbing trees, lions (especially females) will readily climb after prey, to steal a leopard's kill, or to escape insect pests. By Mary Plage/Bruce Coleman, Inc. Pages 90–91: Three-month-old leopard in a thorn tree, Masai Mara, Kenya. By Norbert Rosing/Animals Animals.

nightwalkers, moonlight hunters whose spotted coats render them almost invisible in dappled shadow.

From her airy perch she could survey the entire length of the gorge. Beyond the figs and cactus-like euphorbia trees which sprouted from its rim, the ground rolled away in a stony, tsetse-infested waste of whistling thorns until it joined the open plains. Even from so great a distance, the leopard could see that the grasslands were devoid of game. Within the last two weeks the herds had left for the Serengeti. Once more the vast concourse of wildebeest and zebra had gone south in a cloud of dust, leaving the Marsh lions to hunt pig and buffalo, or to scavenge kills from the…hyaenas. But the seasonal movements of the plains game scarcely affected the leopard. Unlike the lions, whose lives swung between glut and famine, she could depend on an inexhaustible supply of smaller prey. She preferred impala and Thomson's gazelle; but she would also eat hares, dik-dik, hyrax, genets, rock pythons, guinea fowl—

even the bright metallic-blue starlings whose chattering throngs sometimes shared her larder trees.

Once the sun had plunged behind the escarpment, night came swiftly in the eastern sky. The leopard stretched; her claws unsheathed. With forelegs flattened and hindquarters raised, she scratched the bark until it bled. Then, turning easily in her own length, she leapt to a lower branch and balanced, black against the sky, her long tail curved in an elegant question mark. From its perch in a tree on the opposite wall of the gorge, an eagle owl caught the sudden movement. The owl came regularly to the gorge to kill hyrax which lived in holes amongst the rocks. A faint sound behind it caused the bird's head to swivel sharply. When it turned back again, the leopard had gone. She had come down the tree in a series of zig-zag bounds, her paws barely touching the bark as she flowed soundlessly into the shadows.

BRIAN JACKMAN
The Marsh Lions

Nov. 1999
Rick, Debbie,
Chelsea   10
Justin   4
Blake   1

Feline Landscapes

A serval treads delicately through the tall grass stems of Kenya's Masai Mara, barely disturbing them in his passage…a jaguar crouches by a stream bank in Brazil's water-laced Pantanal, waiting for a fish to swim into range…in Alberta, a lynx dashes through snow-laden firs after a long-legged hare…a margay hugs a tree limb in the Paraguay rain-forest, eyes riveted on a preening bird…A Pallas' cat emerges from a marmot's den on a rocky slope in the Siberian Altai, fluffs its thick fur, and scales a nearby rock face for a better view of the mountainside.

The most widely distributed terrestrial carnivores, cats can live in an extraordinary range of habitats. The basic cat shape has proved suitable for life in many climates and kinds of terrain, from the ocean shores to high mountains, and from sandstone canyons to lush jungles. Coloration usually varies according to how a cat's landscape is colored or patterned. Beyond this, many cat species have refined their physical equipment to work optimally with their habitats: the cheetah's lanky build and long legs endows it with supreme speed over flat ground; the margay's shortened legs, extra-long claws, and huge lemurlike eyes provide an edge for hunting in the trees.

However, the cat world's generalists may be more successful than its specialists. The two most widely distributed species are the mountain lion in the Western Hemisphere and the leopard in the Old World. Both are somewhat under maximum cat size, take prey ranging from deer and antelope to small rodents, and can live in habitats varying from wet to dry, and from sea level to highlands. Neither favors the open plains and both manage to live fairly close to human habitation—a useful adaptation in today's world, though a risky path for any wild cat to choose. 🐾

Bobcat (Lynx rufus) *on a sandstone cliff, Uinta National Forest, Utah. By Kevin Schafer/Peter Arnold, Inc.*

Above: Caracal (Lynx caracal) in the Okavango Delta region of Botswana, southern Africa. Despite being sometimes called the "desert lynx" caracals tend to live in dry woodland, hilly steppe, and savannah habitats rather than true desert. This medium-sized cat can take prey as large as impala. By Dave Hamman/ABPL. Facing page: Florida panther (Felis concolor coryi), by Tom & Pat Leeson/West Stock.

The lynx shows a preference for old, high-timbered forests with dense under-growth and windfalls. Like many other cats, however, it is adaptable enough to colonize a variety of other types of habi-tat. In the Coto Doñana of Spain, for instance, it has established itself very successfully in the fairly open forests of pines, junipers, and pistachio scrub covering old sand-dune areas, as well as in the almost impenetrable bush along the swamps. In Mongolia and the Gobi Altai, the lynx is a rock dweller, partial to places where stony outcrops alter-nate with shrubs.

CHARLES A. W. GUGGISBERG
Wild Cats of the World

CATS IN THEIR PLACES

As the true cats spread themselves over the earth, they managed, for the most part, to adjust so per-fectly to one another by keeping their distance, by hunting different prey, and by moving around at different times of day that now different kinds of cats can coexist on the same bit of ground. Three square miles of national forest in Idaho might, for instance, support a puma, a bobcat or two, and per-haps a few feral housecats, with the puma hunting deer and the bobcats and housecats hunting birds and small rodents and keeping well out of the puma's way. A few square miles of tropical rain for-est might similarly support a jaguar, a puma, an ocelot or two, and one or more varieties of the smaller spotted cats. In a European forest, to the consternation of roaming housecats, a lynx's range might also support some wildcats, and in the Asian jungles, a tiger's range would probably support a leopard and possibly also one or more kinds of the small, rare, and beautiful jungle cats. Finally, the range of a pride of lions on the African savannah could support up to five other feline species, most

of them in slightly different settings. One might find a black-footed wildcat, a serval (Africa's version of the ocelot), and perhaps a caracal (Africa's ver-sion of the lynx). Larger cats might live there, too, perhaps a leopard to hunt in the long grass and thickets and a cheetah to course the open plains. Such cats are competitive and mutually hostile; they seek and destroy one another's kittens but otherwise avoid one another at all costs. Even so, by overlapping the distribution of their species, the cats have so perfectly arranged themselves that virtually everything that creeps or flies or walks can be used by one or another of them in almost every situation.

ELIZABETH MARSHALL THOMAS
The Tribe of Tiger

THE BOREAL FOREST

"We'll come to it just ahead—true boreal forest. Excellent lynx habitat."

We let the bright slash of the cutline lead us farther north. Sure enough, the forest is different here. No more poplars, only spruce, and the air is spiced and cool. On both sides of the trail the trees rise like a wall. When I peer in among them, my eyes lose their way in a prickly darkness. A few minutes farther along the trail, the gloom gives way to an open lakeshore. This varied landscape— dense conifers (for denning and shelter) inter-rupted by burned areas or brushy breaks (for hunting)—is the lynx's home.

In the winter the northern forest is deep-snow country, and more than most other predators, lynx are adapted to meet this difficulty. Their legs are extra long to help them through the drifts, and their feet are broad and padded with hair to serve as snowshoes....

It is exhilarating to think that there are lynx nearby. In my mind's eye I see them padding silent-ly along fallen logs; slinking, bellies to the ground, through the willows. Some are bedded under trees and lie dozing, licking their toes. One sits on its haunches in a small clearing and calmly watches us ski past. I scan the forest expectantly, allowing myself to half believe I'll catch a lynx looking back.

CANDACE SAVAGE
Wild Cats

THE EVERGLADES

The land Ponce de León named Florida in 1513 contains today the last true wilderness in the nation. The Everglades, a roadless waste of swamp and hammock, sawgrass and palmetto, of orchids and strangler figs and poisonous manchineel, rolls south a hundred miles from Lake Okeechobee to the mangrove estuaries and shallow flats of Cape Sable, Florida Bay, and the inner Keys. The Cape Sable area is also vast and virtually all uninhabited, and Okeechobee itself is twenty miles across. To the north of the lake lies a different wilderness, broad distances of long-grass prairie, the Kissimmee, some wild birds of which are not again encountered anywhere east of the coastal plains of Texas. Cypress swamps and limestone springs provide other distinct habitats, and far out in the Gulf the Dry Tortugas, named for the green turtles that once abounded there, support tropical sea birds seen nowhere else in North America.

Much of Florida's flora and fauna is peculiar to this four-hundred-mile peninsula, a fact not surprising when one considers that much of it is tropic, remote biologically from the temperate land mass to the north and remote geographically from other areas in the same latitudes. Its waters, fresh and salt, still swarm with fish, and its wildernesses, resistant to man, shelter a variety of life unmatched elsewhere on the continent. Florida can claim today almost all its original land mammals, including significant populations of the bobcat, river otter, and black bear, and a few cougar.

PETER MATTHIESSEN
Wildlife in America

Cheetah (Acinonyx jubatus) on a rocky outcrop, Serengeti National Park, Tanzania. Cheetahs favor flat, open habitats where their great speed can best be used. They are sight hunters, often perching atop rock outcrops or ant-mounds to survey the surrounding plains; they can climb trees but do so rarely. Fires that sweep across the savannahs contribute to high mortality among cheetah cubs, often hidden by their mothers in the grass. By Mark Deeble & Victoria Stone/Animals Animals.

THE BUSHVELD

Bushveld is a word that describes an area containing a myriad of habitats. Some areas are totally dominated by mopane scrub veld for hundreds of square kilometres with skylines dominated by the massive baobab tree, some are mostly grass and others are dominated by sandveld tree communities....Its strength is habitat diversity.

The reserve covers 45,000 acres of gently rolling country more or less bisected by the perennial Sand River, the most important source of water....Away from the river the country falls away in a series of low, rolling hills.

The valleys in-between these ridges support delicate grassland communities, based on clay soils, that are known as seeplines. These areas are very important to the large grazing species such as rhino, wildebeest, buffalo and zebra who feed on the red grass, buffalo grass and other nutritious grass species that thrive in the wet summer months....

Throughout the reserve there are intermittent rocky outcrops and some large granite *koppies* or hills. These are an important component of the landscape—not only for their different vegetation types but also for the cover and vantage points they provide....

This great diversity of habitat supports a wide range of animal and bird species, from the tiny but ubiquitous termite to the majestic elephant, from the busy nectar-feeding sunbirds to the ostrich of the grasslands. Insects and reptiles abound and it is as fascinating to watch a dung beetle roll his mate along on a ball of fresh dung, or a black mamba exploring nests and holes in a leadwood tree, as it is to watch a lion stalking or two buffalo bulls duelling over a female.

GERALD HINDE AND WILLIAM TAYLOR
An African Experience

SIBERIA TO SOUTHEAST ASIA

Somewhere in Siberia millions of years ago a flow of molten lava from the depths of the earth formed the crater of what is now an extinct volcano. Slowly, over the centuries, it cracked and congealed to form a multitude of boulders. The area was cold, dark and inaccessible, and the first descriptions of it were written by travellers less than 200 years ago: "Rugged mountain jaws opened upon us in all their grandeur. This was a terrific rent: the dark purple slaty rock had been riven asunder by granite and heaved up into craggy precipices of enormous height....Deep ravines have been cut in the mass by torrents which come tumbling down."

Once exploration became possible, a discovery was made in the heart of Siberia: it revealed the earliest known information on the origins of the tiger. Fossil records dating from the Pleistocene period were found deep within the Chigar caves of the New Siberian islands, indicating that a sabre-toothed tiger existed there millions of years ago. This tiger became extinct only about 10,000 years ago, and its descendants, the true tigers, began to extend their range, moving southwards in search of more suitable habitats as successive phases of the ice age made northern Asia uninhabitable.

Today, deep in the snows of the Soviet Far East, the Siberian tiger still roams. Its territory is a spectacular combination of plains and mountains, a coast facing the Sea of Japan and the River Amur flowing through startling landscapes. The plains of the Ussuri region stretch westwards, encompassing larch and dark conifer forests and copses of dwarf pines peep from the summit of the mountains. Temperatures can sink as low as -35°C and the winters are bitterly cold.

VALMIK THAPAR
The Tiger's Destiny

In the high plateau of the Moi hinterland lying in the centre of Indo-China where Vietnam, Cambodia and Laos all meet, the forest clearings are always covered with pines and other conifers. In South Vietnam, in the neighbourhood of Phaurang, the general desolation of the scenery is enhanced by the fantastic bare silhouettes of stunted trees standing up gaunt in the grassy plain. This kind of country crops up again at Son Phan, an area near the border of South Annam which is very rich in game of all kinds, especially the big grey ox and the little red one. In Cambodia, these clearings are often visited by cow-prey and in Laos by a smaller species of gaur. Deer, goats, muntjacs, wild boar and agoutis are usually to be found in the forest clearing; so also is the tiger, who comes here to escape from the wood-leech, elsewhere so abundant.

M. DURAND
Imagerie Populaire Vietnamienne

Above: Track of a Siberian tiger in mud. By Erwin & Peggy Bauer. Below: Bengal tiger (Panthera tigris) leaping from rocks to a reedy river bank in the Ranthambhore reserve, India. By Gunther Ziesler/Peter Arnold, Inc. Tigers occasionally hunt in water, and for many cats water is not just for drinking but a place in which to cool off, play, or find relief from pests.

The Fine Detail

Forests of pines, firs, and spruces laced the landscape according to subtle patterns of rain, rock, soil, and slope....It was good country for lions, too. Forests and rock-strewn hillsides afforded plenty of cover and den sites. High and low seasonal pastures of the northern Yellowstone ecosystem seem to have supported plentiful prey in the form of mule deer, bighorn sheep, antelope, bison, and especially elk for at least a millennium.

CHRIS BOLGIANO
Mountain Lion

North American lynx (Lynx canadensis) *hunting a snowshoe hare, the mainstay of this cat's diet. By Tom & Pat Leeson.*

Cats are woven into their habitats intricately, often inseparably. First and foremost, their predation helps control the populations of local plant-eaters, so that these do not overmultiply and overgraze the available plant resources. And as they go about their lives, cats interact with particular details of their landscapes in many ways. Terrain features such as hills, rocks, and caves provide them with vantage points, shelter from pursuit by hunters or other predators (a wolf pack, say), and nurseries for their young. Grasses, reeds, and trees offer cover from which to stalk prey; trees are also hunting grounds for the arboreal cats. Trees serve as receptors of cats' territorial scent-marks and as tools on which they hone and exercise their claws. Cats often chew and swallow grasses or leaves as a digestive scour, and many species avidly consume catnip *(Nepeta cataria)* or other related plants, which apparently produce an odor similar to a cat's own pheromones.

Cats play a vital role in their ecological communities from their spot atop the food chain. Plants synthesize sunlight and inorganic matter to create food for herbivores, which are killed by predators. In addition to controlling and improving the prey species, predation returns nourishment to the soil from the decomposing flesh and bones of the herbivores, along with the feces of the carnivores who consume them—thus renewing the most basic cycle of life on earth. 🐾

THE LYNX-HARE PARADIGM

North American lynx are specialists. Although they can kill grouse, ducks, mice, beavers, squirrels, even deer, they are critically dependent on a single food—the snowshoe hare. When hares increase in number, North American lynx populations climb. When hare numbers dwindle, the cats follow them into decline. As Ernest Thompson Seton put it, in a typically toothsome phrase, the lynx "lives on Rabbits, follows the Rabbits, thinks Rabbits, tastes like Rabbits, increases with them, and on their failure dies of starvation in the unrabbited woods."

Over the past fifty years, the lynx's changing fortunes have provided ecologists with a major perplexity. The lynx's ups and downs don't occur at random; instead, they are cyclic. A complete pattern, from peak population down to the trough and back up to the peak, generally takes from eight to eleven years, with an average of about ten....

Why would the life of a forest go through such a pulse?…Current thinking describes a dynamic interaction amongst the inhabitants of the northern forest. The story begins with willows and other woody plants that produce juicy shoots and bark. Hares eat this nutritious winter browse and have big litters of bunnies, which grow up, eat and have more bunnies, and on and on.…Where there are thousands of snowshoe hares, there will be dozens of lynx, enjoying the easy hunting and raising their own large families.

But this widespread abundance depends on the trees and shrubs, which soon somehow determine that they have taken enough. Willows and alders, two of the hare's favourite foods, respond to aggressive browsing by putting out new shoots that contain bitter, indigestible compounds related to turpentine. This change puts the hares into a double bind. Not only has their food supply been reduced in quantity by thousands of gnawing teeth, it has also been diminished in quality by an act of herbal angst. Under these conditions, many hares starve and the survivors reproduce slowly.

By the time the hares reach bottom (at a scant 5 per cent of their top numbers), the lynx have hit hard times, too. The prosperous dozens of the good old days dwindle to a handful of gaunt survivors and footsore wanderers. It's the darkness before dawn. Granted a reprieve from browsing, the shrubs soon begin producing succulent young shoots. Within a couple of years the woods are full of bunnies, and lynx start to raise young kits. The forest's ten-year cycle is on the upsurge again.

Everybody knows, with no-nonsense certainty, that willows, lynx and snowshoe hares are different kinds of creatures and entirely distinct. Willows are bushes. Lynx are cats. Hares are lagomorphs. But this perception of separateness is partly illusory. We can perceive the surfaces that keep things apart, but not the interactions that hold them together. The connections within the forest are real, as substantial as the nerves and arteries that unite our own bodies.

CANDACE SAVAGE
Wild Cats

THE BOBCAT TREE

From a distance, the dark green juniper appeared shrublike, though it was a twelve-foot-tall tree. Its feathery foliage, hugging twisting stems, gave it the dense look of a bush. Its lowest boughs grew close to the ground and spread wide, like some great sage hen's wings awkwardly trying to shelter the round-bodied rabbit brush that grew around its base.

For more than a century, the juniper had stood alone, a single tree surrounded by desert brush. Boring beetles invaded its dead branches, sage thrashers ate its silver blue berries, winter mantled it. Still it lived on. Its solitariness was awesome. Shoshone hunters long ago had made camp near the tree and, moved by its presence, imbued it with a spirit god. Then they passed from the scene. Still the tree stood, untouched by the sweep of such human events. Since then, wind, silence, and time weighed on the ancient tree, and no person heard the creak of its branches or watched it put forth green fingers.

The tree was known to a bobcat, however. It was, in fact, an important feature on her home range. Frequently, she visited it to sharpen her claws, shredding its fibrous trunk down to vulnerable cambium. After each assault, the tree slowly

The bobcat is much more ubiquitous than the Canada lynx, inhabiting sagebrush country, semi-desert regions, bare mountain-sides, the dense tangles of West Coast chaparral, and woodlands of many types, including subtropical swamp forests and the heavy, humid forests of the Cascade Mountains. In the arid Southwest, it shows a preference for foot-hill bush, but is also quite abundant in open, barren, and rocky areas.

CHARLES A. W. GUGGISBERG
Wild Cats of the World

Cutaway view of a bobcat natal den, with the mother about to enter and rejoin her kits. Bobcat dens usually are very well hidden in a dense thicket, a hollow tree, or a rocky cavity, often in the midst of a tangle of windfall trees. Females with young kits mark the area around their den with droppings to warn other bobcats away.

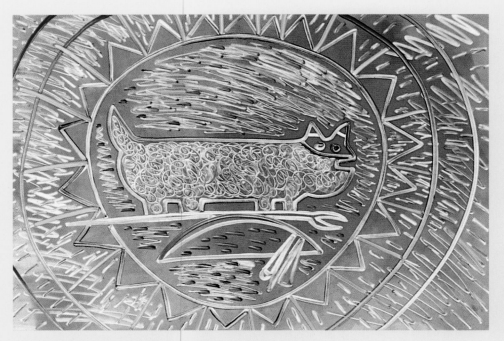

Mountain Lion Series, #2, *monoprint by Linda Lomahaftewa, 1988.*

THE FIRE CAT

In August of every year, according to legend, a large puma appears as the great Fire Cat, jumping from the Olympic mountains to the Selkirks, to Baker, to Rainier, and back to the Olympics, setting fires. It is said that many moons ago a chief of the Lummi Indians on the islands in Puget Sound acquired great wealth and stored it in a huge cave. He captured a large female puma and trained her to live in the cave and guard his treasures. The chief told his two sons that if misfortune should come to them after his death, they should go with fifty men to the cave and tie a fawn at the entrance to lure the big cat out. They then could slay the animal and recover the riches stored inside the cave.

One of the sons grew greedy and gathered fifty warriors with him to steal the wealth. They followed the directions of the chief and killed the puma as it bounded out of the cave. In their greed and haste, they did not realize they had killed a kitten of the big female. While rejoicing over their kill, the great guardian cat charged from the depths of the cave and killed the son of the chief with one swipe of her massive paw and then pursued the warriors into the timber, seeking them out one by one until she had killed them all. The beast was so enraged that she clawed the huge tree until the pitch burst into flames and the forests roared with fire. Since then, the great Fire Cat is supposed to return annually in all her fury to fire the mountains in August.

Tribal tale of the Yakimas and Lummis
in the Puget Sound area

repaired itself, building a new shield of bark. Then the bobcat would return and repeat the mischief.

It was necessary for the old cat to hone her talons, to keep them razor sharp. They were her grappling hooks, her means of escaping up trees, of scaling rock faces. They were also her carving tools, used to rip open prey she killed. And most important, sharp claws were the bobcat's best defense against enemies....

Such vital equipment required maintenance. To prevent them from wearing blunt, the cat walked with her claws withdrawn, protected in sheaths of skin....Moreover, because they never ceased to grow, their old and worn outer layers frequently had to be scaled away, a task best accomplished by dragging them down a stump or a tree.

For that purpose, the old female often made use of the juniper, and had done so for many years. Like the tree, she was a survivor....

HOPE RYDEN
Bobcat Year

LION IN THE GRASS

Two hours before sunset, a new breeze came sighing over the grass. Scar awoke and lifted his head. As the sun slid down, animals emerged from the shadows and began to feed again. Zebra and topi moved slowly along the horizon. A stormcloud bloomed above the escarpment, bearing rain from Lake Victoria. Above it the sky became an immense applegreen cupola, clear and empty except for the specks of orbiting vultures. The cooling air revived him. Leisurely he stood up and walked out into the plain. The grass enveloped him, closing behind him as he moved through the gently bending stems. He felt the brush of its plumed seedheads along his flanks, smelled its dry odour crushed beneath his heavy pads as he sniffed at the sharper taints where Thomson's gazelles had scent-marked individual

spikes of grass with special glands on their cheeks. But when he paused to test the wind, lifting his muzzle above the tops of the grasses, he heard the familiar grunting of wildebeest and padded silently towards the fig tree forest. The trees lay across the lower end of the Marsh in a ragged crescent. Normally they provided excellent cover which enabled the lions to approach the reeds unobserved; but, as he slipped through the leafy shadows he was seen by a troop of Syke's monkeys. Their coughs of alarm alerted the wildebeest so that, when Scar stepped out into the open, they were already scattering before him in a rush of tossing heads. Panic spread across the Marsh. Birds flew up, crying wildly. Zebra and topi burst from the reeds and splashed to the safety of the open plains. The lion ignored them all.

BRIAN JACKMAN
The Marsh Lions

Now the great cloud cat,
darting out its lightning tongue,
licks the creamy moonlight
from the saucepan of the sky.

YOGESVARA
translated by Daniel H. H. Ingalls

Male lion stirs and yawns as a rainbow touches down on the Kalahari Desert, Botswana. By Charles G. Summers, Jr.

Fellow Creatures

Below: A troop of baboons routs a leopard, Masai Mara, Kenya. These large primates have been known to kill a small leopard by mobbing it. By Jonathan Scott/Planet Earth Pictures. Pages 102–103: Mountain lion in the sand dunes of Little Sahara, central Utah. By Daniel J. Cox.

Cats, with their global distribution, share their home ranges with a large portion of the animal kingdom. Their relations with most other creatures can be grouped according to the questions: "Can I eat it?" or "Will it eat me?" The feline diet of meat includes flesh of almost any kind, as we'll see in the next chapter. But relatively few animals can kill an adult wild cat; the young are far more vulnerable, of course.

Relations with fellow creatures aren't always a life-and-death matter. Young cats play with smaller animals that they will one day kill. Some cats appropriate the dens of smaller mammals for their young, and all larger cats provide food for other meat-eaters with their kills.

The adversaries of cats include dogs of all kinds; and hyenas, which steal kills and prey on the young of African cats. Competition among the formidable predators of the savannahs is especially intense, with hyenas, wild dogs, and big cats equally capable of killing each other or stealing kills, depending on circumstances. In North America, cougars and bears seem to avoid each other, though bears chase cougars from kills at times, and a female puma was seen to chase a bear from her den. Cats also steer clear of the biggest herbivores such as elephants, rhinos, and hippos, unless a calf appears vulnerable. The only creatures wild cats seem to serenely ignore are the birds that scavenge their kills—giving the lie to felines' supposed craving for birds, or perhaps revealing some understanding of these scavengers' role in completing the cats' work.

A LEOPARD SCORNED

Normally all animals flee in silence. But not baboons. It is rather as though you are a policeman breaking up a noisy political meeting. Even before they reach the trees both the young and old are turning their heads and hurling threats, hisses and screams at you. Once they are in the branches the uproar redoubles, and there is a note of mockery in the cries as you pass beneath. An awful smell of dungeons hangs in the air. All this is mildly embarrassing and even a little annoying—after all, you have done nothing to the baboons except disturb them—and it's much better fun when a leopard, the chief object of the baboons' hatred, is the centre of the abuse. The leopard walks by with a pained look and an elaborate air of

paying no attention, but somehow as an act it doesn't quite come off. The leopard has, however, better means of redress than an actor being booed from the gallery; he will return at night when the moon is down, and with one noiseless pounce through the branches will tear some sleeping baboon to pieces.

ALAN MOOREHEAD
No Room in the Ark

Wildebeests, hartebeests, Thomson's and Grant's gazelles not only stare at it, but follow in its wake. From time to time one group or another wheels around and canters away, only to stop and approach again. Four blackbacked jackals suddenly

turn up. One of them barks as it becomes aware of the cheetah, two trot along behind it. The wildebeests and hartebeests snort, while the gazelles eventually take flight. The hartebeests are particularly excited, galloping to and fro, gambolling around. Two crested cranes fly over the cat, land nearby and keep pace with it on foot. They jump with uplifted wings when it once turns towards them. At times a regular procession is moving over the plain—the cheetah in the lead, followed closely by the two jackals, with eight or ten hartebeests forming the main body. The cheetah only loses its "retinue" when it finally crosses a deep valley.

CHARLES A. W. GUGGISBERG
Wild Cats of the World

Young lionesses investigate a pair of porcupines, Gemsbok Park, Kalahari Desert, Botswana. Lions (and other wild cats) like to eat porcupines and some learn to flip the creature over with a paw to get at its vulnerable underside—but some earn this experience painfully. Quills in the face or tongue can mean a slow death for a cat unable to eat, and Charles Guggisberg reports, "In the Tsavo National Park I once saw a lioness with about six to eight porcupine quills sticking out from her side." By J & B Photo/Animals Animals.

COYOTE IMITATES MOUNTAIN LION

Coyote was going along and he saw a rock rolling down the hill. It rolled down toward some deer and they jumped. Coyote wondered who was rolling stones and looked up at the top of the hill. Another stone came rolling down past Coyote toward the deer and the deer jumped again. Then a third stone came down and the deer jumped only a little. They knew it was only a stone.

The next moment another stone came by Coyote. But this was a soft rock. It was Mountain Lion who had rolled himself up like a rock and was rolling down the hill.

"What a funny rock," thought Coyote. "It doesn't make any noise when it rolls."

Mountain Lion rolled right up to the deer who were not suspicious of the rolling rocks by this time. Then Coyote saw Mountain Lion get up, jump on a big deer and kill it. Mountain Lion picked up the deer and carried it up to a cliff where he could eat it and see the country all around. The rest of the deer ran off around the hill.

Coyote thought this would be a good way to get deer.

He rolled a stone down the hill to where the deer were and they jumped. He rolled another stone and they did not jump as far. When he rolled the third stone they only looked around to see that it was just another stone. Then Coyote rolled himself up in a ball like Mountain Lion and rolled down the hill. When he got there he jumped up and tried to get a deer but he couldn't. He was too dizzy. He just fell over and the deer ran away.

Zuñi tale, retold by BARRY LOPEZ
*Giving Birth to Thunder, Sleeping with his Daughter:
Coyote Builds North America*

Above: Mountain lion (Felis concolor) keeps a wary eye on a coyote (Canis latrans) passing by at the foot of a small bluff. By Michael Francis/The Wildlife Collection. Facing page: Gray wolf (Canis lupus), Rocky Mountains. By Jim Dutcher.

Cat Versus Dog

The famous antipathy between domestic cats and dogs holds true in the wild world as well, often with far more serious consequences. Except for wolves, members of the canid family—wild dogs, jackals, coyotes, foxes and their relatives—are rarely the largest or most dominant carnivore in their ranges. But because they sometimes travel in packs, they can harass even big cats off their kills, chase them up trees, and generally make themselves detested by their feline cohabitants. Tigers have been harried and even killed by the huge packs of wild dogs that once roamed India. Wolves in any number can easily drive a cougar off its kill, and some cougar deaths have been attributed to wolves. By the same token, a big cat can kill an individual canine with a swipe of its paw or a bite to the skull. Smaller canines rarely pose a threat to full-grown cats; they are more likely to scavenge food from them.

Such interspecies competition has not been well studied. But even if cats and dogs did not compete for prey resources in the wild, their very different styles of social interaction would no doubt put them at odds—as Hope Ryden illustrates in one of the excerpts that follows. 🐾

Snow clouds come up over the mountains, and the shining river turns to black, over black rocks. A lone black *dzo* nuzzles the stony earth. GS [George Schaller] has picked up scat of a large carnivore and turns it in his hand, wondering aloud why fox sign, so abundant at Black Pond, is uncommon here at lower altitudes. "Too big for fox, I think...."

As GS speaks, I scan the mountain slopes for bharal: on these rolling hills to the east of Somdo, we have not seen even one. Abruptly, he says, "Hold it! Freeze! Two snow leopard!" I see a pale shape slip behind a low rise patched with snow, as GS, agitated, mutters, "Tail's too short! Must have been foxes!"

"No," I say. "Much too big—!"

"Wolves!" he cries out. "Wolves!"

And there they are.

Moving away without haste up an open slope beyond the rise, the wolves bring the barren hills to life. Two on the slope to northward frisk and play, but soon they pause to look us over; their tameness is astonishing. Then they cut across the hill to join three others that are climbing a stone gully. The pack stops each little while to gaze at us, and through the telescope we rejoice in every shining hair: two silver wolves, and two of faded gold, and one that is the no-color of frost: this frost-colored wolf, a big male, seems to be leader.... "That's why there's no sign of fox or leopard!" GS says, "and that's why the blue sheep stay near the river cliffs, away from this open country!" I ask if the wolves would hunt and kill the fox and leopard, and he says they would. For some reason, the wolves' appearance here has taken us by surprise; it is in Tibet that such mythic creatures belong. This is an Asian race of *Canis lupus,* the timber wolf, which both of us have seen in Alaska, and it is always an exciting animal: the empty hills where the pack has gone come to life.

PETER MATTHIESSEN
The Snow Leopard

Above: North American lynx (Lynx canadensis) in a defensive posture, Bangtail Mountains, southwestern Montana. By Daniel J. Cox. Right: A coyote, sometimes known as the "song dog," howling in response to the howl of another. By Tom Bledsoe/DRK Photo.

The dogs had spread themselves around the tigress, who was growling ferociously. Every now and then one would dash in from behind to bite her. She would then turn to attempt to rend asunder this puny aggressor, when a couple of others would rush in from other direction. In this way she was kept going continually, and I could see she was fast becoming spent....

Quoted by GEORGE SCHALLER
The Deer and the Tiger

A FAILURE TO COMMUNICATE

In this episode of her fictionalized account Bobcat Year, *Hope Ryden describes how a coyote pup might have wandered away from its family and encountered a young bobcat.*

Facing him was an animal larger than any prey he had yet seen; it was the same size as himself, yet it was not a coyote. The pup responded by opening his mouth to its full flex and exposing all thirty-two of his sharp baby teeth.

The bobcat kitten was not impressed by this gape, for the body signals of a coyote were not in his feline vocabulary....[H]e advanced toward the coyote pup.

The young coyote hunched and rounded his spine in the manner of a Halloween cat. But even this posture, so well understood by coyotes and foxes and, indeed, by most species of the world's cats, failed to deter the oncoming kitten. The bobcat's threat posture was different. The bobcat expressed aggression by raising his shoulders and presenting, not an enlarged view of his side, but his full face, which, at maturity, would be enhanced by wide muttonchops. In this, he behaved like a maned lion. So the bobcat did not take offense at the coyote's behavior. His mood, in fact, was genial, a fact that could easily have been discerned by another bobcat, for he walked boldly, with his stubby tail held erect.

Now it was the coyote pup who misread the bobcat's mood. He understood the cat's posture in terms of his own species' behavior. To the coyote, a stiffly held tail signaled hostility. A coyote who wished to communicate friendly intentions did so by carrying his tail in a low, swinging, relaxed position. Accordingly, the pup's hostility now escalated, and he tipped his head to one side the better to expose his long double row of teeth. But even this exaggerated display of dentition did not deter the oncoming kitten, whose unshakable confidence unnerved the coyote. The pup rolled onto his back and assumed a posture of abject submission.

In the more social world of the wild coyote, this act of surrender would have been understood for what it was—a ritualized gesture of appeasement, a technique for defusing aggression. Nick Ear, however, did not understand this conciliatory language...[He] responded by backing away.

The coyote pup, now satisfied that his gesture of surrender had disarmed the stranger, sprang to his feet and prepared to participate in friendly greeting. His amicable move greatly alarmed the bobcat, and when the young canid raised his paw in typical canid invitation to play, Nick Ear went on the offensive. To the bobcat, a raised paw was a dangerous weapon, something to be respected. Nick Ear hunched his shoulders and ventilated his annoyance in a long, low, rumbling growl.

This unexpected response startled the pup, causing him to back away and sit down. He did understand a growl. He too employed that signal on occasion. For several minutes the two animals eyed one another, neither daring to make a move. Then the pup, feeling amiable again, expressed this attitude by wagging his ropy tail. The lashing appendage sent the kitten sprinting. In the bobcat's world, twitching tail suggested mounting tension and aggressive intent.

The kitten took refuge on a high rock, and from that vantage place he hissed and spat at the coyote.

The standoff between the two species might well have lasted...had not a faraway wail alerted the young coyote that his clan was gathering for its evening howl.

HOPE RYDEN
Bobcat Year

THE WILDCAT AND THE TREE-CLIMBING JACKAL

Jackal was well-known for playing tricks on his fellow creatures; so they mistrusted him; but in spite of this, he fooled them time and again. The animals also disliked Jackal because he was a most annoying boaster.

Now one day, while out hunting for food, Jackal met Wildcat, who was lounging elegantly on the branch of a tree. Jackal was jealous, as this was something he could not do.

"Why do you climb trees, Wildcat?" he asked.

Wildcat replied that it gave her an excellent view, so that she could see friend or foe coming from a long way off. Also, climbing trees was a handy way of escaping from the dogs which were forever chasing her.

"Oh, what a coward you are, Wildcat!" sneered the jackal. "Only cowards, snakes and silly birds hide in trees."

Wildcat's feelings were hurt, but she kept her temper, knowing that Jackal was a nasty trickster, and thinking it would be better to keep on the right side of him.

"Do not forget," she replied patiently, "I cannot run as fast as you, and dogs are my natural enemy."

"I can run faster than any creature in the land," boasted Jackal. "Let those scruffy old dogs come—I'm not afraid of them—anyway, I could outrun them any day."

"That may be so," replied Wildcat gently, "but the art of climbing trees has its use in times of trouble, you know. Would you like me to teach you?"

Jackal considered this generous offer. "Hmm…Well, knowledge can never hurt one," he replied airily, "and I've nothing better to do at the moment." Secretly, he was rather anxious to learn.

African wildcat (Felis lybica) in a tree, Kalahari Desert, South Africa. By Ronald S. Rogoff/Planet Earth Pictures.

Wildcat came down from her branch, and Jackal was given his first lesson. But alas, he was not a very good pupil because his claws were too blunt to grip the bark. He kept slipping, and falling on his back in the dirt.

Polite as she was, Wildcat could not help laughing at the sight of Jackal, the oh-so-clever one, scrabbling furiously up the trunk of the tree and falling in a heap every time.

Jackal was getting angrier and angrier, and suddenly he flew into a rage. He turned and snapped at poor Wildcat, grabbing her leg and snarling that he would kill her for making him look ridiculous.

That would most certainly have been the end of Wildcat, but, fortunately for her, a pack of dogs suddenly appeared, barking furiously. Jackal took one look and instantly was no longer the brave animal of his boasting.

He let go of Wildcat's leg and, as she scrambled up her tree to safety, Jackal put his tail between his legs and ran. He dived down a nearby anteater hole just as the dogs were about to catch him. The dogs tried to dig him out, but they could not reach him, so after a while they gave up and went away.

Now Jackal crept out of the hole and, to his shame, saw Wildcat grinning down at him from her perch. She burst out laughing as he slunk away to mend his wounded pride.

From that day on, whenever Wildcat happened to see Jackal, she took refuge in the nearest tree, for Jackal never forgot how she had seen his cowardice, and his desire for revenge was truly something to fear.

A story from Swaziland

Dangerous to Cats

Below: A sand cat (Felis margarita) hunts a sand viper, Sahara Desert, Niger. By Alain Dragesco/Planet Earth Pictures. Facing page, top: Alert lionesses on a stream bank, Hwange, Zimbabwe. By Bruce Golden/Photonica. Bottom: A hippo in the Okavango Delta shows his impressive, and dangerous, tusks, Botswana. By Frans Lanting/Minden Pictures.

As formidable as wild cats are, they can be vulnerable to injury or death from a variety of hazards. Downturns in prey populations can cause feline mortality to rise, especially in species that rely heavily on one kind of prey animal. A few cat-specific viruses can be fatal, and parasites ranging from intestinal worms to ticks can make their lives miserable.

Some cats, especially lions, are killed trying to bring down large, well-armed prey such as zebra and Cape buffalo, or maimed so that they cannot hunt. A bobcat they preys on fawns can well meet death at the hooves of a defending mother doe. Certain reptiles are a hazard: poisonous snakes can inflict a fatal bite, and cats that hunt in water sometimes fall prey to a crocodile or caiman (though jaguars also prey on the latter). Predation by other carnivores—hyenas, canids, mustelids, raptors, and larger felines—can be a factor, depending on the size and age of the cat.

But by far the greatest threat to cat survival, individually and as species, is human beings. Through hunting, trapping, destruction of habitat, prey disruption, and the trade in wild pets, our species has proven to be the most dangerous animal most cats will ever face. 🐾

Raised in India, Jim Corbett gained fame as the world's leading hunter of man-eating tigers. In this account he waits in a tree near the corpse of a victim, while the tiger meets his doom through a different agent.

I do not think I could have borne the gruesome sight much longer, when there was a roar and a brindled mass sprang at something which was invisible to me. Instantaneously, a vast speckled body coiled itself round the brindled matter, there was a struggle, bones seemed to be crunched to bits, the tiger gave a feeble roar or two, and then all was still except an occasional convulsive heaving.... That long, long night at length terminated and thankful I was to see the dawn of day and hear the jungle fowls proclaim that sunrise was at hand. Losing no time, I descended to solve last night's mystery. The sight that met my eyes was marvellous. A huge rock snake, a python, just over twenty-one feet in length, lay coiled round the body of the tiger whose fangs in turn were imbedded in the back of the snake's head, while the reptile's folds, after enveloping the tiger, had got a purchase by lashing its tail round the adjoining sapling, and so assisted the vast muscular power it possessed in crushing the tiger to death.

JIM CORBETT
The Man-Eaters of Kumaon

LORD OF THE MARSH

When the lions appeared on the bank above him, the hippo gave an ill-tempered snort. His nostrils forced a fine spray of water into the air as he tried to sink out of sight. Yet even with his short legs doubled under him and his belly touching the muddy bottom, the sun still shone on his back. His vulnerability nagged at him, causing his absurdly small ears to twitch angrily, flicking away beadlets of water.

The lion cubs were eager to drink but could sense their mother's caution and kept well behind her as she walked towards the water. Halfway down the bank she stopped and stared back at the pair of frog-like eyes watching her from midstream. Her tail lashed from side to side as she hesitated, sensing how dangerous a cornered hippo could be. When he did not move, she padded forward again with the cubs tumbling after her, and lowered her head to lap at the water's edge.

This was more than the hippo could endure. Water swirled off him as he lifted his huge angry bulk and shook his head. Then, with a cavernous yawn of rage, he turned and faced her. The startled lioness took one look at the gaping pink maw, the wickedly jutting ivory teeth, and fled. The hippo gave a triumphant snort and sank back into the pool, but no sooner had the ripples subsided than a new problem arrived.

The big pride male had lagged behind his females. Now he was hot and thirsty. He moved slowly, his great heavy head lolling, dry-tongued and panting. One of the lionesses rubbed her cheek against his mane, but he ignored her attentions and padded imperiously down to the river; the pride turned to follow.

For a moment the hippo seemed to shrink back into the pool. Unable to submerge, his tiny brain was wrestling with the possibilities of escape. Behind him, the bank rose in a twenty-foot vertical wall. Upstream, he knew to his cost, was another pool with many hippos, and his presence there would almost certainly provoke an attack. Downstream, the river ran noisily over rocky shallows. There was only one way out.

He gave no warning. The lion saw the pool erupt, saw the water part in two crashing bow waves as the hippo ploughed straight for him. He came with head down and, despite his enormous balloon-like girth, he moved with the speed of a charging rhino. He pounded up the bank, blunt mouth slightly parted to reveal a gleam of ivory, scattering the Paradise pride in all directions. But he did not pursue them far. At the edge of the bushes he stopped, defecated with furiously wagging tail, then turned and trotted back to his pool. As the cool waters closed around him, he felt again the soft attentions of the fishes. The lions faded from his memory as his nostrils flared and a deep, mirthless guffaw shook from his throat.

BRIAN JACKMAN
The Marsh Lions

At the center of a wild cat's existence is the hunt. Except for sleeping, nothing occupies more of a cat's lifetime; when it is not resting, mating, or caring for young, it is probably hunting—a skill cats are superbly evolved to practice. Cats occasionally steal or scavenge the kills of other predators, but in general do their own killing, and most competently. ❧ Hunting has shaped the feline body, from its lethal claws and canines to its silent, padded feet. Cats are the masters, probably the inventors, of what Elizabeth Thomas calls the "lurk-and-leap" method, creeping up on their prey through cover in a noiseless stalk, then overtaking it with a final rush and/or leap. With variations, such as the cheetah's longer-than-average rush, all cats hunt in much the same way, whether their quarry is a butterfly or a buffalo. The mere sight of prey provokes great emotional excitement in cats, which they may express in

The Way of the Hunter

remarkable ways: patting or licking recently killed prey, or (with pet cats) pouncing on a person or fellow cat as a "prey substitute." ❧ Opportunistic predators, cats will hunt and eat almost anything catchable that crosses their path. Most do favor certain kinds of prey— size is a factor, with big cats specializing in ungulates and smaller ones concentrating on rabbit- and rodent-sized prey. But some cats are known to take prey three times or more their own weight: bobcats regularly prey on deer, and Africa's tiny black-footed cat is said to kill sheep. Contrary to belief, young cats can recognize and kill prey without benefit of their mother's training—though surely this helps. ❧ Cats, like all predators, have suffered from the notion that predation is bad for the lovely hoofed herd animals (which humans, not coincidentally, also like to hunt). We now know that predation is vital to the health of prey populations; indeed, cats "co-evolved" along with their chief prey, each pushing the other to greater refinements of strength, speed, reflexes, and social skills over generations of natural selection. ❧ The cats' prowess as hunters has long been acknowledged by hunting cultures that share habitats with them. Though big cats can and do kill humans, a kind of mutual respect seems once to have existed between native peoples and wild cats, as skilled predators and worthy adversaries—and in some places survives. ➻

THE BLUE PRIDE GOES HUNTING

We were following Star, our favorite brown hyena, across the riverbed one night when she suddenly stopped and began to bristle, every hair standing out from her body. Suddenly she bolted westward: The Blue Pride was on the prowl. Sassy and Blue trotted to the truck and stood peering over the half door at us. At times this made us a little uneasy wondering if their mood might suddenly become dangerous. But no matter how close they came, they were always playful.

After their initial investigation, Sassy and Blue apparently tired of trying to spook us. Without warning, they launched a mock attack on Spicy, bowling her over and then chasing her in circles around the Land Rover, their big feet drumming on the ground. Their mood was infectious, and the two male cubs, Rascal and Hombre, joined in the fun, all the lions romping in the bright moonlight, except for Chary, who remained aloof as usual.

Abruptly the nine lions stopped their play and lined up shoulder to shoulder, looking north. I swung the spotlight and saw Bones charge into the beam with a powerful stiff-legged trot, his massive head and mane swinging side to side. He strutted to the waiting pride and stood there while each female greeted him in a fluid fusion of her body with his, beginning cheek to cheek, then rubbing along his length until she sidled off his ropey, tufted tail. After their exuberant greetings, the pride lay together quietly, Bones a few yards away. The master of the Blue Pride had come home.

Bones's arrival seemed to have changed the mood of the females. Their playfulness had given way to a calm sense of business as they stared intently into the night, hunting even as they lay there. Sometime later Chary stood and moved off silently, followed soon by the two youngsters, Spicy and Sassy. Then Blue and Gypsy were gone, and finally the entire pride had slipped away into the growing darkness, a long procession, with Rascal, Hombre, and Bones bringing up the rear. The moon was setting toward West Dune.

The pride moved along the riverbed to Last Stop, a small group of trees on the edge of North Pan, where they often scent-marked and rested before leaving the valley. In the early light of dawn they walked slowly toward a herd of seven red hartebeest browsing on silvery catophractes bushes on the west slope of North Dune. An old bull, the tips of his horns worn to shiny nubs, stood a little apart, licking the minerals from a termite mound. Lowering themselves for

Lionesses (Panthera leo) on the hunt, Tanzania. Lions, the only big cats to live in groups, often hunt cooperatively, some holding back to intercept fleeing prey that may change course. Females take the lead, as they are faster and less conspicuous than males. By Erwin & Peggy Bauer.

Above: Lioness pursues a herd of wildebeest, Serengeti National Park, Tanzania. When the enormous herds of wildebeest make their annual migration through East Africa, lions (and other predators) enjoy some of their most fruitful hunting. Lions find watercourses no obstacle and frequently cross rivers in their travels. Page 112: A male lion takes down a young wildebeest. Calves are most vulnerable to predation, but lions can kill adults as well, the only cat that regularly preys on these big ungulates. Both by Mitsuaki Iwago/Minden Pictures.

the stalk, the lionesses fanned out toward the herd, gliding through the brush, ears drawn down beside their heads. Nearly an hour later they were moving abreast, in a line about 100 yards long, still seventy or eighty yards from the hartebeest but moving toward them. Rascal and Hombre stayed far to the rear with Bones. But while the lionesses were stalking north, the hartebeest had turned east; they would miss their chance unless adjustments were made. Chary and Sassy pulled from the line and, slipping behind their pride-mates, they disappeared in the grass to position themselves in front of the

antelope. Liesa, Blue, and Gypsy began stalking slowly forward.

Waiting...then moving from bush to grass clump to hedge...then waiting some more, the pride worked its way toward its target. The hartebeest sensed something. Staring back at the lions, they began prancing and blowing their alarm calls. Then the herd cantered away.

The old bull was in the lead. As he dodged an acacia bush, Chary's thick arm flashed out and hooked over his shoulder. He disappeared into the cover, groaning harshly, his feet flailing wildly. The other hartebeest dashed to the top of the dune and stood looking down, snorting and flicking their tails. Within seconds all the lions were tumbling toward the kill. We could hear their throaty rumblings and the tearing of flesh.

Bones heard the commotion too, and trotted past us on his way to join the others, Rascal and Hombre scampering through the tall grass behind him. At the carcass he rushed forward, snarling and scattering the lionesses, and clamping his wide paws over the hartebeest, he began to feed alone. The females, with Rascal and Hombre, watched him from ten yards away.

But Blue began to edge closer, watching Bones and sinking to the ground whenever he shot a glance at her. At about eight yards, she made a slow arc toward the carcass. Bones stopped feeding. A deep rumble grew in his throat and his lips rose to expose his three-inch canines. Blue spat at him. He roared across the carcass, shoveling sand as he charged, and clubbed her across the nose with his paw. The lioness bellowed, her ears pressed to her head as she flattened to the ground again. Bones went back to the carcass, and twenty minutes later the females, followed by Rascal and Hombre, slowly walked away. That night, while their male was occupied with his hartebeest, the lionesses killed and consumed an eighty-pound springbok on South Pan.

MARK AND DELIA OWENS
Cry of the Kalahari

Lions feeding on a fresh kill. Male lions usually take precedence at kills, though it's the females who do most of the hunting. The pride males may not have caught up to them yet in this case. By Guido Alberto Rossi/Image Bank.

BUSHMAN SONG

I went out into the veld
to look for melons
and on the way, what do you
think I saw?

I saw a blue Wildebeest
But the blue Wildebeest just
flicked his heels at
me and ran away.

I went on and on across
the veld, and what do you
think I saw?
I saw a Hartebeest and called
out: 'Oh! Hartebeest, come to me.'
But it just flicked its
heels and ran away.

Then I saw a Gemsbok,
and I cried: 'Oh! Gemsbok, I am
hungry, come to me.'
But it just flicked its heels
and ran away.

Translated by DABÉ
from LAURENS VAN DER POST
The Lost World of the Kalahari

The Well-Armed Hunter

This beast [the cat] is wonderful nimble, setting upon her prey like a Lion, by leaping, and therefore she hunteth both Rats, all kind of Mice, and Birds, eating not only them, but also fish, wherewithal she is best pleased. Having taken a mouse, she first playeth with it, and then devoureth it, but her watchful eye is most strange, to see with what pace and soft steps, she taketh birds and flies....

EDWARD TOPSELL (1607)
The Historie of Foure-footed Beastes

The cat's main killing weapons are its teeth and claws, but to employ these effectively, its entire body comes into play. Conducting a successful stalk calls upon the cat's superb muscle control, keen eyesight, and cushioned footpads. To speed its final rush, the cat bows and extends its flexible spine for a ground-covering stride; to launch itself at the quarry, it springs from exceptionally well developed hind legs and haunches. Before actually getting a grip with claws and teeth, a pursuing cat may swat its prey off balance with a paw blow, backed by the power of the shoulder muscles.

Because those curving claws are such vital equipment, they are held when at rest by ligaments inside a sheath of skin, so their sharpness is not blunted by contact with the ground. The cat must voluntarily extend its claws to use them, leading some to say they should be called "protractile" rather than "retractile." Cats have four toes on their hind feet and five on the front—though the "thumb" digit, or dewclaw, is positioned slightly up the leg, where it doesn't touch ground but comes in handy for climbing or gripping prey.

Cats seize prey with their long, sharp canine teeth, and killing can occur in several ways. Some cats, like cheetahs, try for a grip on the front of their prey's throat to suffocate it. Smaller prey are sometimes killed with a bite to the skull, but in general cats avoid biting directly on bone with the canines, which contain sensitive nerve endings. Instead, they actually feel with these talented teeth (and related jaw muscles) for the spaces between the prey's vertebrae, forcing them apart and killing by severing the spinal cord. Other teeth are specialized for feeding: the small incisors for stripping off fur or feathers (they are also used when carrying small cubs), and the shearing carnassials for chewing. 🐾

A male lion yawns, offering a fine view of his teeth. Clearly visible is the space just behind the fearsome canines, before the other teeth emerge; this lets the canines penetrate to their maximum extent. Along the side of the jaw are the shearing carnassials; this lion appears to be a missing an upper incisor (in front). Photographed in Ngorongoro Crater, Tanzania. By Kennan Ward.

Cats, by their deepest nature, are elusive. To understand why, just watch Puss in the vegetable patch. When a bird flutters down from the trees, she crouches low and shields herself behind a screen of leaves. Instead of walking, her supple body flows forward, as if her bones and muscles have changed to a slow liquid. Her footfall is silent. A few seconds away from her prey, she stops, gathers her legs underneath her and fidgets her hind end. On the other side of the bean row, the bird goes on feeding. And then the cat is on it in a single well-aimed leap. Her soft paws are suddenly armed with claws, and her strong jaws are biting.

With variations of prey and place, this is the way most wild cats make their living.

CANDACE SAVAGE
Wild Cats

A BODY SHAPED BY MEAT

Cats resemble each other because, so far, they have had no reason to change. Good hunters since the lynxlike Ur-cat of the Miocene from whom the modern cats descend, the cats have had no need to adjust their bodies or their diets in response to major changes in the world's climate. Why not? Because, unlike the diets of other animals, the diet of cats didn't change. The vegetarian menu listed everything from bananas to pecans, from seaweed to eucalyptus leaves, items so different from one another that completely different organisms were required to find, chew, and digest them, but the cat menu listed only one item: meat. From a cat's point of view, the difference between a bird who eats cherries, a fish who eats algae, and a giraffe who eats acacia thorns is mainly one of quantity. All three are meat, and a cat can benefit from any one of them if he can catch it. So while while the glaciers came and went, while the vegetarians struggled

against all odds trying to digest new plants and adapt themselves to overwhelming global changes, the cats simply kept on hunting, waiting to pounce on whoever managed to survive into the next epoch. The limber cat body that hunted successfully in the Pliocene hunts just as successfully today.

Hence, meat-eating has formed cat bodies, beginning in the mouth with daggerlike eyeteeth suitable for fastening their owner to a victim, and with strong, triangular cheek teeth, capable of severing the victim's spine and shearing his flesh into bite-sized chunks for passage down the cat's throat. Meat-eating has caused the shortness of the cat's intestine, since meat is easy to digest and doesn't require a long, heavy gut that would weigh a cat down and keep him from accelerating quickly—a basic requirement for the feline lurk-and-leap style of hunting. Meat-eating explains the short digestive period, the rapid passage of food through the cat, and the nutritional residue in a cat's feces, which is why dogs forage in cats' litter boxes and why cats mark with spray.

ELIZABETH MARSHALL THOMAS
The Tribe of Tiger

Leopards attacking a spotted deer, by Louis A. Sargent, 1909. This illustration, while dramatic, perpetuates the myth that leopards (and other cats) typically hunt by leaping from trees onto the backs of their prey. In fact, this is a risky and inefficient approach that cats rarely if ever take. Leopards actually spend most of their time on the ground. Mary Evans Picture Library.

lets herself go and swiftly grabs more leaves. If the drop is only about 20 feet or less she just bails out.

Having witnessed her perform all these gymnastics there were no more doubts in my mind that pumas can, and do, catch monkeys up in the trees.

STANLEY BROCK
Leemo

Cats enhance their vision by special behavior. A cat about to pounce from one tree limb to another or upon a hapless mouse is likely to sway its head from side to side. That gives the animal's brain an opportunity to make a final and extremely refined assessment of distance before the action takes place. The closer a cat is to its prey or landing place, the greater the displacement caused by the head-swaying trick. Cats are accurate animals. They are designed to be. Since cats need only about one sixth of the amount of light we do to see quite well, the head swaying is used at any time of the day or night when precision is needed. Cats appear to take their extraordinary accuracy for granted. When a cat misses, it looks downright amazed.

ROGER A. CARAS
A Cat Is Watching

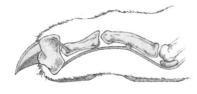

A cat's claws work like a natural jackknife. Normally they are withdrawn into sheaths between the toes, held there by contracted muscles and ligaments (top). To use them, the cat must extend these tissues so the claw protrudes, rather like unfolding the blade of a jackknife.

THE ACROBATIC PUMA

One of Leemo's favourite games is to chase a bird about, as it hops from limb to limb in the top of a tree. She never catches the bird, but the speed and agility with which she goes about it is ineffable. She scampers along the slenderest of branches that under the stationary weight of her body would have collapsed, and bridges two trees simply by springing the gap that separates them....On several occasions I have seen her spring from the branch of one tree into the foliage of another, knowing full well that there was no firm bough for her to land on. She merely grasps a handful of leaves in her forepaws, and swings on them like a trapeze artist, kicking with her hind legs feeling for support. Sometimes she doesn't find it, so she hangs there on outstretched forearms and looks over her shoulder down at the ground. If it looks too far she swings her body again and then

The rakish, loose-limbed cheetah with its sway-backed racing frame is the culmination of an ancient and inseparable bond between hunter and hunted. It has evolved stride by stride with the gazelles, the slenderness and quicksilver pace of the one being matched by the feline grace and devastating acceleration of the other. The small round head, the deep chest and the elastic backbone slung like a hammock between its haunches, everything about it is designed for the short fast rush. In the precarious world of the cheetah, every day is a race for life. Without its speed it would simply starve. That is why it has become the fastest animal on earth, said to be capable of reaching seventy miles an hour.

BRIAN JACKMAN
The Marsh Lions

CHEETAH

Indolent and kitten-eyed,
This is the bushveld's innocent
The stealthy leopard parodied
With grinning, gangling pup-content.

Slouching through the tawny grass
Or loose-limbed lolling in the shade,
Purring for the sun to pass
And build a twilight barricade

Around the vast arena where;
In scattered herds, his grazing prey
Do not suspect in what wild fear
They'll join with him in fatal play;

Till hunger draws slack sinews tight
And vibrant as a hunter's bow:
Then, like a fleck of mottled light,
He slides across the still plateau.

A tremor rakes the herds: they scent
The pungent breeze of his advance;
Heads rear and jerk in vigilant
Compliance with the game of chance

In which, of thousands, only one
Is centred in the cheetah's eye;
They wheel and then stampede, for none
Knows which it is that has to die.

His stealth and swiftness fling a noose
And as his loping strides begin
To blur with speed, he ropes the loose
Buck on the red horizon in.

CHARLES EGLINGTON

The cheetah is a glorious hunter—in that flash of spotted gold, one sees an animal performing what it has evolved for thousands of years to do so well, and somehow in that moment it is in essence the logical conclusion of natural selection.

CYNTHIA MOSS
Portraits in the Wild

Below: A cheetah (Acinonyx jubatus) races after an impala, Masai Mara, Kenya. The cheetah's full-out dash after its prey rarely lasts more than a few hundred yards; it is most successful if it can first get within fairly close range. By Anup & Manoj Shah/Animals Animals. Facing page: The Cat, by an anonymous American artist, c. 1850–1899. National Gallery of Art, Washington.

The Art of the Stalk

S talking their prey is how cats have survived over the eons, and they stalk almost obsessively. If no prey is at hand, housecats will stalk a fluttering leaf, their owner's feet, even a loaf of bread, as one writer observed. It's likely that the earliest cats evolved in forested habitats, where an abundance of hiding places and lack of running room encouraged this approach to capturing prey. As cats spread and diversified, they managed to transfer the stalk to wide-open environments, using even the scantiest cover—though savannah cats like the lion and cheetah have enhanced their pursuit options, with cooperation on the one hand and flat-out speed on the other.

The mechanics of the stalk flow from the cat build, with typically shorter forelegs and great flexibility in the spine as well as the pelvic, knee, and elbow joints, allowing the cat to creep forward with its belly low to the ground. Tails are held low or straight out while stalking, but sometimes quiver with suppressed excitement and give the cat away. In walking, cats extend their paws up and ahead and set them down gently, outer edge first—then rolling inward, testing for safety and sound before shifting weight to that foot. Discretion, in all aspects of the stalk, is of the essence.

The stalk ends in a final rush, which ideally is brief. Cats can muster great speed over a short distance but have little endurance. This dash often climaxes with a well-judged leap, bringing the cat down on top of its prey, front paws extended and claws ready to grasp. 🐾

CASTING A SPELL ON PREY

One day we came on an immaculate little female [leopard] prowling across the wet grass and the behaviour of a group of topi and Grant's gazelle nearby was very strange. They stood and stared at the leopardess with wide straining eyes, and trotted forward towards her—that is to say towards death. The topi is a fairly mad animal anyway, a large brown gleaming antelope with gun-metal blazes on its legs and an air of continual stage-fright, but these topi outdid themselves. They snorted and snuffled, they stamped with their fore-feet on the turf, and they kept trotting nearer and nearer to the leopardess. Most antelopes prefer to keep a

A leopard (Panthera pardus) *crouches low while stalking prey, Etosha National Park, Namibia. Some observers claim that leopards are the most skilled stalkers of any cat, with an unparalleled talent for sneaking close to prey with no hint of their presence. By Daryl Balfour/ABPL.*

hunting lion or leopard in view and will often approach in this manner, leaving themselves just enough distance to get away in an emergency. But with these topi, and to a lesser extent the Grant's gazelle, it was something more than that. They were in an extremity of fear and they simply could not bring themselves to run away. It almost seemed that some kind of mesmerism was at work upon them, that the dreadful danger had broken down their will, and that something in the nature of a death-wish was luring them on towards the leopardess not thirty yards away. She took no notice either of them or of us for a while, until suddenly the breeze carried our scent in her direction. Then she was up and away like a ballet dancer and with that the spell was broken: topi and gazelle wheeled together and went galloping down the valley.

ALAN MOOREHEAD
No Room in the Ark

THE STALK OF THE TIGER

A stalking tiger uses every available piece of cover. It approaches cautiously, carefully placing each foot on the ground. It crouches behind small bushes or rocks, or hugs the edge of a riverbank, all the while remaining focused on the prey. With its striped coat effectively breaking up its outline, the tiger moves slowly forward, patiently closing the distance or waiting for the prey to move closer. Having got to within 10 to 20 meters (about 30 to 60 feet) or less of the prey, the tiger gathers itself up and suddenly rushes its victim, covering the final distance in a few bounds.

The attack is usually from the side or rear so that the first contact is often on the prey's hindquarters. The impact may knock the prey off its feet or unbalance the fleeing animal to the extent that the tiger can get a grip with its claws. Keeping its hind feet on the ground, the tiger tries to bring the prey down or into a position where a killing bite can be delivered quickly.…Speed, experience, and concentration are essential—an estimated one stalk in twenty results in a kill.

MEL SUNQUIST AND FIONA C. SUNQUIST
Great Cats

WALK LIKE A CAT

Stalking is merely another form of walking. The pace slows down; the body is lowered into almost a crouching position. Movement is light and deliberate. If you've ever seen a common housecat stalking a songbird, you'll get some idea of how you should go about stalking. The cat crouches low, keeping its eyes upon its quarry. It steps forward lightly, one foot at a time, placing that foot in just the right position before putting any weight on it. Then it eases forward…very slowly and deliberately. The entire stalking movement is beautiful to watch. There are no finer stalkers on the planet than members of the cat family. I've seen tigers and lions stalking big game, cougars and bobcat sneaking up on smaller animals. The intensity of the stalk, the beautiful poetic movement, are the same with all cats.

BILL THOMAS
Talking with the Animals

For some of these,
It could not be the place
It is, without blood.
These hunt, as they have done,
But with claws and teeth grown perfect,
More deadly than they can believe.

They stalk more silently,
And crouch on the limbs of trees,
And their descent
Upon the bright backs of their prey

May take years
In a sovereign floating of joy.…

JAMES DICKEY
from "The Heaven of Animals"

*Bengal tiger (*Panthera tigris*) hunts sambar deer in a lake, Ranthambhore National Park, India. Tigers commonly hunt along the banks of rivers and lakes, though not many individuals actually pursue prey far into the water. By Gunther Ziesler/Peter Arnold, Inc.*

Right: A domestic cat (Felis catus) stalks through the grass. Domestic cats are unique animals in that they exploit manmade environments while retaining many of the predatory skills of their wild relatives. Much of a domestic cat's hunting consists of waiting patiently by a hole (in a wall, the ground, or a tangle of vegetation) for prey to emerge, then pouncing on it. But often it needs to stalk, which it can learn to do very well. The stalk is most effective when the prey animal scuttles away on the ground; birds that leap immediately into the air usually cause the cat to misjudge its leap. By Peter Kaehler/Image Bank. Facing page: A cougar (Felis concolor) crouches in a meadow. Cougars, like leopards, are master stalkers, able to virtually disappear in grass less than a foot high. By Tom & Pat Leeson.

THE PROCESS

As I stood hoeing in the garden,
the cat appeared carrying a gray treasure
and dropped it near me, perhaps to show me,
though he said nothing. And he sat
in the perfect arrogance and calm
of one who has the upper hand,
and who has complete confidence
in both his reflexes and his motives.
The one caught—mouse or vole,
thick, soft, velvety—lay still,
and when it moved it moved badly,
its forequarters damaged already,
maybe a broken neck, or shoulder.
The cat watched, then didn't watch,
gazing around the garden,
looking off into the woods,
but all the time knowing, I think,
just what the rodent was doing,

and when it made a short, hobbling scurry,
he pounced, cuffed him with his paws,
held him down with his jaws a few moments,
released him, went back to looking.
This went on for several minutes,
and then, suddenly, the cat decided
this part of things was over;
I could almost hear him say
with a subtle, clear change
in the attitude and intent of his body,
"All right, enough of this…."—
and he moved forward and crouched
and lowered his mouth to the
     trembling body,
and grasped it by the head, and began to chew.
And soon he had chewed the head off,
a delicate crunching the skull made,
as the breaking and splintering of small bones

made equally delicate music
     all the way through.
He licked the red, decapitated place.
He lifted the body, limp and tender
as it dangled while he gnawed off
another section, of which there were four.
And then it was done , the small creature,
chewed apart, swallowed, had disappeared.
The cat sniffed the empty place
where the rodent had been, as if to say,
"Hmm, I wonder what happened
     to him…"—
where there were two, now there was one
(what greater mystery is there?)—
and his whiskers bristled and his fur
     twitched a little,
glints of magnificence and satisfaction,
and he sauntered off into the tall grass alone.

HOWARD NELSON

THE COUGAR METHOD

The kill distills two million years of evolution to a single sequence of attack, defense, death. Hidden behind a rock or tree or shrub, cougars watch and listen. Their round pupils are adapted to both daytime and nighttime hunting and set close together for binocular vision with superb depth perception, most sensitive in a range of fifty to eighty feet. Small, rounded ears move together or independently to pick up sounds, including ultrasonic frequencies. Smell is less acute than in dogs and seems to be less important for hunting than for interpreting scrapes and other social signals from neighboring lions.

With prey in sight, cougars crouch like housecats, creep, wait with twitching tail, creep again until they are within fifty feet of the rear or side of the victim. Then they sprint, mobilizing a body of tensing muscle and flexing sinew hung on a light skeleton. Hind legs are longer than the front, facilitating forty-five-foot-long bounds and fifteen-foot-high leaps. The tail, long and heavy, balances the split-second pivots. Cougars have brought down pronghorn antelope, the fastest animal in North America. The majority of the carcasses...found in northern Yellowstone were elk calves. Across North America, deer seem to have been the favorite food, but cougars also eat a wide variety of small prey, including squirrels, snowshoe hares, marmots, beaver, birds, mice, raccoons, and porcupines. Small prey are especially important to cougars in tropical latitudes where jaguars compete with them for deer.

Large prey are generally killed by bites to the neck or throat. Before biting, cougars embrace their prey around the neck and shoulders, claws extended and raking. Whiskers help to feel where canines should pierce to sunder the vertebrae and break the spinal cord. When everything goes well, death comes in an instant. Sometimes, especially with large prey or inexperienced cougars, the cougar is forced around to the throat. Asphyxiation takes longer and allows flailing hoofs to injure and sometimes kill the cougar.

CHRIS BOLGIANO
Mountain Lion

Lionesses close in on a giraffe, Masai Mara National Park, Kenya. Lions are the only African cats that can take on prey this imposing, thanks to their size, strength and (sometimes) teamwork. By Karl & Kay Ammann/Bruce Coleman, Inc.

Lionesses may use quite sophisticated techniques when hunting together, each one watching the others and then patterning her actions to suit the situation.

Cooperation may...involve several lionesses. These may fan out and advance silently in a broad front toward their quarry. Animals startled by one lioness may then rush into the arms of another. A herd may even be encircled, a strategy implying that lions are aware of the consequences of their actions in relation to both the other pride members and the prey. Once, for example, a small herd of Thomson's gazelle had congregated on an island of short grass

surrounded by tall dry stalks....Four lionesses—The Old One, and lionesses A, B, and H—spotted the herd. Lioness A immediately advanced with her body held low, not directly toward the gazelle but to one side of them, until she was just beyond them in the high grass. She waited. Long association had taught the others to anticipate her maneuver, and lioness H encircled the herd from the other side; lioness B also crept slightly ahead, but then crouched motionless. The Old One lagged, watching the proceedings with only the top of her head raised above the level of the grass. Sensing danger, the gazelle became agitated and suddenly bolted toward lioness B. She lunged and missed, which caused several animals to flee back in the direction from which they had come, only to be met there by lioness A. She grabbed and clutched a male, ending his life with a bite through the back of the neck. In their panic to escape several gazelle veered toward lioness H, who was still waiting patiently. Spotting her at the last moment, they swerved around her but she leaped straight up, twisted around in midair, and after a few huge bounds bore a gazelle to the ground.

GEORGE SCHALLER
Golden Shadows, Flying Hooves

I was watching a herd of ibex through a powerful telescope, and a snow leopard suddenly raced across the hollow in which they were feeding and made an attempt on a buck, which started away just in time. The leopard's outstretched claws raked a great lump of hair from the ibex's coat as it wheeled away, and the whole herd bolted to the edge of the hollow, halting on a small ridge, 100 yards away, and staring back at the leopard, which stood waving its great tail in the middle of the hollow. After a minute or so both the parties departed in opposite directions.

C. H. STOCKLEY
Stalking in the Himalayas and Northern India

One sultry summer's evening, I was returning home in my boat at the approach of a thunderstorm, when my companion, an Indian, noticed a jaguar on the edge of the river. We drew nearer and took cover under the overhanging willow trees in order to observe his actions. It was sitting crouched on a spit of land, where the water was running rather more swiftly, the kind of place favoured by a predatory fish known in Paraguay as "dorado." Occasionally it bent forward, its eyes fixed on the surface of the river as if it wished to penetrate the depth below. After about a quarter of an hour, I saw it slap the water with its paw and throw a large fish on to the bank. It was fishing in exactly the same way as our domestic cat.

J. R. RENGGER (1850)

A bobcat, an animal about twice the size of a domestic cat, actually can take down mature ungulates. It is as if Puss gave up on birds and started dragging home freshly killed golden retrievers. Not surprisingly, a deer-hunting bobcat is often in for a very rough experience. By studying tracks in the snow, cat researcher Gary Koehler reconstructed one episode in the Salmon River Mountains of Idaho, in which a female bobcat—probable weight 8 kilograms (about 20 pounds)—leaped on the back of a deer and hung on, ride-'em-cowboy style, as "the deer bounded down the rugged slope, dodging around bluffs, bolting through bushes and up against trees. The ride ended some 300 feet below at the foot of the slope, where perhaps the deer stumbled, giving the cat time to grasp the deer's throat in its mouth for a suffocating bite." Needless to say, deer are not the bobcat's preferred prey, though they can form a critical part of its wintertime fare in some regions.

CANDACE SAVAGE
Wild Cats

Above: Jaguar, drawn from a Mayan stone carving, by Cal Roy, from The Serpent and the Sun: Myths of the Mexican World. *Below: Jaguar (Panthera onca) with a fish, Brazil. Jaguars hunt in water not only for fish but for caimans and river tortoises. They may use waterside habitats in part to avoid competition with pumas, which dislike water. By Gerard Lacz/Peter Arnold, Inc.*

CAT MOVES

Many species of cat treat prey species with which they are so far unfamiliar very cautiously with a mixture of "restrained play" and "catch and throw": They grasp the animal by its fur with their teeth, usually toward the rear of its back, and often only after long hesitation and many intention movements, pick it up, and then toss it away either sideways or upward. Some species, and of those I have observed the Asian golden cats and the servals in particular, intensify this "tossing game" to such a degree of violence that the prey animals may be killed simply by their impact against trees, stones, or the walls and floor of the cage. However, as soon as the cat has grown familiar with that particular prey species, it too will be grasped and killed in the usual manner.

Another example is the paw blow: All cats strike with a paw at a prey animal which turns and defends itself against the attack or seeks shelter in a corner where it is then difficult to grasp with the teeth. Often the cats wait with paw half raised to see whether the prey animal gives them an opening before they strike. They will sit and wait on a riverbank with a paw raised in the same way when they want to strike fish out of the water. It is, therefore, not surprising that the fishing cat performs this behavior pattern more pronouncedly than other species: It raises the paw higher, often beyond ear level, and perseveres in this posture much longer before striking.

A still more extreme development is the paw blow of the servals: As if they were using a truncheon, they reach up very high and strike down with a stiffly outstretched paw onto a prey animal that has stood up in defense. A blow such as this can kill a large golden hamster or a rat....

Finally, let me mention the "capriole." All cats occasionally jump in the air taking all four paws off the ground at the same time—over another animal in play, for example, or sideways onto a branch and so on. With the exception of the servals, however, I have never seen any cat do it at full gallop, as, for example, many antelopes do when in full flight. With this jump servals grasp birds with their two forepaws as they flutter up in the air, then draw in their hind legs, and land only on these, while continuing to hold their prey between their forepaws, and take a grasping bite only after they have landed. In this way one of my servals catches moths with great reliability from heights of up to a meter.

PAUL LEYHAUSEN
Cat Behavior

Left: Photo sequence showing a fishing cat (Felis viverrina) capturing its prey, in Dudhwa National Park, Uttar Pradesh, India. All by Belinda Wright/DRK Photo. Above: A hunting serval (Felis serval) performs the "capriole" leap described by Paul Leyhausen, Ngorongoro Crater, Tanzania. By Kennan Ward.

THE TENDER CARNIVORE

The most important fact about meat-eating…is that it explains a cat's emotions, or some of them. Many expressions of a cat's feelings seem deeply related to the capture of live prey. An excited, happy, or much relieved cat may ambush and pounce upon whatever triggers its pleasure—something worth considering before getting a large cat all worked up.…

Conversely, a committed meat-eater may express affection and even gratitude toward his or her prey—a touching and thoroughly appropriate emotion in a creature for whom captured animal protein is the only source of food. Or so that emotion should seem to us, since in many human societies people do exactly the same thing when thanking or venerating an animal who has been killed for food. In a tender scene I happened to witness on the African savannah, a lion and some lionesses were rendering the carcass of a female kudu. The lion took the intact but severed head of the kudu between his paws and, holding it upright so that she faced him, slowly licked her cheeks and eyes intimately and tenderly, as if he were grooming her, as if she were another, beloved lion. Rigor mortis had not yet stiffened her muscles—under his tongue her eyelids opened and shut in a lifelike manner. An infant lion pushed up under his father's elbow and helped to wash the kudu's face.

ELIZABETH MARSHALL THOMAS
The Tribe of Tiger

There can hardly be an animal within the lion's habitat that does not fall prey to it at one time or another. With a quick blow of a paw, it catches the hare that jumps up at its feet. It likes to kill porcupines and sometimes receives nasty wounds in doing so. Dur-

ing lean times it does not disdain to eat grass-rats, cane-rats, and gerbils. At Seronera I once saw a lioness flush a quail and catch it in midair. I have come across lions at ostrich kills in Nairobi National Park and know of a whole brood of young ostriches being gobbled up shortly after hatching. From Uganda and Lake Rudolf come reports of crocodiles being killed and eaten. The lion is also known occasionally to crack open a tortoise. In the Kruger Park, a lion was seen approaching a python, cleverly avoiding the snake's immediate attack. When the python went for him a second time, the lion jumped forward and practically bit it in two.…Fish, especially cat-fish, living in shallow, muddy pools, are thrown out of the water with a swipe of the paw. Lions also feed on locusts and termites.

CHARLES A. W. GUGGISBERG
Wild Cats of the World

The African panther is like a lion, but with longer legs, and a more slender body. It is completely white, spattered with black spots like rosettes. Its beauty delights the other animals, which would all flock to it were it not for the panther's terrible stare. Aware of this, the panther lowers its eyes; other animals approach it to drink in such beauty, and the panther pounces on the nearest of them.

LEONARDO DA VINCI

A lioness in Botswana licks the skull of a Cape buffalo, probably to remove with her hooked tongue papillae any remaining flesh. Cats have been observed, however, to lick, face-rub, or pat their dead prey before beginning to feed on it—from motives we can only speculate about. By Frans Lanting/Minden Pictures.

WHY THE LEOPARD HIDES HIS FOOD UP A TREE

The Ndebele tell their children that long ago, there were three friends: the beautiful leopard, the jackal and the hyena. They went everywhere together. Whenever Leopard killed an animal, he would always leave part of it for his friends so that they could have a good feed too.

One day it happened that Leopard was ill, and so he could not hunt. "Jackal," he said, "Please catch some food for us, for I am not well."

But lazy Jackal said, "No. I am too weary. Ask Hyena."

So Leopard said, "Hyena, please hunt for us today, for I am not well enough to do so."

But Hyena, too, made an excuse: "No, I have a sore foot."

At this Leopard roared in anger, "I thought you were my friends, but you are a no-good, lazy pair. Never again will I leave you meat when I make my kill. From this day on, I will make sure of it. I shall take what is left and hang it in a tree, when I have eaten all I want. Then neither of you will be able to get at it."

Leopard was true to his word—for since that day he has never left any meat for his selfish friends. Up into a tree it goes, high out of reach of jackals and hyenas. They have become scavengers now instead, and they eat the scraps that other animals leave behind. It was a sad day for them when they lost Leopard's friendship.

A Ndebele story
from South Africa

Of the big cats, the leopard has the most varied diet. It will hunt and eat just about anything that moves, from small birds to animals three times its weight, and it will also scavenge. The leopard is an opportunist—its diet varies with the habitat and the prey available in that area.

Small prey are usually eaten on the ground where they have been caught, although occasionally they are first moved to a more secluded spot. Larger prey animals are often stored in the branches of trees. It is fascinating to watch a leopard carry its prey up into a tree. Pound for pound, leopards are considered to be the strongest of the big cats; this is certainly the impression one gets when watching a leopard carry an animal that weighs over a hundred pounds straight up a tree trunk. (Leopards usually weigh only about 80 to 120 pounds themselves)....Once up the tree, the leopard carefully wedges the carcass in the crook of a branch so that it will not fall out. The leopard can feed on the carcass for several days without being disturbed by other predators and scavengers. Vultures find it more difficult to spot a kill amid the branches of a tree, and if they do, the leopard's presence keeps them away. Lions sometimes smell the carcass, and they have been seen to stand under a tree with a carcass in it, gazing up into the branches somewhat perplexedly. Lions can climb trees, too, but it seems that leopards do not lose their kills to lions in this way very frequently.

CYNTHIA MOSS
Portraits in the Wild

At the Kill

How and when a cat consumes its kill depends on how big it is, how many cats get to share it, how vulnerable it is to theft, and a species' sense of discretion. Lions typically fall to wherever their prey is downed; not even a pack of hyenas is going to rob a strong pride of its kill. Cheetahs are more the losers in confrontations with other predators over kills, and pumas, though dominant carnivores, dislike feeding in the open and usually drag their kills off into hiding. Some cats scratch leaves over a kill and return to it later, if they feel threatened.

Lions and tigers can eat prodigious amounts, 50 pounds or more of meat in a single feeding, and may feed on one kill for several days. Small cats, hunting even smaller prey, must kill more often. Most cats share kills only with their young (if females), and then readily. Lions are famously contentious over kills—and often leave little for their cubs. This trait has wrung the hearts of human watchers, but without high cub mortality, there would be too many lions. 🐾

Food was usually brought back to the barn. Even slices of bread and some chocolate cake from Edith's dustbin were carried home and, in most cases, eaten or hidden away for future attention. All cats, including the large ones, prefer to take their prey to the core area of their range—to their 'dens'—to eat it. [Behavior of feral English cats in a long-term study.]

MICHAEL ALLABY *and* PETER CRAWFORD
The Curious Cat

Below: Mother cheetah grooms her young to remove blood from feeding, Masai Mara reserve, Kenya. By Mark Newman/ West Stock. Facing page: Canadian lynx and grouse, watercolor by an unknown American artist. Superstock photo.

THE GOOD MOTHER

When a mother and her cubs feed on a kill, even when the prey is small, there is not the fierce competition over the carcass that one sees with lions. After making the kill, the mother cheetah usually sits down and rests, but also keeps watch for other predators while the cubs eat, showing little antagonism toward one another. A few growls may be heard and there might be a tug of war—rarely lasting more than a few seconds—over a single piece, but on the whole, feeding is carried out very peacefully. No female cheetah has ever been known to take a carcass away from her cubs and consume it herself, as a lioness is apt to do.

CYNTHIA MOSS
Portraits in the Wild

POSSESSING PREY

Sometimes [mountain] lions feed only once or twice, then abandon the remaining meat. Spoilage of the meat may be one reason, although in cold climates like Yellowstone this is fairly insignificant. It appears more likely that they are preempted from their meals. Lion kills attract many kinds of life. Cougars seem to play the role of provider, not at all an advantageous one for the cougar. Relationships among predators is one of the frontiers of wildlife science, and as yet little is known in quantified ways about interactions among cougars, wolves, bears, bobcats, and coyotes. There is however, a growing body of field observations. "Many times I've seen a lion leave a kill abruptly after only a day," Kerry said, "and I've found black bear tracks at the kill. I'm sure the bear has driven the lion away. I haven't noticed grizzlies doing that, but that's probably only because there's so few grizzlies around, and even fewer wolves." In Glacier National Park, where wolves have filtered down from Canada, a colleague of Kerry's had just started a new study. Already, there was clear evidence that both wolves and bears were following cougar tracks. Wolves were treeing collared lions there and had even killed three of them. In Yellowstone, Kerry once found a young cougar treed by coyotes, and an assistant had seen coyotes harass a lion off a kill. Another of Kerry's helpers watched a mother cougar confront a startled black bear that was coming too close to her den. There was a snarling, growling, and throwing of punches; both animals danced around the bushes, separated, and came together again. In the end, the bear ran away wailing, with the cougar close behind.

CHRIS BOLGIANO
Mountain Lion

DREAM OF THE LYNX

Beside a narrow trail in the blue
cold of evening the trap is sprung,
and a growling deep in the throat
tells of life risen
to the surface of darkness.

The moon in my dream takes the shape
of animals who walk by its light
and never sleep, whose yellow eyes
are certain of what they seek.

Sinking, floating beneath the eyelid,
hairy shape of the slayer appears,
a shadow that crouches
hidden in a thicket of alders,
nostrils quivering;
and the ever-deepening track
of the unseen, feeding host.

JOHN HAINES

Cultures of the Hunt

It comes alive
It comes alive, alive, alive.
In the north mountain
The lion comes alive
In the north mountain, comes alive.
With this the prey animal
Will have the power to attract deer,
  antelope;
Will have power to be lucky.

Acoma Pueblo

Everywhere humans have come into contact with wild cats, we have recognized them for the skilled, powerful hunters they are. Few societies today center on hunting, but in the historical record—and the few places where hunting cultures survive—is much evidence of the respect accorded these beasts.

Lions have always been associated with might, probably as far back as the fearsome cave lions of prehistory. They surely figured in the lives in early humans, as competitors and perhaps exemplars of the hunting arts. This relationship between lions and hunting peoples in Africa endures today, as illustrated in accounts of the Kalahari Bushmen. In Assyria and the Near East as well Africa, lions became linked with royalty and the privilege of hunting them was reserved for rulers—as was true of great cats elsewhere. Guatemalan potentates were once referred to as "Jaguar," and West African chiefs appropriated the skins or other parts of any slain leopard for their personal aggrandizement.

All over Central and South America, jaguars and pumas have represented powerful spirits—sometimes dark and threatening, sometimes protective, always chief among hunters. A pair of Mayan hero-twins named Little Jaguar and Blowgun Hunter were famed for their ability to "hunt like jaguars." Amazon tribal shamans were said to turn into jaguars after death or temporarily assume their form, becoming "were-jaguars."

North American peoples of the Southwest created a vivid body of lore about pumas. The lion was carved in stone by the Cochiti Pueblo as a guardian shrine, and incarnated as a kachina spirit by the Hopi. *Tuju,* as the Hopi call him, is seen as the strongest and bravest of animals, and the best hunter. And the Navajo recognize the Mountain Lion Way of hunting, also called the Tiptoe Way; the puma's Navajo name translates as "walking silently among the rocks." Other Native Americans used cougar skins for quivers, to speed their arrows; as saddle blankets; or to swaddle male infants. The most direct way to incorporate the powers of the cat, practiced in the Americas and Africa, was to eat it—especially the heart—in ceremonial fashion. 🐾

Mountain Lion Kachina, by Oren Poley, Jr., c. 1960s. The Mountain Lion kachina, in Hopi ceremonials, may appear in a mixed kachina dance with Deer or Antelope kachinas, whom he leads, for he is always in the front and never caught. Photo by Jerry Jacka.

The old Bushman took up his assegai and walked to and fro in front of a bush where an imaginary lion was supposed to be tearing to pieces a zebra or an antelope. Brandishing his weapon, he called out to the "lion": "What have you come here for? Have you got anything to eat? You made such a noise I thought you had something. Don't think to come here and quarrel with me, but go off now and get meat." Thus talking he walked around for a while and finally sat down. The puzzled animal usually withdrew, he said, leaving the remains of its prey to him. Another Bushman then started up, spear in hand, and fifty yards in front of the bush sprang about with great animation, shaking his weapon and exclaiming to the imaginary lion: "What have you got there? Cannot you spare me some of it? Be off, and let some stand for me, or I'll do you an injury."... Some of the Bushmen Alexander came across derived almost their whole sustenance from the lions.

CHARLES A. W. GUGGISBERG
Wild Cats of the World

BUSHMAN AND LION

What drew me so strongly to the Bushman was that he appeared to belong to my native land as no other human being has ever belonged. Wherever he went he contained, and was contained, deeply within the symmetry of the land. His spirit was naturally symmetrical because, moving in the stream of the instinctive certainty of belonging, he remained within his fateful proportions. Before we all came to shatter his natural state, I have never found true evidence that he exceeded his proportions. His killing, like the lion's, was innocent because he killed only to live. He never killed for fun or for the sake of killing, and even when doing it was curiously apprehensive and regretful of the deed. The proof of all this is there in his paintings on his beloved rock for those who can see with their hearts as well as their eyes. There the animals of Africa still live as he knew them and as no

European or Bantu artist has yet been able to render them. They are there not as quarry for his idle bow or food for his stomach, but as companions in mystery, as fellow pilgrims travelling on the same perilous spoor between distant life-giving waters....

The Bushman would, for example, use the lion as his hunting dog. When his normal methods of hunting failed him, he would frighten the game in the direction of a hungry lion. He would let the lion kill and eat enough only to still its hunger, but not enough to make it lazy. Then the Bushman would drive the lion off with smoke and fire, and move in to eat the rest of the kill. In this way he would follow a favourite lion about from kill to kill, and it was extraordinary how he and the lion came to respect their strange partnership.

LAURENS VAN DER POST
The Lost World of the Kalahari

Above: Lion at dawn with a wildebeest kill, Masai Mara, Kenya. By Heather Angel/Biofotos. Below: Leopard prestige chair of carved wood from Cameroon, West Africa. Seattle Art Museum.

I went out deer hunting. My older brother went with me. He made a sound like Mountain Lion: ho-o! Mountain Lion is the hunter. His cry makes the deer nervous; it stops running. In this way deer can be hunted even without weapons.

Zuñi account

THE MASAI STRIKE BACK

Cattle thefts by lion cannot all be avenged, for they go on so steadily that the clans would not be equal to the task. Only when the lion's killings become very flagrant, and include, perhaps, a man—the chief calls upon the clan to go into action....When a lion is started they pursue; the lion in flight does not travel much faster than his pursuers; he is not accustomed to running long distances and cannot do so without becoming winded; for, with all his strength, he is muscle-bound. The hunters can run much farther than the lion; inside half a mile, the animal halts. Before he is rested the hunters are upon him again. Generally, but not always, he will run a second time but not so far. He has very little breathing space until the hunters are upon him once more, and he will very occasionally run a third time, but that is his absolute limit. He then stands to fight it out.

The hunters know from experience exactly what to expect; they close in on the quarry in a circle. The lion threatens in several directions, but the circle narrows; since the lion crouches in the highest and thickest grass available, the hunters hold their spears until he exposes himself. One of the most powerful and experienced hunters coaxes him by venturing closer than any of the rest. He knows precisely how far the lion can leap and remains just beyond this distance. The lion's attention becomes fixed upon him; he awaits an opportunity to leap; the other hunters edge closer, every spear poised. When all is ready, the man who is holding the beast's attention leaps forward, and the lion springs at him. As the beast flies through the air the hunter hurls his spear, and instantly dodges, his shield upraised to receive the lion's charge. A rain of spears flashes in the sun, and the lion is pierced by one or several blades; still he fights....Rarely is a man seriously hurt in these encounters; but sometimes one is killed.This does not deter the others; they hold a brief ceremony over the body of the fallen monarch, and are off after another.

W. R. LEIGH
Frontiers of Enchantment

A party of Masai hunters (in what is now Tanzania) surrounds a lion who has raided their cattle. As shown in this illustration, one hunter draws the lion's charge, then tries to protect himself with his shield while his companions rain spears toward the lion. Drawing by W. R. Leigh, in his book Frontiers of Enchantment, *a reminiscence of the artist's travels in Africa in the 1930s.*

DIALOGUE WITH LIONS

In terms of hunting success, it seemed to me, the Ju/wa men were probably more or less equal to the other large-sized hunters of the Kalahari—especially those who hunted large-sized game cooperatively. In those days, the most important of the other large-sized cooperative hunters in the western Kalahari were, of course, the lions.

Whatever large animals the people hunted, the lions also hunted.....A meat meal big enough for the people was also big enough for the lions.

Perhaps partly for this reason, the lions and the Ju/wasi helped themselves to each other's kills.

[Once] my brother, John, was present when lions tried to rob people. He and four Ju/wa hunters had been following a wildebeest that one of the hunters, days before, had shot with a poisoned arrow. When, at last, they caught up to the wildebeest, it was lying down on folded legs in a clearing in heavy brush, very ill from the poison and surrounded by an unusually large pride of lions and lionesses—about thirty of them....The four Ju/wasi took in the situation, then slowly advanced on the lionesses. Speaking firmly but respectfully, they announced that the meat belonged to people. The lionesses rumbled unpleasantly. Some stood their ground. But others turned tail and retreated to the bushes. And then, although the bushes seemed alive with huge, tan forms pacing and rumbling, the Ju/wa hunters descended on the wildebeest, tossing clumps of earth at the lionesses, speaking firmly and respectfully as they did so. At last, the lionesses slowly, unwillingly, backed off. As soon as the lions and lionesses were screened by the bushes, the Ju/wa hunters seemed to give them little further thought and turned their attention to the wildebeest....

ELIZABETH MARSHALL THOMAS
The Tribe of Tiger

THE JAGUAR CULT

The Mojo tribe of eastern Bolivia regarded jaguars with religious awe and made them the object of a cult. Killing a jaguar brought unusual honors to the hunter; the event was celebrated with dancing and beating of drums. Men who had been wounded by a jaguar formed a special group of shamans called *camacoy* and performed the rites connected with jaguar spirits.

The belongings of a person killed by a jaguar were consecrated to that animal, and it became the rightful owner of them. Whoever kept for himself even a small part of these possessions was sooner or later doomed to be devoured by a jaguar. Killing a jaguar gave great prestige to the successful hunter and was followed by elaborate ceremonies in which the tribe danced, beat drums around the slain animal during the whole night, then ate its flesh. The paws and cleaned skull were trimmed with cotton ornaments and displayed in the drinking hall among other trophies. The hunter then retired for several days to a temple where he observed many taboos. The jaguar-shaman offered libations on his behalf to the Jaguar god and revealed to him the secret name of the jaguar—which the hunter bore thenceforward.

The Mojo also believed in a celestial jaguar, who ate the moon and was father of all earthly jaguars. In their stories, the sky jaguar pursued and attacked the celestial deer.

Adapted from a chapter by ALFRED METRAUX,
in The Handbook of South American Indians

Tepeyollotl, "Heart of the Mountain" (the god Tezcatlipoca in jaguar guise). Probably Tlaxcala, Early Colonial period. Bibliothèque Nationale.

When People Become Prey

Below: A British hunter and his unimpressed quarry, ivory miniature from Patiala State, c. 1892. Victoria & Albert Museum. Facing page, left: In Bengal, India, fisherman have learned that wearing a mask on the back of their head can sometimes deter a tiger attack; the animal prefers to stalk unwatched. By Raghu Rai/Magnum Photos, Inc. Right: Undated illustration of a leopard, Senegal. Corbis-Bettmann.

Big cats rank fairly high among animals that pose a danger to humans (though not as high as crocodiles or even domestic dogs). Lions, tigers, leopards, jaguars, and pumas are all capable of killing people, and have, though only the first three in any significant numbers. Tigers, living in close proximity to humans in densely populated southern Asia, have constituted the greatest threat as man-eaters. Various circumstances can precipitate man-eating, including old age or injury that renders a cat unable to catch its normal prey, and the practice in India of leaving corpses unburied, sometimes in large numbers as a result of famine or epidemics. But man-eating nearly always occurs in places where humans have altered the balance between cats and their natural prey, causing food shortages for the cats. The larger question to consider is not why cats sometimes kill people, but why they don't do so more often, since they are so eminently capable of it. George Schaller speculates about this in one of the excerpts below.

Tigers live at peace when they are not hunting. They are quiet, solitary animals when well fed, and they are assiduously avoided by most jungle creatures. When one enters an area, birds twitter and the alarm spreads. Wherever the great cat goes, the alarm spreads before it. Finally, the kill is made and all is quiet for days until the tiger is hungry again and starts to move. A great traveler, it may cover twenty miles or more before feeding again. This pattern, or any other, may not hold, however, when the great striped cat turns man-eater.

A man-eating tiger can disrupt dozens and sometimes hundreds of square miles of countryside. The whole normal parade of life changes to adjust unwillingly to the appetite of one cat. Religious festivals are canceled to keep pilgrims from traveling the roads and making camp in forest clearings. Markets are closed, and harvests rot on the vine. Cattle are not taken to pasture, firewood is not collected, and, in the extreme, villages isolated from the main roads are abandoned. Doctors refuse to travel at night to treat the sick and injured, and people who fail to turn up before dusk are not searched for. One single great cat, wandering silently through the forest, can turn whole vast areas into ghost regions. A human being, unless armed and well qualified, is helpless against attack. Tigers, once turned man-eater, become even more wary and alert, and frequently abandon a kill after one meal. The result is more kills than normal.... The most highly skilled of hunters can spend months, even years, in tracking down a man-eater.

At the height of the terror, the cat takes to raiding villages, ripping open thatched roofs, and clawing down barricaded doors. A cat that has reached the point where it will enter a village and ignore the screams and wailings of the inhabitants, has gone too far, and is usually killed soon after. However, as long as the cat keeps to the forest, it is nearly impossible to destroy. It avoids traps and poisoned bait with almost supernatural cunning. Once hunters think they have discovered a pattern to its behavior, the cat switches and does the unpredictable. If a man-eater happens to be a female with cubs, the situation can be even worse. First, it will require more food to feed itself and its family, and the cubs may grow up to be man-eaters themselves. It is not clear whether cubs raised on human flesh become man-killers once they start to hunt on their own.

ROGER CARAS
Dangerous to Man

Leopards that become man-eaters are even more dangerous than lions since they don't fear entering human settlements. Jim Corbett here chronicles an incident from his long quest for the notorious Rudraprayag leopard.

The woman had now stopped wailing, and in all the world there appeared to be no sound. This was as I had hoped it would be, for all I had to warn me of the leopard's arrival were my ears....

The straw that had been provided for me was as dry as tinder and my ears, straining into the black darkness, first heard the sound when it was level with my feet— something was creeping—very stealthily creeping, over the straw on which I was lying. I was wearing an article of clothing called shorts, which left my legs bare in the region of my knees. Presently, against this bare skin, I felt the hairy coat of an animal brushing—it could only be the man-eater, creeping up until he could lean over and get a grip of my throat. A little pressure now on my left shoulder— to get a foothold—and then, just as I was about to press the trigger of the rifle to cause a diversion, a small animal jumped down between my arms and

my chest. It was a little kitten; soaking wet, that had been caught out in the storm and, finding every door shut, had come to me for warmth and protection.

The kitten had hardly made itself comfortable inside my coat, and I was just beginning to recover from the fright it had given me when from beyond the terraced fields there was some low growling, which gradually grew louder. Then it merged into the most savage fight I have ever heard. [A]nother male leopard, who looked upon this particular area as his hunting ground, had accidentally come across him and set on him....

My chance of getting a shot had now gone, for even if the man-eater succeeded in defeating his attacker, his injuries would probably prevent him from taking any interest in kills for some time to come.

JIM CORBETT
The Man-Eating Leopard of Rudraprayag

To my puzzlement, man is not an important food item of lions even though no other large mammal is as defenseless and easy to kill. Perhaps man's upright stance baffles the uninitiated lion, who is accustomed to attacking animals that are built on a horizontal plane; perhaps lions are conservative, preferring the prey they learned to hunt as youngsters in a pride; or perhaps man's ancient ability and predilection to defend himself has imbued lions with caution. Lions readily capture and eat baboons and other monkeys, showing that they are not averse to primates. When lions face man they growl and snarl, behaving as they do toward a hyena or other predator, not as they do toward prey. Lions act as if they recognized in man his predatory past, and this after all is not surprising, because the two have competed for the same resources for several million years.

GEORGE SCHALLER
Golden Shadows, Flying Hooves

LEOPARD

Jeremiah said we cannot change.
I would like to get my jaws around
    Jeremiah,
and then we would see who can
    change faster.

At certain times I have dreamt

I tunneled under the ground
and looked for visionaries who were
    discarded many years ago.

When I found them, I rescued them,
    let them see
the light then ate them.
More than one prophet of the
    Second Coming
have been surprised that way.

If the twenty-four buddhas were to
    wander under my tree,
discoursing on the Eightfold Path,

I would show them the instant teeth
of Maya.

RICHARD GROSSMAN
The Animals

…The sleek musculature of tawny long-tailed jungle cats uncoiling in the foreground of your mind….

DANIEL HOFFMAN

from To the Maker of "A Peaceable Kingdom"

"Exalted and denigrated, admired and despised…" is how zoologist and author George Schaller describes humankind's attitude toward the great cats—and such contradictory emotions can apply to our feelings for just about all cats. Since our hominid forebears first laid eyes on the great cats of prehistory, or heard their roars in the dark night, these animals have stimulated our awe at their gracile beauty, our envy of their hunting skill and general air of seeming on top of their world, and our fear and wonder at their ability to appear and vanish as if by magic. From south African deserts to Indian jungles to European palaces and ancient American city-states, we have made of them deities and symbols of puissance and authority. ❧ Since a certain small wildcat became our valued companion (first in the grain barn and later at the hearth), our relationship with the feline clan has deepened, and

Catkind and Humankind

we have learned something of the still-wild cats' ways from observing the domestic version. Yet even housecats, once revered by the Egyptians, have been subject to human persecution at darker times in history. And our species' ever-expanding presence into almost every wild place on the planet has had a fearful impact on wild cats, as it has on every predator. We have killed them for taking too many deer and rabbits (which we also like to hunt), for eating our cattle after we have settled on their lands, and for the thrill of sport. Among the less laudable emotions cats have provoked in us has been lust for their gorgeous skins, a craving that countless cats have died to satisfy. ❧ Slowly, over the last several decades, we have come to realize the extent to which our activities have imperiled the wild felines. Pioneering field studies by biologists such as Schaller and Maurice Hornocker have enlarged our understanding of how wild cats go about their lives and the vital ecological roles they play. Animal writers like Roger Caras and Hope Ryden have dramatized their lives and discovered their histories for us, bringing us closer to these elusive and reticent animals. More and more, we are coming to appreciate wild cats as the embodiment of a world we stand in danger of losing, and our own domestic cats as a living pathway to that world— a way for us to experience a little wildness close at hand. ⋙

A COGAR STORY

The day was perfect, with the deep, stark clarity of the Southwest that strikes you speechless. As the morning warmed, orange-and-black-and-white butterflies burst from beneath the mules' hooves and zigzagged around us like electrons run amok. By the time the day was well heated, we arrived at the foot of the final rocky outbreak beneath the long chain of peaks. The nearest cliff was fractured into squat hieroglyphic blocks, like Mayan writing. A tendril of mountain flung out from it, and here we waited as Charley went down one last canyon. The breeze came in tufts. The buzz of an oncoming insect sounded for an instant like a dog howling. A raven sailed over me, very close and then closer, almost within reach, circling and looking directly at me with black shining eyes. In many Native cultures the raven is a powerful spirit, creator of the world. Even Theodore Roosevelt welcomed the raven's company in the desolation of the wild. What the hell, I thought, and made a prayer to the raven: Grant us a glimpse of the lion. We mean him no harm. The raven wheeled around my head, black eyes darting, slowly gaining altitude, then floated away.

Ten minutes later the dogs opened. The wind played with the howls until they sounded like Indian war whoops in an old western. We waited, tensing. In twenty minutes they had treed a lion. Although lions can run extremely fast for short distances, they have little stamina or sporting instinct and rarely run far. It took us an hour to reach them, maneuvering through a forest of burned mountain mahogany that arched over us in black and white, then up into thickening bouldery brush on a knuckle of mountain. Finally the scrub was too dense even for the mules. We dismounted to claw frantically through the last hundred yards up to a huge, lone ponderosa pine that stood like a beacon above us. My heart was racing and my lungs were pushed to extremes. This excitement, this frenzied dance to the rhythm of howling dogs, is what lion hunters sing of. "In cougar hunting the shot is usually much the least interesting and important part of the performance," wrote Theodore Roosevelt. Zane Grey hoped for a prolonged chase "because the race was too splendid a thing to cut short." The very language that Charley and Karen and all hunters use affirm this—they never "take" or "shoot" or "kill" or even "harvest" a lion, but always "catch" one.

At the foot of the tree the dogs were barking furiously and Charley lay stretched out against a rock, grinning. The lion lay draped along a sturdy branch forty feet up. She was a mature female and nearly perfect as a picture, her pelage marred only by a nick in her left ear. She was the color of oak leaves bleached by winter. With one hind leg and her tail dangling, she looked nonchalantly down as we emerged one by one from the thicket. Her expression was grave but sleepy. I stood open-mouthed, gaping, feeling limp and breathless and bursting, all at once. With binoculars we were eye to eye. Hers were golden and the pupils were medallions of light. She gazed at the dogs, at us, at the mountain, with a sort of absent-minded composure. Along the top of her nose was a line of froth from running hard on this hot, dry day. Forgive me, I said silently. She snarled once at the dogs, her lips lifting to show white canines, then put her head on her paws and blinked her eyes as if she could hardly keep them open. In fact, she couldn't; she closed them to slits, rested her head on her paws, and dozed. This was typical treed lion behavior, Charley said.

Charley did not like to kill cats under two years of age; he would tell a client that any cat without spots was legal, but he would prefer to let the animal grow up. Mothers accompanied by kittens were not legal. This was a paper prescription that blew away in the field. Kittens younger than six months don't usually travel with their mothers, so hunters can't tell from the tracks that the lion has young who will starve unless she returns. Yet mothers with young to feed travel in search of prey more often than usual, leaving many tracks. In heavily hunted areas, nearly half of the female lions killed probably leave behind doomed kittens. Occasionally the dogs

will track up to a litter of kittens still too young to climb trees, and tear them apart. This is a serious consideration for camera hunters. It has happened to lion researchers. It happened to Theodore Roosevelt, much to his regret, for he would have liked to keep the kittens, although he didn't say why. Lions that are chased repeatedly by camera hunters may also suffer permanent lung damage. On her last hunt, Sue suspected that the female she treed was pregnant, and felt badly enough about it that she doubted she would hunt much longer.

CHRIS BOLGIANO
Mountain Lion: An Unnatural History of Pumas and People

Page 142: Bengal tiger (Panthera tigris), Ranthambhore, India. By Gunther Ziesler/Peter Arnold, Inc. Facing page: Cougar (Felis concolor) scales a rock face, western North America. By Joe McDonald/Animals Animals. Above: Cougar cubs find shelter in a tree after an adult male kills their littermate, White Cloud Mountains, Idaho. By Jim Dutcher.

In her splendid treatise on the mountain lion, Bolgiano interviews scientists, Native Americans, ranchers, wild cat breeders, and hunters, for a broad perspective on the American cat. Leaving no doubt where her own sympathies lie, she here recounts the experience of searching for a puma with dogs—as do researchers and photographers as well as hunters—and coming face to face with one.

STALKING THE FLORIDA PANTHER
Everglades National Park

**Oh, the beautiful, splendid, supple,
graceful, powerful, silent puma!
I would rather watch and draw and
dream about it than about any other
living thing.**

CHARLES LIVINGSTONE BULL

*Above: On the prowl—cougar, pencil drawing by Todd
Sherman, 1996. Preceding page: Feline figurine from Key
Marco, Florida, one of the oldest wooden artifacts found in
the Americas, c. six to eight centuries ago. Smithsonian
Institution. Facing page: Bushman rock painting of a lion hunt,
Coerland rock shelter, South Africa. Photo by Paul Bahn.*

Camped near fresh tracks, we wait.
Such blackness—the leafy horizon
closed shut like a fan.

The fire burns in whispers.
All night it has eaten itself
like a trapped animal

down to glowing red bones.
We lie on separate hummocks
in this river of grass,

the water moving
as stealthily as I imagine
the cat—its plush paws

dimpling the black muck
as it hunts. What I know:
that desire spreads like light ·

without doctrine. By morning
the sawgrass will shatter
the swamp to a million

glittering shards. Now,
moving for each other
in the darkness, our skin shines

like flares. I want to think
the cat is watching as our bodies
pull the wilderness in.

ENID SHOMER

Early Cats and Early Humans

On the Africa savannah, a group of early hominids huddles together on a rock outcrop, intently watching the movements of the local lions. It's a scenario that must have taken place often in the days when our species was smaller, not very well organized, and armed only with sticks and stones. And not just in Africa, but surely in Europe, Asia, and the Americas. If we sometimes display a kind of "sixth sense" about someone coming up behind us, it may well be a vestigial survival mechanism from the days when cats preyed on humans.

On the other side of the equation, early humans probably scavenged and/or stole kills from big cats; even a rudimentary form of organization would have helped. One researcher believes that leopard kills stored in trees were a prime target. The present-day relationship of leopards and baboons suggests that leopards may also have preyed on these hominids.

In some parts of the world, humans probably moved into dens belonging to cave lions or other large predators, driving them out with fire if necessary. Although prehistoric artists depicted carnivores less often than the "sacred game" such as bulls and deer, spectacular Ice Age images of lions (or other cats) have been found in France, Siberia and China, in caves and as open-air petroglyphs. Rock art from a later era abounds in South Africa, and pumas are found on canyon walls throughout the American Southwest. 🐾

In his ceaseless pursuit of game, Palaeolithic man must often have found himself in direct confrontation with other predators, including wildcats, lynxes, leopards, giant tigers, and cave lions. We can be fairly certain that as far as possible he avoided direct encounters with the big cats, while the latter may usually have kept away from the strange, upright creature which went about in hordes and was capable of throwing things. When game was plentiful, there probably existed something like a state of armed neutrality. In times of scarcity, however, hungry cats must have taken the occasional human, while the humans are sure to have done a considerable amount of scavenging from their feline competitors.

CHARLES A. W. GUGGISBERG
Wild Cats of the World

Suddenly there appeared to my eyes the head of a roaring lion, drawn with wonderful realism. This head, more than natural size, is uncannily lifelike in its expression. There are the wrinkles around the gaping maw, fangs, eight centimetres long, protrude from the jaws, the eye is half-closed because the mouth is wide open. All this gives the brute an utterly savage appearance. The great artist who, with a pointed flint, scratched this masterpiece into the rough ceiling of the low corridor has faithfully rendered the impression of an encounter with the terrible predator!

ARMAND DENIS
Cats of the World

Above: Rendering by Léon Pales of an Ice Age cave pictograph, possibly of a cave lion (Felis speloea), La Marche, France. Pales asks, "Quel est ce grand Félin: Panthère, Tigre ou Lion?" But tigers never inhabited Europe and the massiveness of the creature depicted argues for the lion. Below: Lion guardian of the temple of Dagon, Mesopotamia, bronze sculpture from early in the second millennium B.C. Louvre/RMN Photo.

THE CAVE CATS

Saber-toothed tigers were found in both Americas, the forests of India, and Europe. Few could survive, however, during the Ice Age that closed the Tertiary era. When the glaciers crept back to the North Pole, and the Quaternary era—the Age of Man—came upon earth like Spring, saber-toothed tigers were making their last stand in England. Soon they were gone also, leaving the lynx, leopard, and wildcat to uphold the honor of the cat family there. These evidently adapted themselves to living in caves, which the saber-toothed tiger could not do. He was literally frozen out.

Man lived in caves to keep warm then too, and by necessity he discovered fire. So he had a hearth; now where was the cat? The most famous cat of caves was *Felis speloea,* the Latin words for "cave cat." Certain it is that man would not share a cave with this pussy cat. Those cave lions, as they were more often called, were twice the size of modern lions. They became living legends. Cave lions disappeared north of the Alps, when man entered the New Stone Age. A few lions stubbornly clung to the Balkan Peninsula, or southeastern Europe, until Xerxes laid crafty plans to conquer Greece. That Greece also was a refuge for cave lions is proved by the early Minoans, who lived there. The lion (so far away from the knowledge of Africa) was their crest. Their famed Lion Gate at Mycenae dates from about 1400 B.C. The stone beasts are headless now, but they guard the remains of the greatest city of prehistoric Greece and prove that the city's inhabitants were proud of the great cat's prowess.

JEAN CONGER
The Velvet Paw

148

PROTO-LIONS

Few animals...have ever been as successful as the lions. The most recent of the Panthera, lions evolved on the African savannahs only 700,000 years ago, probably to the consternation of our ancestors, and soon thereafter—long before our ancestors thought of doing anything similar—the lions colonized the rest of the planet. Until very recently lions were almost everywhere that glaciers were not. They lived in North and South America, all across Asia and down into India; they lived in Europe and on the British Isles; they lived in the Middle East and throughout the continent of Africa, where of course they remain to this day. (Australia and the Pacific Islands were about the only places the lions hadn't found.)

In keeping with the tendency of animals to be very large in the northern parts of their ranges, the northernmost lions were enormous. These were the cave lions. Having survived the Ice Age, their hair would have been longer than the hair of their southern relatives. They may have been quite fluffy. Only recently extinct, they certainly coexisted with people in Europe, Asia, and the Americas...

ELIZABETH MARSHALL THOMAS
The Tribe of Tiger

FROM SCAVENGER TO HUNTER

The early contacts between man and the larger cats may have been dramatic and frequently must have been tragic. Drama and tragedy aside, one cannot help imagining that food played an important part in prehistoric encounters.

We are still unsure about how soon man discovered the pleasures of meat. Perhaps his first experience of it came in the course of fires, which drove small animals towards him, or delivered them to him part-cooked....

No matter how the first meat meal came, man

must soon have discovered a carnivorous animal's kill, and have been tempted to steal it. I believe that in this way the first hunting of the great cats must have come about. Firstly man would have been a straight-forward thief, "irish" as that might sound. He would have been on a par with lower scavengers, scuttling away at the earliest grunt or roar of rage from the rightful owner. Later, desperate for food, probably nagged by more than one wife, man would have attempted to stand-up to the killer, changing from petty thief to armed robber. Disasters may have followed, but eventually animals must have been killed as well as driven-off. It is probable that man then found that not only was the cat-meat good to eat, but that the skin—while no warmer than that of less formidable creatures— created prestige and admiration for the successful hunter. Possibly the modern cult of the fur coat dates from such prehistoric days, although I suspect that prehistoric man sensibly kept the best skins for himself.

PETER TURNBULL-KEMP
The Leopard

Male lion (Panthera leo) *with a full belly, at sunset, Botswana. By Frans Lanting/Minden Pictures.*

I have just emerged from the depths of the great wide open spaces, from the life of prehistoric times, today just as it was a thousand years ago, from meeting with the great beasts of prey which enthrall one, which obsess one so that one feels that lions are all that one lives for....

ISAK DINESEN
Letters from Africa

How Cats Came Inside

Cats and Mice, illustration on a page from a 12th-century
English bestiary, possibly from Lincoln or York. Cats are the
only felines, besides lions, that often live in groups; domestication encourages social behavior in animals. The Pierpont
Morgan Library/Art Resource.

I n Rudyard Kipling's *Just So Stories,* "The Cat Who Walked by Himself" is lured by a clever woman
into a life of domesticity. But Kipling's tale may err in implying that humans deliberately
domesticated cats. A truer view, some think, is that cats domesticated themselves, choosing to live
around human habitations because it suited them. And it suited them because we had domesticated grasses, which produce grain, which attracts rodents, which are a primary food for cats.

It's generally accepted that Egypt was the first place where cats commonly lived with people,
starting around 6,000 years ago. The species involved was almost surely the African (or desert) wildcat, *Felis lybica.* Without question the Egyptians were the first to produce a body of records and myth
about their cats, revealing a passion for the creatures to match that of any current cat devotee.

From the southern Mediterranean we can trace the exodus of cats to other parts of the
Middle East and southern Europe, and via the imperial might of Rome through the rest of the
Continent and into the British Isles. These tamed African cats mated with the larger, furrier
European forest wildcats to produce generic tabbies, and eventually an array of specialized
breeds. Meanwhile, in central and southern Asia, another race of wildcats was becoming the
cherished pet of royalty; this eastern strain gave rise to the modern Oriental breeds.

Despite our long shared history, some see evidence that the cat has traveled only partway
down the path to domestication. They are still capable of living in a semiwild, or feral state, for
one thing, and they can interbreed with several true wild cats, including bobcats and forest wildcats. Moreover, as animals become domesticated, their brain size usually decreases sharply, but
the brains of *Felis catus* are not much smaller than those of like-sized wild cats.

In contrast to this remnant wildness is the close bond that cats and humans sometimes
form. With their human companions domestic cats often revert from competent predator to

a kind of infantile state, curling close and kneading
with their paws as if on their mother's belly. Conversely, they sometimes treat us like kittens, goes the
theory, by bringing us their prey as they bring it to
the den of their young. They rub against our faces and
bodies as with other cats they are bonded to, and they
enjoy sleeping on clothes that carry our scent.

Over the ages, we have loved, even revered domestic cats. We have admired, pampered, neglected,
and sometimes inflicted cruelties on them, yet the
relationship endures—one of mutual benefit and
cautious mutual attraction—probably in much the
same form as when the cats first chose it. 🐾

CATS DISCOVER MAN

We know for certain that thirty-five hundred years ago the cat was already fully domesticated. We have records from ancient Egypt to prove this. But we do not know when the process began. The remains of cats have been found at a neolithic site at Jericho dating from nine thousand years ago, but there is no proof that those felines were domesticated ones. The difficulty arises from the fact that the cat's skeleton changed very little during its shift from wild to tame. Only when we have specific records and detailed pictures—as we do from ancient Egypt—can we be sure that the transformation from wild cat to domestic animal had taken place.

One thing is clear: There would have been no taming of the cat before the Agricultural Revolution (in the neolithic period, or New Stone Age). In this respect the cat differed from the dog. Dogs had a significant role to play even before the advent of farming. Back in the paleolithic period (or Old Stone Age), prehistoric human hunters were able to make good use of a four-legged hunting companion with superior olfactory and hearing abilities. But cats were of little value to early man until he had progressed to the agricultural phase and was starting to store large quantities of food. The grain stores, in particular, must have attracted a teeming population of rats and mice almost from the moment that the human hunter settled down to become a farmer. In the early cities, where the stores were great, it would have become an impossible task for human guards to ambush the mice and kill them in sufficient numbers to stamp them out or even to prevent them from multiplying. A massive infestation of rodents must have been one of the earliest plagues known to urban man. Any carnivore that preyed on these rats and mice would have been a godsend to the harassed food-storers.

It is easy to visualize how one day somebody made the casual observation that a few wild cats had been noticed hanging around the grain stores,

picking off the mice. Why not encourage them? For the cats, the scene must have been hard to believe. There all around them was a scurrying feast on a scale they had never encountered before. Gone were the interminable waits in the undergrowth. All that was needed now was a leisurely stroll in the vicinity of the vast grain stores and a gourmet supermarket of plump, grainfed rodents awaited them. From this stage to the keeping and breeding of cats for increased vermin destruction must have been a simple step, since it benefited both sides.

DESMOND MORRIS
Catwatching

God has made the cat in order to give man the pleasure of caressing the tiger.

FERNAND MÉRY

A cat hunts fowl in the marshes, detail from a wall painting from the tomb of Nebamun, Thebes, c. 1400 b.c. This cat closely resembles the modern-day African wildcat, Felis lybica, but may be a domesticated Egyptian cat. Oriental Museum Institute, University of Chicago.

least one sexual scruple....Don't flirt with he (or she) who might eat you. A big cat would be more likely to kill and perhaps eat a smaller cat than dally with it romantically. Our domestic at-home cats have always despised lions, tigers and cougars, as you will discover if you ever drag your pet cat to a zoo....

In fact, cats generally are not the manmade animals most of our other domestic animals are. Such extremely varied canines as the Chihuahua and the bull mastiff, the Dalmatian and the bulldog, all belong to one species. The physical variances of cats have proven to be far less elastic genetically, with nothing like that kind of spread in size or shape—or, for that matter, behavioral purpose. Cats would never permit it.

ROGER A. CARAS
A Celebration of Cats

In his detailed studies of domestic cat behavior, Paul Leyhausen came up with the most logical explanation to date for why cats bring prey home to their owners—it may be a displacement activity for cats who don't have young to feed.

It is relatively common to find domestic cats and sometimes even castrated toms which retain this "bringing hypertrophy" for years. It usually finds its expression in their bringing home from their wanderings a large proportion of the rats and mice they catch, laying them out in a neat row and then, for lack of kittens to care for, addressing their coaxing "mouse call" to the human being with whom they are closest. The cat's owner usually interprets this as meaning that the cat proudly wants to demonstrate how clever it is, especially as it often will not let the matter rest until its owner has actually examined the "bag" and praised and stroked the cat. The important thing for the cat, however, is, at least primarily, not the praise but the fact that the human serving as "deputy kitten" actually goes to the prey it has brought home, just as a kitten thus coaxed does.

PAUL LEYHAUSEN
Cat Behavior

Evidence indicates that cats were first tamed in Egypt. The Egyptians stored grain, which attracted rodents, which attracted cats....I don't think this is accurate. It is certainly not the whole story. Cats didn't start as mousers. Weasels and snakes and dogs are more efficient as rodent-control agents. I postulate that cats started as psychic companions, as Familiars, and have never deviated from this function.

WILLIAM S. BURROUGHS
The Cat Inside

Portrait of an African wildcat (Felis lybica), Kalahari Desert, Botswana. By Rita Summers.

WHOSE GENES?

Probably between fifteen hundred and two thousand years before Christ, almost certainly in Egypt, surely from a wildcat known as *Felis lybica* or something close to that scientific designation, our domestic cat arose. It has been straight uphill from there....

One thing seems absolutely certain in all of this: the great cats of the world never figured in it. As much as we enjoy seeing the panther in our puss, the lion in our litters, there is not a shred of evidence that anything like that kind of a mix ever happened. Yet, wildly exotic mixtures could have happened if people had been keen enough to try for them. Today we list the bobcat as genus *Lynx* and our cat as genus *Felis,* so by all odds, as members of different genera, not to mention species, those two cats should not be able to breed. Yet one of our fourteen resident cats of the moment is a cross between a bobcat and a domestic tabby.

The reason there aren't more such cases is that crossbreeding is unlikely to occur in the wild—not unknown but, unlikely. Cats apparently have at

Cat,
Cat,
What are you?
Son, through a thousand generations,
    of the black leopards
Padding among the sprigs of young bamboo;
Descendant of many removals from the
    white panthers
Who crouch by night under the loquat-trees?
You crouch under the orange begonias,
And your eyes are green
With the violence of murder,
Or half-closed and stealthy
Like your sheathed claws.

Slowly, slowly,
You rise and stretch
In a glossiness of beautiful curves,
Of muscles fluctuating under black, glazed hair....

You walk as a king scorning his subjects;
You flirt with me as a concubine in robes of silk.
Cat,
I am afraid of your poisonous beauty,

I have seen you torturing a mouse.
Yet when you lie purring in my lap
I forget everything but how soft you are,
And it is only when I feel your claws open
    upon my hand
That I remember—

Remember a puma lying out on a branch
    above my head
Years ago.

Shall I choke you, Cat,
Or kiss you?
Really I do not know.

AMY LOWELL
from "To Winky"

The Woman Within, *painting by Mira Reisberg, 1996.*

WHY WOMEN ARE LIKE CATS

In this Mexican folktale, the narrator's Uncle Aurelio pokes gentle fun at the ladies by comparing them to cats. Many writers have done so, but in truth it's a compliment to both.

"Well, it is true that it had been God's intention to make Eve from the rib of Adam. Our father Adam was on the operating table, and the rib had been taken from his side. God placed it on a stand nearby, and had turned away to wash his hands when the wildcat came in.

Let it be known, *señoras de mi alma,* that the *gato montés,* during the first days of creation, sported a long tail. He came into the operating room in search of food. You see, God had been too busy with man and had had no time to prepare *comida* for his innocent creatures. Well, God's back was turned, and the cat saw the rib. He pounced upon it and out the door he went. Goodbye ladies! God gave chase. The cat saw he was losing the race and was bustling up a tree when God grabbed his tail. There was so much momentum on the part of the cat that the tail came off.

"And now what have we? *Ahora verán las señoras.* High in the tree, crouching on a limb and snarling with Adam's rib between its teeth, was the *gato montés.* On the ground was Nuestro Señor with a cat's tail in his hand.

"Nuestro Señor is wise beyond wisdom, and furthermore has a fine sense of humor. He smiled and looked first at the rib, well out of reach in a high tree, and then at what he held in his hand.

"At last he said: 'Oh, well, a cat's tail is good enough to make a woman of.' And that, *amigas,* is why women are such cats."

RILEY AIKEN
Mexican Folktales from the Borderland

Thou must be married to no man but me for I am he and born to tame you Kate. And I bring you from a wildcat to a Kate, conformable as other household Kates.

WILLIAM SHAKESPEARE
The Taming of the Shrew

Cat Cousins

For he is of the tribe of Tiger.
For the Cherub Cat is a term of the Angel Tiger.

CHRISTOPHER SMART

Catlore contains many stories of the relations between big and small cats. The goddess Diana, it's said, mocked her brother Apollo for creating the lion by creating the cat, so these two represent the sun and the moon. Here's another tale of cat cousins.

TIGER'S SISTER

Cat was Tiger's sister and they lived together in perfect harmony and accord. One day, however, Tiger got sick and began to shiver all over. Cat grew alarmed when his chills continued, and although she didn't like to leave him she decided she'd have to get some fire to warm him.

Man was the only one who had fire so she went to his house to ask for some. No one was at home. She went inside to get the fire herself, but what did she see as soon as she entered but some rice and fish on the noon. And how good they tasted!

In the meantime Tiger began to wonder what was keeping Cat. When his teeth stopped chattering long enough he called and called to her. Cat finally heard him. With her stomach comfortably full she had curled up at the hearthside to enjoy its pleasant warmth. Guiltily she took some fire and ran back to him with it. But she had found indoor life so much to her liking that she decided to live that way from then on. She told her brother of her decision and ran back to the house.

Tiger was so angry that he forgot how sick he felt. He ran after her, and prowled around the house, ready to grab her and eat her if she showed herself outside. But she remained indoors, and the door remained shut.

Since that day cats have lived with the Khasi people, and tigers try to kill cats whenever they can.

CLAIRE NECKER
The Natural History of Cats

HOPI TALE

A long time ago a Hopi boy went out to hunt. It was winter and snow lay on the ground in the valley where he searched for game. To his surprise he found some tracks in it that were like no tracks he had ever seen before, and he followed them. Out of the valley they went, ending at last at a large rock. The boy put his hand into the opening under the rock and pulled out a strange animal by its leg. He tied its legs together and started back with it to his village.

When he reached home and asked his father what the animal was he was told that it was a cat and that it ate mice, rats and rabbits. On hearing this the boy went again into the valley and caught a rabbit which he brought back to the cat.

Keeping it confined in a niche in the wall of his home he continued to feed it for four days. In this way the cat became tame and has lived in Hopi houses ever since.

THE UNCORRUPTIBLE CAT

We tie bright ribbons around their necks, and occasionally little tinkling bells, and we affect to think that they are as sweet and vapid as the coy name "kitty" by which we call them would imply. It is a curious illusion. For, purring beside our fireplaces and pattering along our back fences, we have got a wild beast as uncowed and uncorrupted as any under heaven.

It is five millenniums since we snared the wild horse and broke his spirit to our whim, and for centuries beyond counting we have been able to persuade the once-free dog to fawn and cringe and lick our hands. But a man must be singularly blind with vanity to fancy that in the three—ten?—thousand years during which we have harbored cats beneath our roof-trees, we have succeeded in reducing them to any such insipid estate. It is not a "pet" (that most degraded of creatures) that we have got in our house, whatever we may like to think. It is a wild beast; and there adheres to its sleek fur no smallest hint of the odor of humanity.

ALAN DEVOE
Concerning Cats

Revered and Royal Cats

The self-possessed, dignified bearing of cats readily brings the term "regal" to mind. Add to this the power of life and death they wield over other animals and their almost magical ability to appear and disappear at will, and it's not surprising that people in many parts of the world have raised admiration to reverence, or made cats an emblem of royalty.

The ancient Egyptians were among the first, and perhaps the most fervent, of all cat worshippers. To these Nile farmers their grain supplies were vitally important, which may explain why they elevated to the status of deities the small, tame wildcats who helped protect that grain. Among their many gods, the Egyptians included the local big cat as well, in the form of a lionheaded goddess.

The great cats were always linked with might, none more so than the lion. In styling himself "Lionheart," England's Richard I intended to convey all the kingly courage implied by that name. African tribal rulers generally made sure that any lion or leopard skins obtained by their followers came into their possession, also reserving for their own use the chairs, amulets, belt masks, and other talismans created in the cats' image. Hunting the great cats or keeping them as captives was often a ruler's exclusive province. For the Assyrian king Assurbanipal, for example, killing lions affirmed his own might, and was memorialized by temple reliefs of great artistry and power. Cheetahs, once plentiful in the Near East and India, were cherished by sultans and maharajas for their aristocratic looks and hunting skill, and could actually be taught to hunt for their masters. Smaller wild cats have had their cults, too: the European lynx was considered sacred to the Norse goddess Freya.

In the New World, jaguar gods were often dark deities. The Aztecs associated the animal with one of their two chief creation gods, Tezcatlipoca, who grew tired of darkness and turned himself into the First Sun. The mountain lion was more often a benevolent spirit, sometimes cast in the role of Keeper of all the Animals. In some places, white mutations of cats were accorded special reverence, as in China, where the white tiger Pai Hu ascended into the Milky Way. 🐾

Following death, the body of an Egyptian cat was embalmed with full ceremony, the corpse being bound in wrappings of different colors and its face covered with a sculptured wooden mask. Some were placed in cat-shaped wooden coffins, others were encased in plaited straws. They were buried in vast feline cemeteries in huge numbers—literally millions of them.

The cat goddess was called Bastet, meaning She-of-Bast. Bast was the city where the main cat temple was situated, and where each spring as many as half a million people converged for the sacred festival.

About one hundred thousand mummified cats were buried at each of these festivals to honor the feline virgin-goddess (who was presumably a forerunner of the Virgin Mary). These Bastet festivals were said to be the most popular and best attended in the whole of ancient Egypt, a success perhaps not unconnected with the fact that they included wild orgiastic celebrations and "ritual frenzies." Indeed, the cult of the cat was so popular that it lasted for nearly two thousand years.

DESMOND MORRIS
Catwatching

Thou art the Great Cat, the avenger of the Gods, and the judge of words, and the president of the sovereign chiefs and the governor of the holy Circle, thou art indeed...the Great Cat.

Inscription on the royal tombs at Thebes

Mummy of an Egyptian cat, possibly from Abydos, Roman period, after 30 B.C. Smithsonian Institution.

CAT DEITIES

No one knows when the cat was first sanctified in Egypt and as far as the records so far uncovered show, it was never officially listed as a god. It was, however, perceived as one—at the least, that is, as an animal sacred to the gods—a perception that went on for at least two thousand years. There are carvings, papyri, statues and engravings that show priests kneeling before bejeweled cats, clearly praying and making offerings....The Egyptian goddess Isis was believed to have held the cat sacred. In fact, cats were often considered incarnations of Isis. When Isis's daughter married the sun-god Osiris she gave birth to the catheaded goddess Bastet or Bast,... There were lionheaded goddesses, too, Tefnut and Sekhmet, and their provinces overlapped with Bast's domain.

ROGER A. CARAS
A Celebration of Cats

Since I have succeeded to the throne of my father, Adad, the Weather God, has sent torrents of rain, Ea, Lord of the Waters that are under the Earth, has opened the fountains of the deep, the forests have grown enormously, the reeds have shot up in thickets, so that nobody can enter them any more. In there, lions have bred in mighty numbers. Through the killing of cattle, small stock and man they have become bold. The mountain shakes with the thunder of their roars, the game of the plains has fled. They constantly kill the livestock of the fields and they spill the blood of men and cattle. The herdsmen and the supervisors are weeping; the families are mourning. The misdeeds of these lions have been reported to me. In course of my expedition I have penetrated their hiding places and destroyed their lairs. For my regal amusement I have caught the Desert King by his tail, and on the instruction of my helpers, the Gods Nusib and Nergal, I have split his head with my two-handed sword.

ASSURBANIPAL

On every occasion of a fire in Egypt the strangest prodigy occurs with the cats. The inhabitants allow the fire to rage as it pleases, while they stand about at intervals and watch these animals, which, slipping by the men or else leaping over them, rush headlong into the flames. When this happens, the Egyptians are in deep affliction. If a cat dies in a private house by a natural death, all the inmates of the house shave their eyebrows;...

HERODOTUS

Above: Amulet of a seated goddess with a lion's head, c. 1070–712 B.C. Metropolitan Museum of Art. Right: The great lion hunt, detail from an Assyrian limestone relief in the North Palace of Assurbanipal at Ninevah, 7th century B.C. British Museum/Werner Forman. Facing page: Tiger rug from Tibet, by an unknown weaver, c. early 20th century. Only those in authority could own and use such tiger rugs; thrown over luggage on a caravan, they indicated a traveler's importance. Mimi Lipton, Tibet Charitable Trust/Heini Schneebeli.

TIGERS RULE

To the Annamites, tigers, or spirits who dwell in tigers, govern the four corners of space. The Red Tiger rules over the South (which is located at the top of maps); summer and fire belong to him. The Black Tiger rules over the North; winter and water belong to him. The Blue Tiger rules over the East; spring and plants belong to him. The White Tiger rules over the West; autumn and metals belong to him.

Over these Cardinal Tigers is a fifth tiger, the Yellow Tiger, who stands in the middle governing the others, just as the Emperor stands in the middle of China and China in the middle of the World....

JORGE LUIS BORGES
The Book of Imaginary Beings

HOLY CATS

The Goldis [an ancient tribe of Siberia] revered the tiger and the bear as their sacred ancestors. The tiger or *amba* was considered sacred as the guardian of the forest, and never hunted. It was the ruler or god of the wild regions. On the rare occasions when a tiger raided the hunters' snares for trapped deer, or carried off their dogs, or even ate the vital supplies of frozen fish that would see them through the lean periods, it was immediately forgiven. Anyone found killing a tiger was expelled from the tribe for having violated the traditions handed down by their forefathers.

Their religion was a mixture of totemism, nature worship and fetishism. The priests or shamans acted as intermediaries between the living and the supernatural world of the spirits. They had a diversity of duties—healing the sick, making sacrifices on occasions of misfortune or death, conducting prayers and even performing magic. They would bedeck themselves with fur robes, with the bones and teeth of sea animals and metal images of birds and beasts, making them look like a mixture of man and animal.

One shaman described how he was prompted into this service by a spirit who approached him in a dream: "Sometimes she comes as a winged tiger. I mount her and she takes me to show me different countries. I have seen mountains where only old men and women live, and villages where you see nothing but young people, men and women. Sometimes these people are turned into tigers."

VALMIK THAPAR
The Tiger's Destiny

I know of course cat's origin—
　　the incubation of "greybeard."
The cat was gotten on a stove—
　　has a girl's nose, a hare's head,
A tail of snake's venom, claws of a viper,
Feet of cloudberries, the rest of its body
　　is of the wolf's race.

A magic song of the Finns

Above: North American lynx (Lynx canadensis), northern Rocky Mountains. By Ralph A. Reinhold/Animals Animals. Below: Old postcard depicting a leopard tamed and trained to hunt in India. Cheetahs were sometimes conveyed to the hunt on fine horses or elephants rather than a prosaic ox-cart. Mary Evans Picture Library.

CHIEF OF CHEETAHS

It chanced that they loosed a special cheetah called "Chitr Najan" at a deer. Suddenly there appeared in front of them a ravine which was twenty-five yards broad. The deer leapt into the air to the height of a spear and a half and conveyed itself across. The cheetah in its eagerness took the same course, cleared the ravine and seized the deer. On beholding this astonishing occurrence the spectators raised a cry of amazement, and there was great rejoicing and astonishment. The Emperor raised the rank of that cheetah and made him chief of the cheetahs. He also ordered that as a special honour and as a pleasure to men, a drum should be beaten in front of the cheetah.

ABU FAZIL

FREYA'S CAT

The peoples of ancient Europe, living close to untamed nature, could not fail to be fascinated by the lynx, the big secretive cat that lurked in the mysterious depths of dark forests, from which it occasionally emerged to make its presence felt by a quick raid on their flocks of sheep and goats. In Teutonic and Scandinavian folk-lore, this bold freebooter was regarded as sacred to Freya, the goddess of love and beauty, and a couple of lynxes (not wildcats, as is often stated) were supposed to have drawn her chariot when she rode into battle. The authors of the Classical Age represented the lynx as sharing with Lyncaeus of Greek mythology the ability to see through stone walls.

CHARLES A. W. GUGGISBERG
Wild Cats of the World

Celestial Cats

Animals humans think highly of are often placed in the heavens. Leo is there, along with the jaguar as one of the Aztecs' many suns. The Bushmen link the caracal with Venus, and in China the white tiger Pai Hu was incorporated into the Milky Way after living 500 years, from where he protected planet Earth.

LYNX AND THE MORNING STAR

This story is concerned with the morning star or, as he called it far more feelingly, the Dawn's Heart. The old Bushman father in the desert had already described this star to me as the greatest of all hunters in the sky, saying that when it appeared the black night whisked about, the red dust spurting at its heels. In the imagination of the vanished Bushmen of my part of Africa the Morning Star was a hunter too, but it was also a person of the early race. As a person he had come down to earth, fallen in love and taken as his natural bride the Lynx, also at that time a person. This marriage of a star to a Lynx is perhaps the most inspiring example I know of the extraordinary precision of language which the first spirit of life forged in the fire of the imagination. If there is one animal among the multitudes shining like jewels in the grass, bush and sombre forests of Africa more suitable than any other to be married to a star, it is the Lynx.

In the Mountain of the Wolves, after which was named the great farm my grandfather gave my mother as a wedding present, there were several families of lynxes when I was a boy, and I had many an opportunity of observing them. I had even tried to make a pet of one, but I was forced to release it because it preferred dying to becoming reconciled to captivity. In its natural state, the Lynx made an impression of flamelike grace, courage, vitality and instinct which no other animal has ever equalled in my experience. When it appeared in the shadows far at the back of the cave where it lived in the Mountain of the Wolves,

moving towards the daylight opening, it was like a lamp being drawn up from deep down in a dark well. Other cats may have been as vivid and as graceful, but they lacked the starry being of the Lynx. The Lioness, for instance was far too big; the mere thought of her marriage to such a star offended the sense of proportion. The Leopard was all that the Lioness was and nearer the right size, but unfortunately she was spotted: the Dawn's Heart, pure in the stainless black sky of an early African morning, could not possibly have had a spotty bride. Only the Lynx satisfied all the demands of shape, size, and unblemished fiery colour, so that when the marriage of the images was consummated, no wonder the Dawn's Heart loved the Lynx dearly and all other rejected females among the people of the early race were jealous.

LAURENS VAN DER POST
The Heart of the Hunter

JAGUAR SUN

One of the two chief Aztec gods of creation was Tezcatlipoca, god of night and blackness. He grew tired of living in darkness and turned himself into the First Sun, called Smoky Mirror. But the other god, Quetzalcoatl, challenged him to a duel and threw him down from the sky, into the water, where he next turned himself into a jaguar. He ate most of the first race of humans on earth, then went back up into the heavens. As his fur dried, shining spots appeared on his coat and can still be seen as the constellation Great Bear. (Later men decided this star cluster looked more like a bear than a jaguar, but the Aztecs believed it was Texcatlipoca, in his jaguar form.)

Adapted from various sources

The constellation Leo contains nine bright stars including the famous "sickle," with the alpha star Regulus at its base. The Egyptians accorded it power because the Nile came into flood as the sun entered Leo each year. Photo by John Sanford & David Parker/Photo Researchers, Inc. (Science Photo Library), drawing by Miriam Lewis.

King of Beasts

From the temple art of Ninevah to Disney's "The Lion King," no animal has been such a potent and enduring symbol for the aspirations of men. Characterized as mighty, fierce, fearless, noble, magnanimous—that is, everything a king would like to be thought—the real lion has been difficult to locate amidst his symbolic laurels. The many movies evoking lions—"The Lion in Winter," "The Wind and the Lion," "The Young Lions"—are recent manifestations of our ancient habit of using lions to suggest nobility. It climaxed in the heydey of heraldry and the courtly tradition, with lions *rampant* or *couchant* appearing on more crests than any creature except, perhaps, the eagle.

THE LION OF LUXOR

It was during that time that we received from Luxor, away up the Nile, a very superior Barbary Lion. He was big, hairy, dignified, and so handsome in face, form and pelage that the painters and sculptors flocked to him.

…His name was Sultan I, and he looked it. You know Sultans are long on dignity. Once when a keeper suddenly found himself (by a bad mistake) in that lion's cage and at close quarters with Sultan, with only a penitentiary broom between them, Sultan proudly refused to seize the opportunity to kill the keeper. The keeper always had been square and kind with him; it was beneath his royal dignity to take a mean advantage of a mistake, and so the old chap just calmly looked at Schwartz, and never even snarled.

At this point Sultan turned his face toward us, and looked at us with strange intentness of regard. Then we were astounded by hearing deep and solemn tones, saying:

"I am the Lion of Luxor. I look backward through five hundred generations of desert history."…

"My home," continued the Voice, "was within sight of the ruined Temple that stands on the west bank of the Nile," said Sultan. "My Saharan ancestors roared in the streets of Carthage within one month after it became a ruin. Toward the far south, my forbears knew all the secrets of Zimbabwe, the wonderful stone city of Rhodesia. My grandsires were the rulers of the deserts of middle Egypt. They saw the stone quarried for the pyramids of Gizeh, and the Sphinx was modeled from one of my great-grandmothers. They knew the quarries of the Mokattam Hills, as I knew the fields of Luxor."

"I say, Sultan," said I, very gently. "Why did not your people exterminate all the early Egyptians? I think they easily could have done so."

"There was no reason, no incentive. It would have meant a great waste of raw human material, and from the beginning of the Age of Lions we never have killed more food than we could eat, and never wastefully. On the game plains of the poor old Africa of today, each full-grown lion kills only two zebras, or two antelopes, each week. What sense is there in being wasteful? Do we not preserve the balance of Nature, by keeping the hoofed animals down to reasonable numbers?"

"That is all perfectly true. We learned it first from the very keen game-rangers of Kenia and Tanganyika."

"Good!" muttered Sultan. "And you hear very little about the killing of people. After hunting and feeding upon big game, the hunting of men and women seems mighty trivial. It is no sport for kings, I assure you."

WILLIAM T. HORNADAY
Wild Animal Interviews

And first the Lion, greatest of degree,
    Was called there, and he most fair to sene,
    With a full hardy countenance and keen.

Before Dame Nature came, and did incline,
With visage bold, and courage leonine.

This awful Beast full terrible was of cheer,
    Piercing of look, and stout of countenance,
Right strong of corps, of fashion fair, but feir,
    Lusty of shape, light of deliverance,
    Red of his colour, as is the ruby glance,
On field of gold he stood full mightily,
With fleur-de-lis encircled lustily.

The Lady liftit up his clawès clear,
    And let him listly lean upon her knee,
And crowned him with diadem full dear,
    Of radiant stones most royal for to see;
    Saying, The King of Beastes mak I thee,
And the chief protector in woods and straws;
Unto thy lieges go forth and keep the laws.

WILLIAM DUNBAR, 1465–1525
from "The Thistle and the Rose"

THE LION'S SHARE

The Lion went once a-hunting along with the Fox, the Jackal, and the Wolf. They hunted and they hunted till at last they surprised a Stag, and soon took its life. Then came the question how the spoil should be divided. "Quarter me this Stag," roared the Lion; so the other animals skinned it and cut it into four parts. Then the Lion took his stand in front of the carcass and pronounced judgment: "The first quarter is for me in my capacity as King of Beasts; the second is mine as arbiter; another share comes to me for my part in the chase; and as for the fourth quarter, well, as for that, I should like to see which of you will dare to lay a paw upon it."

"Humph," grumbled the Fox as he walked away with his tail between his legs; but he spoke in a low growl—"You may share the labours of the great but you will not share the spoil."

AESOP

The Lion alone of all wild beasts is gentle to those who humble themselves unto him, and will not touch any such upon their submission, but spareth what creatures so-ever lieth prostrate before him. As fell and furious as hee is otherwhiles, yet hee dischargeth his rage upon man, before that hee setteth upon women, and never preyeth upon babes unless it be for extreme hunger.

PLINY (1ST CENTURY A.D.)
Natural History

Above: Portrait of a captive male lion. By Stephen Walker. Below: Lion and Hedgehog, from Villard de Honnecourt's Sketchbook, *early 13th century. Bibliothèque Nationale. Facing page: Lion relief in molded and glazed bricks from the Processional Way in Babylon, 6th century* B.C. *Staatliche Museum, Berlin/J. Liepe.*

Daniel in the Lions' Den, *by Peter Paul Rubens, c. 1613–1615. Rubens and other Renaissance painters had the opportunity to see live captive lions and rendered them with great accuracy. National Gallery of Art/Richard Carafelli.*

Salva me ex ore leonis...

Save me from the lion's mouth...

Psalm XXI

Lions, Christians, and Other Notions

Along with their secular associations with royalty, lions (and other legendary cats) have taken on some religious meanings, especially in the Christian canon. The tale of Daniel in the lions' den is an Old Testament parable on the power of faith. The twelfth-century Latin *Bestiary,* a version of an earlier work by Physiologus, turns the lion and panther into allegories for certain qualities of Jesus Christ. As its translator T. H. White points out, the writers of medieval bestiaries had no personal experience of these animals—what they looked like or how they behaved. They used them as vehicles to write about their chief preoccupation: the nature of their own God. The use of lions in heraldry, on the knightly shields of Christianity's defenders, made the beast by extension a "supporter of the faith." And even before that, the lion had been adopted by the Evangelist St. Mark as his emblem and messenger. 🐾

A PIOUS PANTHER

There is an animal called a PANTHER which has a truly variegated colour, and it is most beautiful and excessively kind. Physiologus says that the only animal which it considers as an enemy is the Dragon.

When a Panther has dined and is full up, it hides away in its own den and goes to sleep. After three days it wakes up again and emits a loud belch, and there comes a very sweet smell from its mouth, like the smell of allspice. When the other animals have heard the noise they follow wherever it goes, because of the sweetness of this smell. But the Dragon only, hearing the sound, flees into the caves of the earth, being smitten with fear....

The true Panther, Our Lord Jesus Christ, snatched us from the power of the dragon-devil on descending from the heavens. He associated us with himself as sons by his incarnation, accepting all, and gave gifts to men, leading captivity captive.

And because it is a beautiful animal, the Lord God says of Christ: "He is beautiful in form among the sons of men."

T. H. WHITE
The Bestiary

It is written that the Lion is of such a nature that when he is hunted he wipes out with his tail the traces of his footsteps as he goes along, so that none can trace him....The track of the Lion typifies the Incarnation. For thus did God lower himself by degrees through the orders of prophets and apostles until he became fleshly man, and thus He vanquished the Devil. If the Devil had known that God was become mortal man, he would never have led him on so far as to crucify Him. So God acted cunningly and without being perceived.

PHILIPPE DE THAUN (12TH CENTURY)
The Book of Creatures

LIKE UNTO A LION

The Lion's second feature is, that when he sleeps, he seems to keep his eyes open.

In this very way, Our Lord also, while sleeping in the body, was buried after being crucified—yet his Godhead was awake. As it is said in the Song of Songs, "I am asleep and my heart is awake," or, in the Psalm, "Behold, he keepeth Israel shall neither slumber nor sleep."

The third feature is this, that when a lioness gives birth to her cubs, she brings them forth dead and lays them up lifeless for three days—until their father, coming on the third day, breathes in their faces and makes them alive. Just so did the Father Omnipotent raise Our Lord Jesus Christ from the dead on the third day. Quoth Jacob: "He shall sleep like a lion, and the lion's whelp shall be raised."

T. H. WHITE
The Bestiary

Above: The famous Lion of St. Mark sculpture on the Orlogio (clocktower), in Venice's Piazza San Marco, late 15th century. Below: Lions and peacocks in a Byzantine-style relief, Cathedral of Santa Maria Assunta, Torcello, Venice, 13th century. Cameraphoto/Art Resource.

> Therefore it must be considered what harmes and perils come unto men by this beast. It is most certain, that the breath and favour of Cats consume the radical humour and destroy the lungs, and therefore they which keep their Cats with them in their beds have the air corrupted, and fall into severall Hecticks and Consumptions.
>
> EDWARD TOPSELL (1607)
> *The Historie of Foure-footed Beastes*

Above: Woodcut of three witches and their cats from a 17th-century broadside reporting their trial. Below: French circus poster, c. 1887, recreating the Roman Hippodrome, where lion–human combats were staged. The Granger Collection.

Darker Meanings

Our relationship with cats has a dark side. If cats have been adored, they have also been feared, hated, and persecuted, for reasons ranging from irrational terror to cold-blooded competition for resources. Superstitions about black cats hark back to the Middle Ages, when cats were first seen as companions of witches and familiars of Satan. The witchcraft mania reached its climax in the sixteenth and seventeenth centuries, when not only hundreds of people but thousands of cats were executed, often with appalling cruelty. Why cats? Surely their stealthy movements and glowing eyes suggested a link with the supernatural to those open to such beliefs. Perhaps, too, killing harmless domestic cats was an unconscious way for people to exert power over the bigger, more dangerous members of the cat tribe.

As for wild cats, they have sometimes been detested out of plain fear for the danger they pose to human life—though people who live near lions and tigers have traditionally incorporated those feelings into an overall stance of respect and tolerance. Where the cats have been seriously persecuted, it usually stems from the perception that they kill too many game animals or too much livestock. Farmers, herders, and ranchers have killed many for these reasons; sport hunters have enthusiastically joined in. Further justification was found in the supposedly bloodthirsty manner in which some cats killed, executing more victims than they could possibly eat, the argument went. Millions of wild cats have also been killed from economic motives, for skins and other body parts used in Asian folk medicine. Underlying most if not all these motives may be a primal fear of the wildness within ourselves, which we see manifested most dramatically in the beasts of prey. 🐾

CAT SLANDER

The South American puma is the most sadistic and bloodthirsty of the cats that roam the jungles of British Guiana, killing indiscriminately for the sheer brute exhilaration it enjoys in its natural conquest of other animals that are either larger or smaller, stronger or much weaker. Most of the puma's skillful violence seems designed not just for food or for self-protection but to satisfy an insatiable taste for destruction. No animal, wild or domestic, ever really feels safe in its company (unlike the lion the jaguar feared by other animals only when they are obviously hunting for food). As a result of its unrestrainable ferocity, man has long been terrified of the puma...

from the book jacket for Leemo, *by Stanley Brock*

THE WILD INSIDE

The tiger was a symbol of all that civilized life rejected. The tiger represented not control but its loss. The tiger stood for both nature out of control and it also stood for human nature out of control. It embodied the darkest impulses of human beings; it represented the dreadful animal nature that lurked in civilized humankind something that needed to be suppressed if civilization was to continue. The tiger hinted at the dreadful truth: that *Homo sapiens* is a mammal kin to *Panthera tigris*.

SIMON BARNES
Tiger!

Of common wild cats I need not speak much, for every hunter in England knows them, and their falseness and malice are well known. But one thing I dare well say that if any beast has the devil's spirit in him, without doubt it is the cat, both wild and the tame.

GASTON PHOEBUS (C. 1391)
Livre de la Chasse

Black Beast, by Darrel Austin, an American painter, 1941. Black leopards or jaguars (and, indeed, black house-cats) have been the targets of many superstitions and legends; but in fact, their melanism seems not to influence their behavior at all. Smith College Museum of Art.

In the excerpt above, a book-jacket copywriter editorializes in melodramatic fashion on the killing habits of the puma; curiously, the book itself gives a much fairer picture. The text below quotes one of several letters on the topic of leopards from a Roman bureaucrat stationed in Asia Minor to Cicero, then preconsul of Cicilia.

In nearly all my letters to you I have mentioned the subject of leopards. It will be a disgrace to you if, when the merchant Patiscus has sent ten to the Tribune Curio, you don't get many more. Curio has made me a present of those ten and of another ten from Africa....

Do please see that you attend to this. In this affair the trouble for you is only to talk—I mean to issue orders officially and to promise commissions. For as soon as the leopards are caught, there are my own people to look after the animals' keep and to bring them to Rome.

MARCUS CAELIUS

The Fate of the Puma

The mountain lion, or cougar, or puma *(Felis concolor)* is a cat that has evoked myriad human reactions, from deification to detestation. The big American cat once figured in a widespread Native American myth as the malevolent Underwater Panther, a force from the underworld that could call up destructive storms but also wield healing powers or reward good behavior. Southwestern tribes took a more positive view, making the puma a powerful hunting spirit or guardian. When Europeans first encountered the cougar they mistook it for the same animal as Africa's lion; then, on realizing the error, propounded the notion that it was a "degenerate" version of the same. During the century of continental expansion, mountain lions were regarded as "varmints," only slightly less despicable than wolves, and consequently eradicated from many areas. Today they represent one of the great challenges of maintaining some kind of ecological balance into the next century: weighing the need for human safety, as we continue to move into lion habitat, against the need to keep wilderness and mountain lions in our world.

When the Puritans came over
  Our hills and swamps to clear
The woods were full of catamounts,
  And Indians red as deer.

OLIVER WENDELL HOLMES

The big horse-killing cat, the destroyer of the deer, the lord of stealthy murder… with a heart both craven and cruel.

THEODORE ROOSEVELT

Mountain lions are not the largest predators in temperate North America, being far outweighed by grizzly and black bears, but bears are omnivores and rely more on plants than on meat. In this, and in the way they use their hands and feet, bears are like humans. Mountain lions are true carnivores, living almost exclusively on animals—preferably deer—that they themselves kill. Wolves have a similar diet, but they procure it through family cooperation in a way that is easily observed and appreciated by humans. Lions live and hunt alone, except for mothers with young.

They seem magically elusive, able to remain invisible even when the landscape is clearly imprinted with signs of their passing. They are agile enough to traverse the roughest country, and strong enough to kill animals much larger than themselves. When Europeans arrived in the Americas, mountain lions ranged from Canada to Tierra del Fuego, from the coasts of both oceans to the peaks of the Appalachians, Rockies, and Andes. The only large mammals more widely distributed throughout the western hemisphere were humans, so every Native culture except those in the Arctic encountered lions—a fact that contributed to the long list of names by which the animal became known to European settlers. Coping with a creature so alien to humans, so physically powerful and potentially threatening, and above all so mysterious must have been a serious exercise for the human psyche.

CHRIS BOLGIANO
Mountain Lion

Left: Mountain lion petroglyph in the Petrified Forest, Arizona. Rock art of pumas is found in many places around the Southwest, typically depicted thus with exaggerated claws and a long, lean body and tail. Petrified Forest Museum Association. Facing page: Puma, color lithograph by an unknown artist, c. 1870. Mary Evans Picture Library.

A young cougar snarls a warning, White Cloud Mountains, Idaho. By Jim Dutcher.

WHAT ARE THEY GOOD FOR?

"Don't get me on my soapbox about predators. You're a tourist, you don't have to make a livelihood on this country," she said softly, courteously. "My living depends on how many calves I send to market."

"How many calves have you lost to lions in your years of ranching?" I asked.

"None," she said. "That I know of. We've had lions to kill some saddle horses. Lion prefer deer to beef but would rather have horsemeat than anything. What are they good for? Coyotes eat some of the small rodents and help keep them down, that's the only thing I could see them do, but I don't see where the lion is important at all. They'd be just fine in a zoo. What right do they have to kill the beautiful deer and antelope I love to see? It's a shame for predators to kill all the good animals."

CHRIS BOLGIANO
Mountain Lion

The woods [of Pennsylvania] teemed with them.... Almost every backwoods kitchen had a Panther [mountain lion] coverlet on the lounge by the stove. Panther tracks could be seen crossing and re-crossing all the fields, yet children on their way to school were never molested.

COLONEL W. H. SHOEMAKER
(EARLY 19TH CENTURY)

The Cat of Many Names

Mountain lion
Puma
Cougar
Léon americano
Plain lion
Gray lion, Silver lion
Onça vermelha
Onça parda
Leon bayo
Leopardo
Tyger, Tigre
Tigre rouge
Deer tiger
Cougouar
Mountain tiger
Cuguacuarana
Panther
Painter
Catamount
Carcajou
Quinquajou
Catawampus
Wild cat
Big cat
King-cat
Long Tail
Pampas cat
Swamp devil
Swamp lion
Sneak-cat

"Let me give him one more name,
and call him the "Story Lion!"

WILLIAM T. HORNADAY

An abandoned stone pavilion, part of an old fortress in what is now Ranthambhore National Park, India, serves as shelter for some of the park's tigers. By Valmik Thapar/Peter Arnold, Inc.

Tigris the Tiger gets his name from his speedy pace; for the Persians, Greeks and Medes used to call an arrow 'tygris'. The beast can be distinguished by his manifold specklings, by his courage and by his wonderful velocity. And from him the River Tigris is named, because it is the most rapid of all rivers.

T. H. WHITE
The Bestiary

Cultivating Cat Power

Peoples around the world have recognized in wild cats a powerful life force, and tried in various ways to share it. Cats, especially the big ones, are clearly potent creatures who dominate their worlds—as humans wish to. One of the chief ways of borrowing some of this power has been to wear an animal's skin; while the practice is deplorable today, it's understandable among traditional people living in an earlier world.

Archeological evidence of leopard skins worn by dancers, found at the Catal Huyuk site in Anatolia, suggests that wearing cat skins for ritual purposes dates back at least to 6500 B.C. Aztec warriors sometimes wore entire jaguar pelts, with the head and tail left attached; this guise endowed them with the cat's power and ability to move unseen. Similarly, the Masai in East Africa often wore lion manes, and the African golden cat was held in such esteem by West African chiefs that they could rarely be persuaded to part with a skin. Dayak warriors on the island of Sarawak wore clouded leopard skins into battle, and puma skins held power for Native Americans.

Other parts of the cat's body, or objects associated with it, carried power as well. Some Africans treasured a magical stone from the stomachs of lions—most likely a hairball. The tiger has more "magical" body parts than any other cat: its whiskers gave power over women; its penis made the best aphrodisiac; tiger fat relieved aches and pains; its teeth and claws conferred power and averted evil. Unfortunately, these beliefs persist and tigers are still dying for them. But Asia abounds with other manifestations of the bond between tigers and people; in India, the Hindu goddess Durga is depicted riding a tiger while fighting demons to bring to new life to earth. The tiger was often regarded as the guardian of the forest and its inhabitants, and some believed that tigers only killed the sinful. Even objects bearing the tiger's image could act as charms.

Shamans and witch doctors in Africa, Asia, and the New World used a kind of totemic merging of themselves with wild cats to cure illness, cast out evil, or restore faith in their tribe's power. Such practices sometimes led to belief in "were-cats"—were-tigers, were-jaguars, were-leopards, and so on—men who could turn themselves into the animal and vice versa, for purposes both benevolent and destructive. 🐾

Food was never mere food to the Bushman. What a person ate, so in a sense he became. A Bushman father, for instance, would never give his son the meat of a jackal to eat because the jackal was a coward and this would make the child cowardly too. He gave the child the heart of a leopard, as he gave its mind the heart of a star, because a leopard was one of the bravest of the brave and would make the child brave.

LAURENS VAN DER POST
The Heart of the Hunter

A pair of nearly life-size leopards, carved from five elephant tusks in 19th-century Benin, West Africa. Copper disks form the spots. Benin's rulers, or abos, *associated themselves with the great cat and made it a symbol of their power.*

In previous centuries, in less humanly crowded, more tiger-filled days, the people who lived in or near the forests of Asia had, as a central concern of life, the need to come to terms with the tiger. Understanding nature, and the place of a person and a community in nature, is a central need of rural people—all the more so when nature is most spectacularly represented by so uncompromising an animal as the tiger. And so, in such communities, one of the first steps towards reaching an understanding of life, and of death, was to come to an understanding of the tiger.

The essential thing was to find a way of coping with life alongside tigers. Coexistence was, after all, the only possible option. Wiping out the local population of tigers was, in the days before firearms, mechanized farming and tree felling, an impossible idea and one that simply would not occur to a village cultivator. They had to accept tigers as a natural, an inevitable and an inescapable part of life. If life was to continue in some sort of harmony and peace of mind, people and their communities had to come to terms in their own minds with the striped killer of the woods.

SIMON BARNES
Tiger!

BLOOD BOND

A blood bond between human and lower animals occurs in both Naga and West African territories. In the West African form the Leopard involved is trapped alive and uninjured. Once bound, the Leopard is treated with religious respect. Penultimately the worshipper or worshippers make a small incision in the lashed up Leopard and use the resulting blood. Some versions tell of drinking the warm blood from the living beast, other speak of a cut being made in the skin of the worshipper and a mingling of the blood of man and bound beast. One account tells of the doubtless frightened and furious Leopard being seated upright, and even of its being capped or crowned for the ceremony. Finally the probably infuriated but certainly entirely unimpressed Leopard is released. It would be interesting to learn how this release is engineered, for the human blood-brother certainly believes implicitly in the close, friendly, or even sacred relationship and might be expected to expose himself to a mildly injured and certainly greatly aggravated Leopard. For what it is worth, and on the most slender rumour, I consider that the beast wisely is drugged with smoke from burning herbs offered for its delection; but this is simply a personal opinion of the obscure and highly secret West African ceremony.

PETER TURNBULL-KEMP
The Leopard

PUMA CHILD

The [mountain lion] was also considered a friend and provider by the Cheyenne Indians who watched crows and buzzards to guide them to the remains of a puma feast for the same purpose. In the Cheyenne tradition is the story of a woman who strayed into the woods mourning the death of her baby. Finding a den of motherless panther kittens, she gently pressed one close to her breast and affectionately stroked the tiny animal. Apparently hungry, it began to suckle. The woman raised the kitten, and in time it repaid her by killing deer and bringing in meat to share. After that, other Cheyenne women raised puma kittens for the same purpose, according to their legends.

J. B. TINSLEY
The Puma

MALDONADA'S DELIVERANCE

The tale of Maldonada, an Argentinian girl who acquired a puma as a guardian, has been told in many versions; this is from the naturalist W. H. Hudson.

The case of Maldonada is circumstantially narrated by Rui Diaz de Guzman, in his history of the colonization of the Plata:…He relates that in the year 1536 the settlers at Buenos Ayres, having exhausted their provisions, and being compelled by hostile Indians to keep within their pallisades, were reduced to the verge of starvation. The Governor Mendoza went off to seek help from the other colonies up the river, deputing his authority to one Captain Ruiz, who, according to all accounts, displayed an excessively tyrannous and truculent disposition while in power. The people were finally reduced to a ration of six ounces of flour per day for each person; but as the flour was putrid and only made them ill, they were forced to live on any small animals they could capture, including snakes, frogs and toads. Some horrible details are given by Rui Diaz, and other writers; one, Del Barco Centenera, affirms that of two thousand persons in the town eighteen hundred perished of hunger. During this unhappy time, beasts of prey in large numbers were attracted to the settlement by the effluvium of the corpses, buried just outside the pallisades; and this made the condition of the survivors more miserable still, since they could venture into the neighbouring woods only at the risk of a violent death. Nevertheless, many did so venture, and among these was the young woman Maldonada, who, losing herself in the forest, strayed to a distance, and was eventually found by a party of Indians, and carried by them to their village.

Some months later, Captain Ruiz discovered her whereabouts, and persuaded the savages to bring her to the settlement; then, accusing her of having gone to the Indian village in order to betray the colony, he condemned her to be devoured by wild beasts. She was taken to a wood at a distance of a league from the town, and left there, tied to a tree, for the space of two nights and a day. A party of soldiers then went to the spot, expecting to find her bones picked clean by the beasts, but were greatly astonished to find Maldonada still alive, without hurt or scratch. She told them that a puma had come to her aid, and had kept at her side, defending her life against all the other beasts that approached her. She was instantly released, and taken back to the town, her deliverance through the action of the puma probably being looked on as a direct interposition of Providence to save her.…

W. H. HUDSON (1892)
The Naturalist in La Plata

The so-called gentle disposition of the animal toward man in Argentina inspired the gauchos of the pampas to give it the appellative *amigo del cristiano* ["friend of the Christians"]. Justifications were based on the passivity of the animal in the presence of man, its curious habit of following man, and the almost uncanny anecdotes of its protectiveness of man on occasion.

J. B. TINSLEY

Embroidered mola panel of a cat from Panama, Kuna Indians, c. 1920s. Panama, San Plas Islands, Mandinga Niranjo Grande. Art Institute of Chicago. Facing page, top: Transformation #4, *by George Littlechild, 1991. Bottom: Bronze incense burner in feline form, Iranian, c. 1182. Metropolitan Museum of Art/Schecter Lee.*

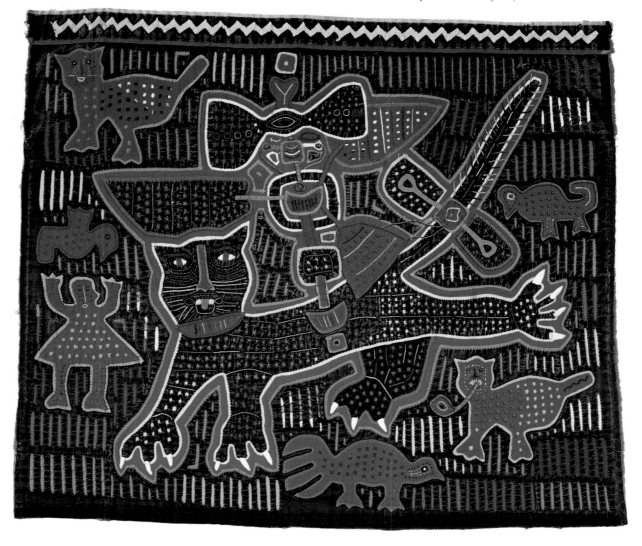

The Tygers of Wrath

The tygers of wrath are wiser than the horses of instruction.
WILLIAM BLAKE

For the people who lived under the umbrella of the forest, the tiger was the most important, most powerful representation of nature that walked the earth. Nature was the giver of life and the tiger seemed to symbolize the force that could provide life, defeat evil and act as an 'elder brother' to man, defending crops and driving out unhealthy spirits. It was the protector, the guardian, the intermediary between heaven and earth.

The tiger evokes myriad images: tigers who carried princesses on their backs; who grew wings in order to travel great distances to cure and heal; who turned white and became part of the Milky Way, keeping a protective eye on the earth and its inhabitants; tigers and dragons who fought to create rain; tigers who guarded their forests against thoughtless woodcutters; who changed into men and back again; tigers who carried people into the next world; who fought evil so that mankind could love and reproduce; tigers linked to man in so many ways, but with a primary purpose of preventing disaster, regenerating life and providing balance, peace and fertility.

All this is irrespective of the fact that tigers sometimes killed people, long before the arrival of the professional hunter. Forest communities accepted the tiger's right to intervene in their lives—that which gave life also had the right to take it away.

* * *

A legend from Nagaland in north-eastern India relates that the mother of the first spirit, the first tiger and the first man came out of the earth through a pangolin's den. Man and the tiger are seen as brothers, one in human shape, the other striped. One stayed at home while the other went to live in the forest, but one day they met in the forest and were forced to fight. The man tricked the tiger into crossing a river and then killed it with a poisoned dart. The tiger's body floated downstream, where it was caught in reeds. The god Dingu-Aneni saw that the bones had come from a human womb and sat on them for ten years; as a result, hundreds of tigers were born, some of whom went to live in the hills and others on the plains.

This legend is typical of the belief that tigers and man are closely connected, being born of the same mother. The concept of the 'tigerness' of man and 'humanness' of the tiger recurs again and again throughout the vast tracts of land where the tiger has roamed.

The tiger was lord of the Malay jungles, always referred to as 'the striped prince' or 'old hairy face', never by the name tiger, which he would have regarded as an insult. When a Malay came across tiger tracks in the jungle, he covered them with leaves and twigs to prove that he has shown due deference. As lord of the jungle, the tiger was very much a part of the ritual and well-being of the people. Seances among the Benua people show how inextricably linked people, forests and tigers are.

The object of the seance is to cure—a shaman, the intermediary between the people and the heaven above, is about to evoke the spirit of the tiger. He sits quietly, completely covered up in the magical circle. His eyes peer out. The drumbeat gets louder and louder, taking over from the sharp sounds of the crickets. A candle flame starts to quiver. The tiger spirit has arrived—this is how it is manifested. It has entered the candle and the shaman's eyes are fixed on the flame, unblinking, unwavering. The tiger spirit has descended on him to provide the cure. The shaman soon shakes with a frenzy, driving away evil and all the demons around. He growls, snarls and leaps much like a tiger, then falls into a state of *lupa* or unconsciousness. He is now in communication with the spirit. The cure has started. This is Malay shamanism, in which the tiger spirit is invoked as the mythical ancestor and initiatory master of the entire area.

A princess waits on the bank of a river, desperate to cross to the other side. The waters of the river rage in front of her. Suddenly, a tiger appears by her side. She climbs on his back and they set forth to cross the waters. The tiger is a powerful swimmer and carries the princess safely to the other side. The princess gives birth to a baby on the far bank. The river is called Tigris and weaves a long course through the land, symbolizing the 'fertile connection' between man and the tiger in the legends of the area.

Early Sufism—the branch of Islam which is prevalent around the Caspian—encompassed a variety of existing doctrines and adopted the image of the tiger in carpets and textiles. It is apparent from these just how deeply the tiger was venerated—it is always depicted as the central figure, surrounded by a variety of other sacred objects.

A story of a compassionate prince giving his body to save a starving tigress and her cubs is told with variations in several Buddhist texts. According to one version, the young prince Mahasattva was walking over the hills with his brothers when they saw near the foot of a precipice, a tigress with two cubs. The tigress was little more than a skeleton, and so mad with hunger that she was about to eat her young. Seeing this, Prince Mahasattva left his brothers and, desirous of saving the animals' lives, threw himself down the precipice and lay still, waiting for the tigress to eat him. But she was too weak and exhausted even to bite. So he pricked himself with a sharp thorn to draw blood. By licking the blood, the tigress gained enough strength to devour the prince, leaving only his bones. When his parents found these, they had them buried and raised a mound above the grave. Prince Mahasattva was then revealed to be the Buddha as a bodhisattva—one of the numerous preparatory stages of existence through which he passed before emerging as 'the Enlightened One'.

All the excerpts above are from The Tiger's Destiny *by Valmik Thapar. Thapar is one of India's foremost "tiger-wallahs," men who have devoted much of their lives to working for the preservation of tigers in their native land. His remarkable book chronicles the shared history of tigers and people throughout Asia, as well as the lives of the remaining tigers in Ranthambhore National Park.*

Above: "The Tyger," by William Blake (1757–1827) from Songs of Experience, *in hand-lettered form with the poet's own illustration. The British Museum. Facing page, top: A holy man with tiger, date unknown. The serene mood of this piece reflects the bond between man and tiger in Indian myth and legend. Victoria & Albert Museum. Bottom: Bengal tiger swimming among water lilies, India. By Roland Seitre/Peter Arnold, Inc.*

Cat Science and Scientists

In the Serengeti, lions spend twenty out of every twenty-four hours resting. Lions are consummate resters; they stretch out in sometimes ridiculous positions, utterly relaxed and apparently without a worry in the world. This quality makes them a difficult animal to study in a way—the scientist is forever in danger of falling asleep with his subjects. At two o'clock in the afternoon, with everything still and warm, it is a tremendous struggle to stay awake; and at two in the morning, during night observations, Schaller admits that he would sometimes succumb to sleep—and, of course, this was always the time that the lions decided to get up and move.

CYNTHIA MOSS
The Big Cats

Wild cats remain among the most familiar, yet little known, creatures on earth. Despite our wealth of stories about them, cats have been seriously studied in the wild only since the mid-1960s, when George Schaller conducted his pioneering research on lions and tigers. Before that, most of our information about wild cats came from the literature of hunting and game management, generally slanted toward preserving game for human use. Paul Leyhausen's groundbreaking work with domestic and captive wild cats took place in the 1950s, but only through long-term field studies can information vital to the survival of cats in the wild be gathered.

Valuable new data has come in on the big Panthera cats from biologists such as Maurice Hornocker and Wilbur Wiles on cougars, Alan Rabinowitz on jaguars, Patrick Hamilton on leopards, Tim Caro on cheetahs, and Rodney Jackson on snow leopards. John Seidensticker and his colleague Mel Sunquist made important advances in radiotelemetry while studying tigers, cougars, and Florida panthers. To them and others we owe our knowledge about the fascinating lifeways of wild cats, and many cats owe their lives. 🐾

A FLEETING EMBRACE

I was hiking near the Barafu kopjes some twenty-five miles east of Seronera, when I saw a cheetah at rest along one of the many erosion terraces in that part of the plains. Slowly moving closer, I finally reclined a hundred feet from her. Casually, as if such meetings were routine, we looked at each other. Suddenly I recognized her: she was one of the sisters. She had severed her ties with her siblings and was now leading a solitary existence typical of her species. We remained there quietly. After some fifteen minutes she jerked to attention and then I too heard the bleat of a gazelle fawn. Four adult gazelle and a fawn swept over a nearby rise closely pursued by two jackals. The cheetah sprinted past me and after a brief chase slapped the fawn and grabbed its neck. She was now an adept huntress. The jackals, deprived of their meal, trotted up to the kill, hoping at least for the scraps. But they saw me and bolted, looking back in a harried manner as if this corner of the plains was becoming rather overcrowded with predators.

The cheetah carried her unexpected kill 250 feet to a small waterhole and there began to eat. Crawling closer on my hands and knees, I was soon within fifteen feet of her. She paused occasionally, glancing at me with guileless eyes, then resumed her meal. I was quite astonished at her acceptance of me. While she had learned to tolerate vehicles, even to the extent of jumping on their hoods and using such vantage points to look around, she must have had few encounters with persons on foot. Thirty-five minutes after making the kill, she finished eating and sat down, scanning the limitless expanse with the wind whipping into her face. Ambling to the pool, she crouched down and lapped some water only ten feet from me. I purred but she ignored this blatant overture. Abruptly she walked up the slope a hundred feet, then returned, drank again, and checked over the remnants of the kill. After that she reclined fifteen feet away, her back to me. Never had I been treated with such studied indifference and it almost rankled. Over 1½ hours had now elapsed since the appearance of the fawn. A hooded vulture wheeled over us, its eyes fixed on scraps of skin and bone. Slowly the cheetah walked away, past the pool, up a slope, and out of sight, leaving me alone to exult over the fleeting embrace of our spirits.

Such meetings are immensely satisfying as token returns to a world from which man has long been an outcast.

GEORGE SCHALLER
Golden Shadows, Flying Hooves

JAGUAR ENCOUNTER

In the evening I took my gun, and strolled along the road a little way into the forest, at the place I had so long looked forward to reaching, and was rewarded by falling in with one of the lords of the soil, which I had long wished to encounter. As I walked quietly along, I saw a large jet black animal come out of the forest about twenty yards before me, which took me so very much by surprise that I did not at first imagine what it was. As it moved slowly on, and its whole body and long curved tail came into full view, in the middle of the road, I saw that it was a fine black jaguar. I involuntarily raised by gun to my shoulder, but remembering that both barrels were loaded with small shot, and that to fire would exasperate without killing him, I stood silently gazing. In the middle of the road he turned his head, and for an instant paused and gazed at me, but having, I suppose, other business of his own to attend to, walked steadily on and disappeared in the thicket. As he advanced, I heard the scampering of small animals and the whizzing flight of ground birds, clearing the path for their dreaded enemy. This encounter pleased me much. I was too much surprised and occupied too much with admiration to feel fear. I had at length had a full view, in its native wilds, of the rarest variety of the most powerful and dangerous animal inhabiting the American continent.

ALFRED RUSSEL WALLACE
(19TH CENTURY)

Above: Mr. Chacko, a ranger in India's Kanha National Park, holds an orphaned tiger cub. By Belinda Wright/DRK Photo. Facing page: A pride of lions in Botswana's Kalahari, after resting through the day's heat, rouse themselves at dusk to begin the evening's hunt. By Frans Lanting/Minden Pictures.

GS [George Schaller] has crossed the river early to look for more fresh signs: he tries not to let the leopard interfere with his study of blue sheep, but the great cats have a strong hold on him, and the snow leopard is the least known of them all. It is wonderful how the presence of this creature draws the whole landscape to a point, from the glint of light on the old horns of a sheep to the ring of a pebble on the frozen ground.

PETER MATTHIESSEN
The Snow Leopard

A female Scottish wildcat (Felis sylvestris grampia) basks in the autumn sunlight, Perthshire, Scotland. The feisty Scottish wildcat, sometimes called "the British tiger," is scarce in its homeland, where primeval forests have largely given way to cultivated land. This cat has been persecuted by hunters and by farmers in defense of their poultry and rabbits, but its value in controlling rodents far outweighs any damage to livestock. By Wild-Type Productions/Bruce Coleman, Inc.

Keeping Cats in Their Places

It's hard to imagine a world without wild cats—yet, as a family, they are among the most threatened land animals on earth. Loss of habitat is the single most critical factor in declining cat populations. And despite increasingly strict international laws, the trade in skins and other cat parts still takes an enormous toll. The solutions to keeping wild cats in wild places are complex but achievable; cats are highly adaptable and have shown they can rebound when given a chance. The primary steps, as outlined by the International Union for the Conservation of Nature and Natural Resources (IUCN) are: building public support, both among urban dwellers and people living in rural areas near the cats; conserving habitat in large enough chunks to separate wild cats from humans and maintain viable populations; continue captive breeding programs that support the survival of cats in the wild; encourage long-term field studies of cat behavior and ecology; and control the trade in wild felines. Since our own survival depends on keeping the world in a healthy balance, our fate and that of the cats is closely intertwined. 🐾

ONCE WERE JAGUARS

The Mexican Jaguars (*Panthera onca veracrucensis,* and *P. o. hernandesi*) have been near extinction since the turn of the century, but it was the large American subspecies, the Arizona Jaguar (*P. o. arizonensis*) that vanished entirely at the beginning of this century. Its habitat was the mountainous areas of eastern Arizona north of the Grand Canyon, the southern half of western New Mexico, and northeastern Sonora. In the early nineteenth century, it could also be found in southern California. The United States authority on mammals, C. Hart Merriam 'was told by an old chief of the Kammei tribe that in the Cayamaca Mountain region in San Diego County it was there known as "big spotted lion" in their native tongue'.

DAVID DAY
The Doomsday Book of Animals

THE LEOPARD-NURSER

Since children hear what they will hear, I heard
a man had gone to nurse the leopards.
"Women go?"
I asked, and "yes" they said, marveling
in admiration. I envied more than I admired.
Ah! the speechless hurt great leopards
in their woe.

I would go. In a round starry cave
of leaves and moss the green-eyed patients lay;
some worse
than savaged, some bloody, some unmarked:
each beautiful, fluid and fatal
to all save me, their skilled
and speechless nurse.

Though I grew up and went my daylight ways
I never lost that cave. I learned;
at secret length,
that any pain, or any love, reminds me:
a leopard-nurser's is a métier
by which a child nurses a dangerous beast
to strength.

JOSEPHINE JACOBSEN

THE LAST PURE SPIRITS

My wilderness wildcats have more than repaid their debt for whatever care I have been able to give, for I have learned far more than mere biological facts from them. In their beauty, independence and natural courage they symbolize what it takes for any living being to be truly free. Shy, proud, faithful in love, their care for their young, for which they will fight fearlessly, is extraordinary. Although relatively small in the feline world, they are not equipped for compromise like the fox. Yet their wild, free natures epitomise qualities which so much of mankind has lost. At last, thankfully, a new wind blows and we realize, through continued study, that, even to man, wildcats are more useful than otherwise. Surely now it behoves us, as the most intelligent, foreseeing species on earth, as responsible custodians of the world about us, to give complete protection to these last pure spirits of our dwindling wild places.

MIKE TOMKIES
My Wilderness Wildcats

Every hunter who feels that he must prove himself by obliterating a lion should first contemplate the animal for a while. As he gazes at his intended victim, a perfect and unique product of evolution, a being with its own aspirations and fears and joys, there may come a time when he suppresses his urge to kill and instead recaptures his sense of wonder and feeling of fellowship.

GEORGE SCHALLER

Mr. A. _____ the well-known big game hunter has been missing for ten days. It is feared that something he disagreed with ate him.

ANONYMOUS

Leopard Bust, *by Todd Sherman, 1996.*

capped, as its hunting depends so much on its speed. (Pippa died as the result of a broken leg; one of her cubs also broke a leg but recovered with the help of veterinary attention.)

Third, being low in the predator hierarchy, the cheetah is at a disadvantage in competition with the other carnivores. It is postulated that where there are many hyenas, cheetahs have a difficult time, because their kills are constantly being stolen and their cubs are often killed. It is interesting that there are few hyenas in Nairobi and Amboseli National parks, places with relatively high densities of cheetahs.

And fourth, wherever cheetahs are safe from poachers, have good open country for hunting and moderate competition from other predators—in other words, in

One can only speculate as to why [cheetahs] are declining. Several factors are probably responsible. First, but not necessarily foremost, the cheetah has been heavily poached in some areas for its spotted skin which, though not so highly prized as the leopard's, is a good status symbol all the same. When spotted skins were the fad in the United States in the sixties, fifteen hundred cheetah skins entered the country each year.

Second, it is thought that the cheetah may have evolved its present way of life and hunting style in open, semiarid habitats that, more and more, have been taken over by humans and their cattle. Cheetahs are nervous, shy animals and cannot tolerate the disturbance of living in close proximity with man; so they have retreated to other areas where the habitat may not be so well suited to them. Joy Adamson speculates that when cheetahs live in less favorable habitats they are more prone to injuries, since it may be necessary to hunt less appropriate prey and in rougher terrain. A cheetah with even a slight injury is badly handi-

national parks and reserves like Nairobi, Serengeti, and Amboseli—they are continually being harassed by tourists. As a diurnal, open plains hunter, the cheetah is easily spotted by tourist guides and pursued while it tries to make a kill. This almost invariably spoils the hunt. When trying to rest in the daytime, the cheetah is surrounded by vehicles with engines running, as each car tries to maneuver into a better position for that perfect picture. This kind of harassment is seen frequently, and although complaints are sometimes made, very little has been done about it. Tourists do not understand what is happening, and the drivers and guides are thinking only about their tips at the end of the game run.

CYNTHIA MOSS
Portraits in the Wild

A lone cheetah crosses the track of a four-wheel-drive vehicle in Kenya's Masai Mara National Park. Cheetahs have become remarkable acclimated to vehicles, but the presence of tourists often interrupts their hunts. By Anup & Manoj Shah/Animals Animals.

Cats in Captivity

Few issues surrounding wild cats are as fraught with emotion as captivity. The sequence of emotions typically begins with the deep thrill of seeing for the first time a real live lion or tiger, albeit through bars in a zoo or circus. Later our feelings often shift toward guilt and sadness that an animal intended for life in the wild must live as a captive.

The news has gotten better for captive cats, however. Zoos have come a long way from the days of cramped cages and concrete blockhouses; large, vegetated enclosures encourage more natural behavior on the cats' part. Nutrition and breeding requirements are better understood, and the cats are protected from constant exposure to curious humans. It would be naive to suggest that life in captivity could truly simulate life in nature, but today's zoos not only provide most of us with our only chance to encounter wild felines, they serve a vital function in carrying out captive breeding programs, critical to some species' chances of surviving in their native lands.

Cats in circuses can arouse even stronger reactions, many people believing that animals shouldn't be compelled to entertain us. On the other hand, the life of a performing cat may be considerably more stimulating than that of a zoo animal. They often truly bond to their human trainers, some of whom develop an exceptional understanding of the creatures. These cats, too, have something to teach us. 🐾

THE PANTHER
Jardin des Plantes, Paris

From seeing and seeing the seeing has
    become so exhausted
it no longer sees anything anymore.
The world is made of bars,
    a hundred thousand
bars, and behind the bars, nothing.

The lithe swinging of that rhythmical
    easy stride
that slowly circles down to a single point
is like a dance of energy around a hub,
in which a great will stands stunned
    and numbed.

At times the curtains of the eye lift
without a sound—then a shape enters,
slips through the tightened silence
    of the shoulders,
reaches the heart and dies.

RAINER MARIA RILKE
Translated by Robert Bly

TOO MUCH LEOPARD

I was sitting with my husband Robert, a tall logician, in a waiting room on Ventura Boulevard in Sherman Oaks. With us were Dr. Max MacElroy, D.V.M., and Cinder, a black leopard six months old, who weighed around forty-five pounds and was leaping for Robert's back as Robert was trying and failing to figure out what was happening to him. (Exactly how scholars and philosophers end up in such enviable situations is a trade secret.)

I knew what was happening to him. Cinder, like any good kittycat, is intensely interested in people, and especially in figuring out which person in a given situation would be the most interesting one to unsettle. Robert qualified because he's tall (the big cats are especially alert to height: tall people read as enemies and short people read as prey) and because he was the only one in the room who had never before found himself suddenly in the presence of a young, energetic, and intelligent leopard, so he

Above: An African leopard (Panthera pardus), *black color phase. By Erwin & Peggy Bauer. Preceding page: Turning the tables, tigers inspect (captive) tourists at Samsung Electronic Company Safari Park near Seoul, Korea. By Paul Chesley/Photographers Aspen.*

THE LION

O lion, mournful image
Of kings sadly brought down,
You are born now only in cages
In Hamburg, among the Germans

GUILLAUME APOLLINAIRE
Translated by Robert Bly

was sending out brain waves that made Cinder curious—logicians, especially deep ones, have brain waves the rest of us wot not of. You know about cats and curiosity? The old saying has it wrong. It is usually the mouse that is killed by the cat's curiosity, not the cat, and even if the mouse is a scholar, satisfaction doesn't bring him back.

Robert wasn't killed, and in fact lost his heart to Cinder. This sort of thing happens with leopards, which is why Dr. MacElroy has big cats in the first place. It started with Rocky, a lion who was brought to him with virtually every bone in his body broken—"pathological fractures caused by rickets." There was a bobcat with a similar story, and Cinder's mother was another. Dr. MacElroy fixes them up, and that's how they become his pets. I was interested in Dr. Max and his leopard cubs because Cinder is well handled and didn't eat up Robert. An enormous amount of attentiveness is required in order to end up with a mentally and physically healthy leopard in captivity.

Leopards, I was told by Bob Wagner at the

American Association of Zoological Parks and Aquariums, are considered the most cunning of the big cats. They are unlike lions, for example, in that they spend a lot of time in trees and can carry their kills—up to forty-five pounds, about half their adult size—into treetops and consume their dinner in the branches. "Cunning" is, of course, the sort of term you use if you are a zookeeper worried about staying whole, but I am uneasy with the adjective because most people have forgotten its true meaning, which is "knowing," not "dishonestly knowing," though I must admit I had the feeling there were a minimum of two or three leopards in the room all the time, and when Cinder's brother was brought out, it seemed like a herd of leopards.

What Cinder is like to look at: The paws express Cinder the mischievous kitten, playing innocently, and the eyes and mouth reveal the lovable kittycat, the one who wants to sit in your lap, and the whole leopard reveals something else. The affectionate kitten is real, the mischievous kitten is real—and so is the leopard....

The usual fate of a captive leopard is a small cage or a zoo, when it isn't rickets and early death, or so I am told by people who may know. Cinder's fate, thanks to Dr. MacElroy, was not so bleak. In fact, she was slated to be a working cat, an actress, so you may have seen her on movie and television screens, though the big cats rarely get decent credits. She may one day play the part of a lovable pet, and you may be moved to want a leopard. Don't do that. Leave the big cats alone.

If you are tempted, then look at the extraordinary intelligence in Cinder's eyes, at how dangerously that intelligence flames there. Think of the thinness of your own skin, the thinness of your own mind. Think of the vanity involved in presuming that you could ever own or control what goes on in those eyes.

And then think about the handlers and trainers of the big cats—people who can collaborate with that flame.

VICKI HEARNE
Animal Happiness

Imagined Cats

Lions are experiencing a swinging pendulum effect at the moment, although they are blissfully unaware of it. Public opinion on the lion is either positive or negative; rarely do feelings fall in between. Throughout history the lion has been the symbol of power and nobility, but an actual lion met face to face may elicit other emotions. The early hunters and settlers in Africa considered the lion vermin, without the dignity of a game animal. Lions were simply shot on sight. Their reputation deteriorated even further when they became famous for man eating, as described in J. H. Patterson's book *The Man-eaters of Tsavo* (1907). During the 1920s and 1930s their status was raised somewhat, as they became suitable ferocious prey to be stalked by intrepid white hunters.

Then in 1960 the pendulum swung dizzily to the pro-lion side with the advent of Elsa, the pet lion made famous in Joy Adamson's books *Born Free, Living Free,* and *Forever Free* and the popular films based on them. The lion became the best-loved animal in America and Europe, and Elsa Clubs sprung up by the hundreds. The emphasis in the books was on the lion's intelligence, its happy family life in the wild, and, of course, the kindness and affection in the relationship between this lioness and her understanding owners.

For more than ten years hardly a word was spoken against the lion. Then the results of scientific studies began to appear, and journalists started characterizing lions as lazy, selfish, scavengers, murderers, bad mothers, rotten fathers, etc. Nevertheless, these reports have not really affected the average tourist, who still wants to see a lion more than any other wild animal.

CYNTHIA MOSS
Portraits in the Wild

The Sleeping Gypsy, by Henri Rousseau, 1897. Museum of Modern Art, New York.

Since Cynthia Moss wrote the above, the success of the Disney blockbuster "The Lion King" has swung the pendulum once again towards sentimentalizing lions. But it may soon swing back: a new film about the Tsavo man-eaters is in the works as of this writing. On a more intimate scale, Soseki Natsume's I Am a Cat *is the "autobiography" of a cat who finds a home with a fussy scholar; it's a perennial bestseller in Japan.*

SPEAKING FOR HIMSELF

I would like to take the occasion of this incident to advise my readers that the human habit of referring to me in a scornful tone of voice as some mere trifling "cat" is an extremely bad one. Humans appear to think that cows and horses are constructed from rejected human material, and that cats are constructed from cow-pats and horse-dung. Such thoughts, objectively regarded, are in very poor taste though they are no doubt not uncommon among teachers who, ignorant even of their ignorance, remain self-satisfied with their quaint puffed-up ideas of their own unreal importance. Even cats must not be treated roughly or taken for granted. To the casual observer it may appear that all cats are the same, facsimiles in form and substance, as indistinguishable as peas in a pod; and that no cat can lay claim to individuality. But once admitted to feline society, that casual observer would very quickly realize that things are not so simple....Our eyes, noses, fur, paws—all of them differ. From the tilt of one's whiskers to the set of one's ears, down to the very hang of one's tail, we cats are sharply differentiated. In our good looks and our poor looks, in our likes and dislikes, one may fairly say that cats occur in infinite variety.

SOSEKI NATSUME
I Am a Cat

Cats, Seen and Unseen

The jaguar brushed the leaves
with a luminous absence,
the puma runs through the branches
like a forest fire,
while the jungle's drunken eyes
burn from inside him

PABLO NERUDA

Below: The Beast and the Blackberry, *by Nicholas Wilton, 1995. Facing page: A puma emerges from the shadows in the lowland rainforest of Belize. By Frans Lanting/Minden Pictures.*

Few experiences can quicken the blood like the sight of a wild cat on its own ground. Whether the cat is a lion lounging under an acacia tree on the Serengeti or a bobcat pausing briefly at the margin of a California meadow, something in us responds to any glimpse of these creatures—in part because they are so good at not being seen.

Lions are probably the least concerned of all cats about being seen. This isn't surprising, since of all cats they have the least to fear from other animals. They even seem to include humans in their field of serene unconcern, except in extraordinary circumstances. But most wild cats become aware of our presence far sooner than we sense theirs, and most choose if possible to discreetly vanish before we figure it out. (Our housecats can do the same whenever they choose; they just choose to less often.)

For some who are passionate about wild creatures, the chance to see a great cat is worth much expense, many thousands of miles traveled, and a vast amount of discomfort. The story of one such quest is told by Peter Matthiessen in his book *The Snow Leopard,* where the animal becomes a metaphor for the author's spiritual journey. It's remarkable how often cats seems to serve as a focus for human seeking. Creatures so different from ourselves, they arouse our deepest interest, inspire us to look longer and closer at them, at the world, at ourselves. 🐾

GHOST PANTHER

Years ago I undertook a long-delayed task and began work on a book about the mountain lion or cougar or painter or panther as it is known in Florida. Following my lifelong rule of trying never to write about animals and places that I have not observed first hand...I went to the Everglades and began my search for one of the world's rarest and most elusive cats. I had observed the Florida race (I doubt that it is a subspecies) in captivity often and knew its habitat from experience, but I did want at least to see the cat in that habitat acting out a fragment of its natural life. An animal in its place adds a texture to your knowledge of it that can be gained in no other way. My quest was simply not to be successful.

The Florida panther saw me, however. Lots of times. Of that there can be no doubt. Time and

182

again we would find brand-new spoor in the form of scats, or tracks or pug marks, but the cat always managed to get out of sight just in time. At one point we pointed our airboat, unfortunately a terribly noisy contraption, in toward a hammock or small Everglade island where a cat was thought to be. We jumped off into the muck and waded ashore. In the soft mud of the hammock beach were fresh tracks. They were so fresh the ridges between the pad marks were still stiff and firm. The marks had no water in them although firmly impressed in a matrix of very wet mud. As we hunkered down to examine the evidence, the ridges in the tracks began to crumble and water seeped into the impressions, filling them up, absorbing them back into the island. They were soon history. It all took considerably less than two minutes and then they were no more. They were as irretrievably lost as just a moment ago.

There was no doubt we had missed seeing our ghostlike panther by fifteen seconds, hardly more than that. It had been watching us and almost certainly still was. With a good resident population of water moccasins and eastern diamondback rattlesnakes guaranteed nearby, it didn't seem wise to blindly jump over fallen logs and begin beating our way back into the thick tangle of undergrowth where we knew our panther had gone. The cat would just have moved ahead of us anyway, stopping to look and listen as we flopped and floundered about unable to see the ground beneath our feet. He would have moved in circles for as long as we chose to play his game, rather than moving off the hammock into the open water where he would lose control of when he was being seen. He was calling the shots on his own home ground. Cats like that position of command. It suits them perfectly. They watch you when they want to. You watch them…when they want you to. It is the very essence of being a cat.

ROGER A. CARAS
A Cat Is Watching

The Edge of Wildness

FERAL

On the uncertain border between wild and tame live feral domestic cats. They occupy a spectrum from cats that have been abandoned or left their homes recently for some reason, and haven't found another, to cats that have been feral for several generations. Raised apart from humans, such cats may behave like true wildcats but can usually be tamed, with patience, as author Ellen Berkeley and her husband have found. There's no denying that large populations of feral cats can pose a danger to songbirds in some places—notably islands—though birds form a fairly small part of their diet. Mostly they are themselves in danger: from disease, dogs, and other predators. Programs to round up, vaccinate, and neuter feral cats are spreading, to the benefit of all parties.

I am full of wonder at this creature of the woods who wants to be so close to us.... How can we know what she thinks? And yet we know what she wants, our Turtle from the wild. She wants it all: the in-doors, the outdoors, and us. As she stalks through the weeds, she exhibits all the natural cunning of her species; she is at home there. But as she curls into me on the bed, she exhibits something else natural to her, and she is at home here, too. We give her the protection and attention she must have known only in her kitten-hood. She could not have found this in the wild. And she hungers for it.

ELLEN PERRY BERKELEY
Maverick Cats: Encounters with Feral Cats

THE TOM-CAT

I had a name once, a short, furry name, a Persian Angora's name. But I left it on the roofs, in the gurgling hollow of the gutters, and on the rubbed moss of the old walls. I am the tom-cat. What need have I of any other name? This one satisfies my pride. Those for whom I was once "Sidi," the Lord Cat, no longer call me; they know that I obey no one. When they talk of me they say "the tom-cat." I come here when I please, and the masters of this dwelling are not my masters....

Even when I play I hardly ever smile. When I condescend to break some ornament with my royal paw, I give the impression that I'm chastis-ing it. And if I raise the same heavy paw against that irreverent princeling, my son, you would think it was to cast him into outer darkness. You surely didn't expect that I would simper about on the carpet like the She-Shah, my little Sultana whom I neglect?

I am the tom-cat. I lead the restless life of those whom love has creat-ed for his hard service. I walk alone, bloodthirsty by necessity, and doomed always to be the victor. I fight as I eat, with a controlled appetite, like an athlete in perfect condition who wins without haste or rage.

I never return to your house until morning. Down I drop at dawn, and as blue as the dawn, from the top of those bare trees where a moment ago I looked like a nest in the haze. Or sometimes I glide over the sloping roof until I come to the wooden balcony; then I take up a position on the sill of your half-open window, looking like a winter nosegay from which you can drink in all the scents of a December night, with its tang of a cold graveyard. Later, when I fall asleep, my hot, feverish body will give off an odour of bitter box-wood, dried blood and musk....

I sleep and sleep. Sometimes an electric shock makes me sit up, but after a rumbling growl, like distant thunder, I fall back again. Even when I wake up in earnest towards the end of the day, I seem absent and still haunted by dreams. I have an eye on the window and an ear on the door.

After a hasty wash, with stiff and aching bones, I cross the threshold every evening at the same hour, and off I go with my head down, looking more like an outcast than one of the elect. Off I go, threading my way like a sluggish caterpillar between the icy puddles, and flattening my ears against the wind. I make my way indifferent to the snow. If I stop for a moment it is not because I hesitate; I am listening to the secret rumours of my empire. I consult the dark air, hurling into it those solemn, rhythmic, despairing howlings of the wandering, defiant tom-cat. Then, as though the sound of my voice had lashed me into sudden frenzy, I spring. You catch sight of me for a second on the top of a wall, you have a vague impresion that I'm up there, fur on end, blurred and floating like a shred of cloud, and then you see me no more.

COLETTE, TRANSLATED BY ENID MCLEOD
The Tom-Cat

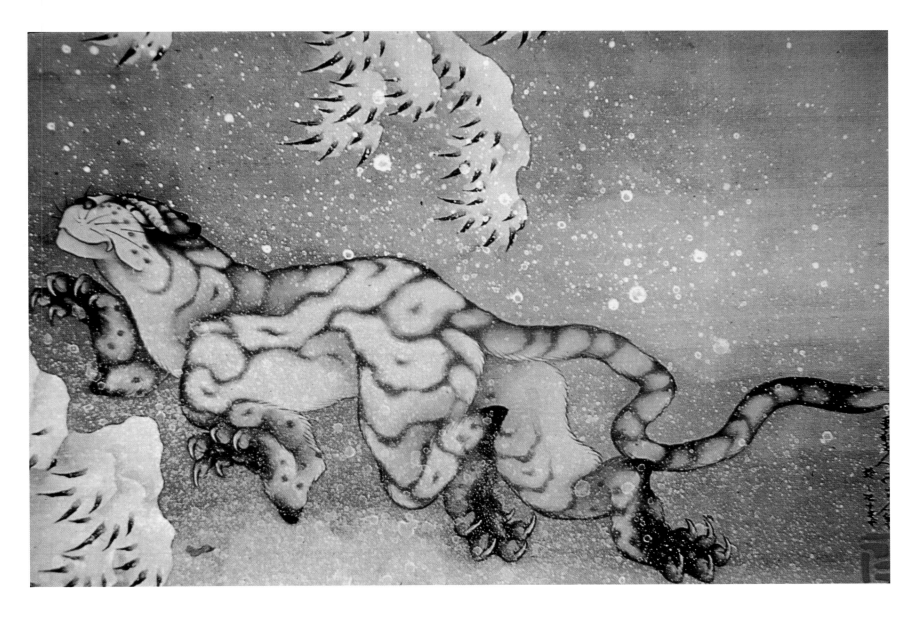

DREAMTIGERS

In my childhood I was a fervent worshipper of the tiger: not the jaguar, the spotted "tiger" of the Amazonian tangles and the isles of vegetation that float down the Parana, but that striped, Asiatic, royal tiger, that can be faced only by a man of war, on a castle atop an elephant. I used to linger endlessly before one of the cages at the zoo; I judged vast encyclopedias and books of natural history by the splendor of their tigers. (I still remember those illustrations: I who cannot rightly recall the brow or the smile of a woman.) Childhood passed away, and the tigers and my passion for them grew old,

but still they are in my dreams. At that submerged or chaotic level they keep prevailing. And so, as I sleep, some dream beguiles me, and suddenly I know I am dreaming. Then I think: This is a dream, a pure diversion of my will; and now that I have unlimited power, I am going to cause a tiger.

Oh, incompetence! Never can my dreams engender the wild beast I long for. The tiger indeed appears, but stuffed or flimsy, or with impure variations of shape, or of an implausible size, or all too fleeting, or with a touch of the dog or the bird.

JORGE LUIS BORGES
Dreamtigers

Tiger, woodblock print by Katsushika Hokusai, 1840. Photo by J. Perno/Explorer. Facing page: Paris Through the Window, by Marc Chagall, 1913. Solomon R. Guggenheim Museum/David Heald.

I long to see the snow leopard, yet to glimpse it by camera flash, at night, crouched on a bait, is not to see it. If the snow leopard should manifest itself, then I am ready to see the snow leopard. If not, then somehow (and I don't understand this instinct, even now) I am not ready to perceive it, in the same way that I am not ready to resolve my koan; and in the not-seeing, I am content. I think I must be disappointed, having come so far, and yet I do not feel that way. I am disappointed, and also, I am not disappointed. That the snow leopard is, that it is here, that its frosty eyes watch us from the mountain— that is enough.

PETER MATTHEISSEN
The Snow Leopard

Snow leopard (Panthera uncia) *portrait. By Stephen Walker.*

THE SPIRITUAL CHALLENGE OF THE EASTERN PANTHER

Sometimes it seems as if I am the only person of my acquaintance who has not seen a cougar in the mountains of western Virginia, where I live. Reports come in from all sides. Lori saw a black one playing at the foot of Little North Mountain not far from here, but she is a poet and a writer of fantasy novels and sees things in the shadows that other people don't. My neighbor Willy was startled the other night by a big, long-tailed cat that ran in front of his car; he is a hunter and said he never saw anything like it in the woods, but it was night and he barely got a glimpse as the animal streaked by....Gil was riding his mountain bike just across the state line in West Virginia and swears he saw one gliding through the green gloom, but he runs a bike touring company, and if tales of eastern panthers spark up his clients' experience, so much the better. Dave is a self-taught woodsman who lives what is called an alternative lifestyle, and he is convinced that the eyeshine and yowling beside his campfire one night was a cougar, though he couldn't find any sign. Larry watched a mother and kitten in his scope for several minutes one brilliant autumn afternoon while he was squirrel hunting. He is a professional biologist, and his story is not easily discounted.

Every year, hundreds of people across the East report that they've seen an animal believed extinct since the early twentieth century....Yet the people who think they've seen a cougar resist the obvious and logical explanations. "It was a dog," I told Lori, Willy, Gil, and Dave, only to be met with angry stares. They want to believe they've seen the rarest and arguably the most dangerous animal possible where they live. Surely these cougars are cultural projections, drawn perhaps from guilt for our collective ravaging of the continent, and from yearning for the exoneration that the survival of cougars would confer. Psychologists say that knowledge of humankind's assault on the natural world is a painful source of modern Angst. Surely, too, there is an element of thrill-seeking in the sightings, in a culture addicted to the fastest, biggest, highest, and fiercest, whether in machines, mountains, or animals. Maybe the image of cat goes deeper than culture. Maybe it has been permanently etched on human consciousness by eons of fear and admiration. Cat sightings may be a primal expression of the human understanding of nature.

In the end, it doesn't really matter whether eastern cougars are out there or not. What matters is that they should be there. Cougars belong in the East by evolutionary birthright. It is the ripening of this idea that makes our time different....Still, it would be difficult to actually turn the idea into reality, to bring cougars back. Unlike bears, which have been teddified for nearly a century, and wolves, whose admirable family life is now well known, cougars offer little on which to hang a notion of kinship. They must be accepted on their own wild terms. To find the humility to atone for past mistakes, to find the greatness of heart to share the woods with a being far beyond our ken—that is the spiritual challenge of the eastern panther.

CHRIS BOLGIANO
Mountain Lion

I used to ask people what would happen if someone met a lion in the bush. If that should happen, I would be told, one should walk purposefully away at an oblique angle without exciting the lion or stimulating a chase. Several times, people showed us how to do this. But at Gautscha we never met a lion. Although among us we spent at least parts of more than fifty person-years in the bush there, we never once had occasion to use the technique we had learned.

We saw it used, though. One day, in the close quarters of some heavy bush in the farthest waterless reaches of the Kalahari, my brother and I met a lion. He was all golden in the sunlight, with a golden mane. He seemed very large and, unlike many Kalahari animals today, he was in beautiful physical condition: he had 110 scars or scratches and had plenty of flesh on his bones. Stupefied, we gazed at him, in awe of his presence and his beauty. He stood still, gazing at us. How long we might have stayed this way I don't know. My brother and

I were too dazzled to do anything. So the responsibility fell upon the lion. Moving calmly, confidently, purposefully, keeping us in view without staring at us aggressively, he walked purposefully away at an oblique angle. The effect of the encounter on us—or at least on me—was memorable. The lion was only a few feet away, and I could have become afraid for my life. Yet his intentions were so clear and his demeanor was so reassuring that I felt absolutely no fear, not even alarm—just interest and wonder. By his smooth departure and his cool, detached behavior, the lion apparently intended to save himself the risks of an unwanted skirmish. A man acting in a similar way under similar circumstances would have been considered refined, gentlemanly, polite. In our species, too, reassuring manners can bring desirable results, for exactly the same reasons.

ELIZABETH MARSHALL THOMAS
The Tribe of Tiger

That night, too, we heard our last lion. He was just at the right distance from us to make the sound of his roar perfect. I have always been grateful that I was born into a world and shall die in one where the lion, however diminished in number, is still roaring. Heard in his and my native setting, it is for me the most beautiful sound in the world. It is to silence what the shooting star is to the dark of the night.

LAURENS VAN DER POST
The Heart of the Hunter

A male lion in the last light, Kalahari Desert, Botswana. By Daniel J. Cox/Tony Stone Images.

Organizations That Work for Wild Cats

American Zoo and Aquarium Association
7970-D Old Georgetown Road
Bethesda, MD 20814
301-907-7777

Represents almost every major zoological park, aquarium, wildlife park, and oceanarium in North America. Its highest priority is the conservation of the world's wildlife and its habitat through programs such as the Species Survival Plan, which helps secure the survival of selected wildlife species.

Animal Welfare Institute
P.O. Box 3650
Washington, DC 20007
202-337-2332

This nonprofit was founded to reduce the sum total of pain and fear inflicted on animals by humans. Supports reform of cruel methods for controlling wildlife populations and the preservation of species threatened by extinction.

Defenders of Wildlife
1101 Fourteenth Street, NW, Suite 1400
Washington, DC 20005
202-682-9400

National, nonprofit membership organization dedicated to the protection of all native wild animals and plants in their natural communities, through education and reasoned advocacy.

EFBC's Feline Conservation Center
HCR 1, Box 84
Rosamond, CA 93560
805-256-3793

Nonprofit research and breeding facility dedicated to saving wild cats threatened by habitat destruction and poaching. EFBC's goal is to promote the growth of the world's wild cat populations and reintroduce felines into natural habitats of the future.

Fund for Animals (national office)
200 West 57th Street
New York, NY 10019
212-246-2096

Founded in 1967 "to speak for those who can't," the fund is very active in campaigning against hunting and trapping.

Fund For Animals (California chapter)
Fort Mason Center
San Francisco, CA 94123
415-474-4020

Campaigned successfully against passage of Prop 197, which would have legalized trophy hunting of mountain lions; works in the political arena on behalf of animals in California; operates a wildlife rehabilitation center in southern California.

Global Tiger Patrol (Charity No. 328126)
The Ranthambhore Trust
PO Box 195, Leatherhead
Surrey KT22 7HB
England
44-(1)83-977-2277

International nonprofit working in all tiger range nations, with emphasis on the dwindling census in India, to avert the crisis of extinction that faces the world's tiger population.

Hornocker Wildlife Institute
University of Idaho
P.O. Box 3246
Moscow, ID 83843-1908
208-885-6871

Founded to conduct long-term research, with emphasis on threatened and endangered species and their wild environments, and to make new knowledge available to the scientific community, agencies that manage wilderness and wildlands, and the public.

The Humane Society of the United States
2100 L Street, NW
Washington, DC 20037
202-452-1100

Committed to securing a lasting home for other species in a world crowded with people. Works to modify human behavior to allow threatened species an opportunity to survive. Applies political pressure to Asian countries to halt poaching of tigers and trade in their parts.

Mountain Lion Foundation
P.O. Box 1896
Sacramento, CA 95812
916-442-2666

Formed in 1986 to protect mountain lions, this organization has since become a leader in protecting and preserving all wildlife species throughout California.

National Audubon Society
700 Broadway
New York, NY 10003
212-979-3000

Educational and advocacy programs to benefit wildlife in general.

National Parks and Conservation Association
1776 Massachusetts Avenue, NW
Washington, DC 20036
202-223-6722

Nonprofit citizens group that works to preserve, protect, and enhance the national parks system. Recently involved in reintroduction and habitat protection programs for the Florida panther in the Everglades.

National Wildlife Federation
1400 16th Street, NW
Washington, DC 20036-2266
202-797-6800

Endangered species protection is a core mission of NWF. Works toward the goal of maintaining and strengthening safeguards for imperiled species, including cats such as ocelots, jaguars, and mountain lions.

The Nature Conservancy
1815 North Lynn Street
Arlington, VA 22209
703-841-5300

International nonprofit membership organization dedicated to preserving plants, animals, and natural communities by protecting the lands and waters they need to survive.

The Predator Project
P.O. Box 6733
Bozeman, MT 59771
406-587-3389

Dedicated to its motto, "North America Needs Predators for Intact Ecosystems," the Project is a grassroots effort to help maintain the natural balance of native fauna by protecting carnivores within ecosystems.

Roar Fund/Shambala Preserve
6867 Soledad Canyon Road
Acton, CA 93510
805-268-0380

Operates and maintains an established wildlife sanctuary for endangered exotic big cats, while educating children and adults through various outreach programs on the danger of extinction of these rare creatures.

TRAFFIC India
172-B Lodi Estate
New Delhi 110003
India

One of the worldwide offices that monitor and investigate traffic in illegal animal parts.

Above: Signpost in Palamam National Park, India. By Stanley Breeden/DRK Photo. Facing page: A serval in the grass. By Galen Rowell/Mountain Light.

Wildlife Conservation Society
100 85th Street & Southern Boulevard
Bronx, NY 10460
718-220-5100

WCS has embarked on an ambitious tiger conservation program, earmarking as a top priority regions for tigers in India, Indochina, Russia, and China.

World Society for the Protection of Animals (WSPA)
29 Perkins Street, P.O. Box 190
Boston, MA 02130
617-522-7000

International animal protection organization representing millions of people through local societies in 75 nations. Helps teach local peoples how to sustain long-term programs that will secure the welfare of animals now and in the future. Operates Project Life Lion, a unique program to vaccinate dogs in villages surrounding Serengeti National Park in Tanzania against canine distemper, which is killing many lions.

World Wildlife Fund
1250 24th Street, NW
Washington, DC 20037
202-293-4800

For more than three decades WWF has led international efforts to slow habitat destruction and halt the illegal trade in endangered wildlife. Its fight for trade sanctions against countries that continue to thwart endangered species protection rules has begun to help the highly threatened Siberian tiger.

European affiliates:

World Wide Fund for Nature (WWF) UK
Panda House
Weyside Park, Godalming
Surrey GU 1XR
United Kingdom
44-(1)48-342-6444

World Wide Fund for Nature (WWF) Germany
Hedderichstrasse 110
P.O. Box 701127
60591 Frankfurt
Germany
49-69-60-50-03-80

TEXT CREDITS

Grateful acknowledgment is made to the following for permission to reprint material copyrighted or controlled by them. Every effort has been made to determine original sources and locate rights holders. We regret any unintentional errors of fact or omission that may have resulted from the complexity of this process and time constraints. Any errors brought to our attention will be corrected in subsequent printings; please write to Walking Stick Press, 1853 Powell Street, San Francisco, California 94133.

Addison-Wesley Publishing Co., Inc.: "How the Leopard Got Its Spots" from *The Magic Horns: Folktales from Africa*, retold by Forbes Stuart. Copyright © 1974 by Forbes Stuart. Reprinted by permission of the publisher.

Alfred A. Knopf: *Golden Shadows, Flying Hooves*, by George B. Schaller. Copyright © 1973 by George B. Schaller. Reprinted by permission of Alfred A. Knopf, a division of Random House, Inc.

American Mercury: "Concerning Cats" by Alan Devoe.

Andrews & McMeel: "Coyote Imitates Mountain Lion" from *Giving Birth to Thunder, Sleeping With His Daughter: Coyote Builds North America*, by Barry Lopez. Copyright © 1977 by Barry Holstun Lopez. Reprinted by permission of the publisher.

Barron's Educational Series, Inc: "How Cheetah Got his Speed," "Why Does the Lion Roar?", "Why the Cheeks of the Cheetah Are Stained with Tears," "Why the Leopard Hides his Food up a Tree" and "The Tree-climbing Jackal" from *When Hippo Was Hairy and Other Tales from Africa*, by Nick Greaves. Copyright © 1988 by Nick Greaves. Reprinted by permission of the publisher.

Charles E. Tuttle Co.: *I Am a Cat*, by Soseki Natsume, translated by Aiko Ito and Graeme Wilson. Copyright © 1972 by Aiko Ito and Graeme Wilson. Reprinted by permission of the publisher.

Crown Publishers, Inc.: *Catwatching*, by Desmond Morris. Copyright © 1986 by Desmond Morris. Reprinted by permission of Crown Publishers, a division of Random House, Inc.

Curtis Brown, Ltd.: *Dangerous to Man: The Definitive Story of Wildlife's Reputed Dangers*, by Roger A. Caras. Copyright © 1964, 1975 by Roger A. Caras. Reprinted by permission of Curtis Brown, Ltd.

Dell Publishing: *The Natural History of Cats*, by Claire Necker. Copyright © 1970 by A. S. Barnes and Co., Inc. Used by permission of Doubleday, a division of Bantam Doubleday Dell Publishing Group, Inc.

Doubleday: *My Wilderness Wildcats*, by Mike Tomkies. Copyright © 1977 by Mike Tomkies. Used by permission of Doubleday, a division of Bantam Doubleday Dell Publishing Group, Inc.

Beacon Press and Editions Gallimard: "The Lion" in *The Sea and the Honeycomb: A Book of Tiny Poems*, edited by Robert Bly. Copyright © 1971 by Robert Bly. Bly's translation of "Le Lion" by Guillaume Apollinaire, extraits de la Bestiare, *Oeuvres Poetiques* de Guillaume Apollinaire. Copyright © Editions Gallimard 1956. By permission of Beacon Press.

Charles Eglington and Oxford University Press (UK): "Cheetah" by Charles Eglington from *The Penguin Book of Animal Verse*, introduced and edited by George MacBeth. Copyright © 1965 by George MacBeth.

Farrar, Straus & Giroux, Inc. and Martin Secker & Warburg, Ltd.: "The Tom-Cat" from *Creatures Great and Small*, by Colette, translated by Enid McLeod. Copyright 1951 by Martin Secker & Warburg, Ltd. Reprinted by permission.

Greystone Books: *Wild Cats*, by Candace Savage. Copyright © 1993 by Candace Savage. Reprinted by permission of Greystone Books, an imprint of Douglas & McIntyre, Vancouver, Canada.

Richard Grossman: "Lion" and "Leopard" from *The Animals*, by Richard Grossman. Copyright © 1983 by Richard Grossman. Published by Graywolf Press. Reprinted by permission.

Harcourt Brace Inc.: *The Spotted Sphinx*, by Joy Adamson. Copyright © 1969 by Joy Adamson. Reprinted by permission.

Harcourt Brace, Inc.: "Why There are No Tigers in Borneo" from *Kantchil's Lime Pit and Other Stories from Indonesia*, by Harold Courlander. Copyright © 1950 by Harcourt, Brace and Company, Inc. Reprinted by permission.

Harcourt Brace, Inc.: *Animals at Play*, by Laurence P. Pringle. Copyright © 1985 by Laurence Pringle. Reprinted by permission.

Harcourt Brace, Inc.: *How the Animals Got Their Colors: Animal Myths from Around the World*, by Michael Rosen. Copyright © 1991, 1992 by Michael Rosen. Reprinted by permission.

HarperCollins, Inc.: *No Room in the Ark*, by Alan Moorehead. Copyright © 1957, 1958, 1959 by Alan Moorehead. Reprinted by permission of HarperCollins, Inc.

HarperCollins, Inc.: *Animal Happiness*, by Vicki Hearne. Copyright © 1994 by Vicki Hearne. Reprinted by permission of HarperCollins, Inc.

Houghton Mifflin Company: *Cry of the Kalahari*, by Mark Owens and Delia Owens. Copyright © 1984 by Mark J. and Delia D. Owens. Reprinted by permission of the publisher.

Howard Timmins (Cape Town, South Africa): *The Leopard*, by Peter Turnbull-Kemp. Copyright under the Berne Convention, 1967.

Ivan Obolensky, Inc.: *The Velvet Paw: A History of Cats in Life, Mythology and Art*, by Jean Conger. Copyright © 1963 by Jean Conger. Reprinted by permission of the publisher.

Kyle Cathie Ltd.: *The Tiger's Destiny*, by Valmik Thapar. Text copyright © 1992 by Valmik Thapar. Reprinted by permission of the publisher.

William R. Leigh: *Frontiers of Enchantment: An Artist's Adventures in Africa*, by W. R. Leigh. Copyright © 1938 by William R. Leigh.

Paul Leyhausen: *Cat Behavior: The Predatory and Social Behavior of Domestic and Wild Cats*, by Paul Leyhausen, translated by Barbara A. Tonkin. Copyright © 1962 by Paul Leyhausen. Reprinted by permission.

Howard Nelson: "The Process" (previously unpublished poem) by Howard Nelson. Copyright © 1996 by Howard Nelson. Used by permission of the author.

New Holland (Publishers) Ltd.: *The Leopard of Londolozi*, by Lex Hes. Text copyright © 1991 by Lex Hes. Reprinted by permission of the publisher.

The New Yorker: "Catalog" by Rosalie Moore. Copyright © 1940, 1968 by The New Yorker Magazine, Inc.

Nicholas Enterprises Ltd.: *The Doomsday Book of Animals*, by David Day. Copyright © 1981 by London Edition/David Day. Used by permission.

Oxford University Press (UK): *Man-Eaters of Kumaon*, by Jim Corbett. Copyright © 1946 by Oxford University Press. *The Man-Eating Leopard of Rudraprayag*, by Jim Corbett. Copyright © 1948 by Oxford University Press. Reprinted by permission of the publisher.

Penguin Books UK: *The Marsh Lions: The Story of an African Pride*, text by Brian Jackman, photographs and drawings by Jonathan Scott. Text copyright © 1982 by Brian Jackman. Reprinted by permission of the publisher.

Penguin Books USA Inc.: *Bobcat Year*, by Hope Ryden. Copyright © 1981 by Hope Ryden. Used by permission of Viking Penguin, a division of Penguin Books USA, Inc.

Penguin Books USA Inc.: *The Book of Imaginary Beings*, by Jorge Luis Borges. Translated by Norman Thomas Di Giovanni in conjunction with the author. Copyright © 1969 by Jorge Luis Borges and Norman Thomas Di Giovanni. Published by E. P. Dutton. Used by permission of Viking Penguin, a division of Penguin Books USA, Inc.

Penguin Books USA Inc.: *The Cat Inside*, by William S. Burroughs. Copyright © 1986, 1992 by William S. Burroughs. Used by permission of Viking Penguin, a division of Penguin Books USA, Inc.

Penguin Books USA Inc.: "The Leopard Cat" from *The Realm of the Green Buddha*, by Ludwig Koch-Isenburg. Copyright © 1963 by Viking Press. Used by permission of Viking Penguin, a division of Penguin Books USA, Inc.

Penguin Books USA Inc.: *The Snow Leopard*, by Peter Matthiessen. Copyright © 1978 by Peter Matthiessen. *Wildlife in America.*,by Peter Matthiessen. Copyright © 1959 by Peter Matthiessen. Used by permission of Viking Penguin, a division of Penguin Books USA, Inc.

Penguin Books USA Inc.: *Testament to the Bushmen*, by Laurens van der Post and Jane Taylor. Copyright 1984 by Jane Taylor and Megasoma Holding B.V. Used by permission of Viking Penguin, a division of Penguin Books USA, Inc.

Penguin Books USA Inc.: Lines from "To Winky" by Amy Lowell, from *The Sophisticated Cat: A Gathering of Stories, Poems, and Miscellaneous Writings About Cats*, chosen by Joyce Carol Oates and Daniel Halpern. Copyright © The Ontario Review, Inc. and Daniel Halpern, 1992. Used by permission of Viking Penguin, a division of Penguin Books USA, Inc.

St. Martin's Press and Boxtree Limited: *Tiger!*, by Simon Barnes. Copyright © 1994 by Simon Barnes. Reprinted by permission of the publishers.

Sierra Club Books: "The Panther" by Rainer Maria Rilke, translated by Robert Bly, from *News of the Universe: Poems of Twofold Consciousness*. Translation copyright © 1980 by Robert Bly. Reprinted by permission of the publisher.

Simon & Schuster: *A Cat Is Watching: A Look at the Way Cats See Us*, by Roger A. Caras. Copyright © 1989 by Roger Caras. *A Celebration of Cats*, by Roger A. Caras. Copyright © 1986 by Roger A. Caras. Reprinted by permission of Simon & Schuster, Inc.

Simon & Schuster: *The Tribe of the Tiger: Cats and Their Culture*, by Elizabeth Marshall Thomas. Copyright © 1994 by Elizabeth Marshall Thomas 1993 Irrevocable Trust. Reprinted by permission of Simon & Schuster, Inc.

Simon & Schuster: *Wild Animal Interviews*, by William T. Hornaday. Copyright © 1928 by Charles Scribner's Sons. Copyright © renewed 1956 by Helen H. Fielding. Reprinted by permission of Simon & Schuster, Inc.

Southern Book Publishers (Pty) Ltd. (South Africa): *An African Experience*, by Gerald Hinde and William Taylor. Copyright © 1993 by Gerald Hinde and William Taylor. Reprinted by permission.

Southern Methodist University Press: "Why Women Are Like Cats" from *Mexican Folktales from The Borderland*, by Riley Aiken. Copyright © 1980 by Riley Aiken. Other copyrights 1935, 1940; and 1957, 1958, 1962, 1964 by the Texas Folklore Society. Reprinted by permission of the publisher.

Stackpole Books: *The Mountain Lion: An Unnatural History of Pumas and People*, by Chris Bolgiano. Copyright © 1995 by Chris Bolgiano. Reprinted by permission of the publisher.

Taplinger Publishing Co., Inc.: *Leemo: A True Story of A Man's Friendship with A Mountain Lion*, by Stanley E. Brock. Copyright © 1966 by Stanley E. Brock. Reprinted by permission of the publisher.

Taplinger Publishing Co., Inc.: *Wild Cats of the World*, by C. A. W. Guggisberg. Copyright © 1975 by C. A. W. Guggisberg. Reprinted by permission of the publisher.

Texas Western Press: *The Puma: Legendary Lion of the Americas*, by Jim Bob Tinsley. Copyright © 1987 by Texas Western Press. Reprinted by permission of the publisher.

University of Chicago Press: *The Deer and the Tiger: A Study of Wildlife in India*, by George B. Schaller. Copyright © 1967 by the University of Chicago Press.

University Press of New England: "Dream of the Lynx" by John Haines, from *Winter News*. Copyright © 1964 by John Haines. Reprinted by permission of the publisher.

University Press of New England: Lines from "The Heaven of Animals" by James Dickey, from *Drowning with Others*. Copyright © 1962 by James Dickey. Reprinted by permission of the publisher.

University of Pennsylvania Press: "The Leopard-Nurser" by Josephine Jacobsen, from *The Chinese Insomniacs: New Poems by Josephine Jacobsen*. Copyright © 1981 by Josephine Jacobsen. Reprinted by permission of the publisher.

University of Texas Press: *Dreamtigers*, by Jorge Luis Borges, translated from *El Hacedor* by Mildred Boyer and Harold Morland. Copyright © 1964 by Jorge Luis Borges. Reprinted by permission of the publisher.

Walker & Company: *Maverick Cats: Encounters With Feral Cats*, by Ellen Perry Berkeley. Copyright © 1982 by Ellen Perry Berkeley. Reprinted by permission of the publisher.

Watkins/Loomis Agency, Inc.: *The Bestiary: A Book of Beasts*, by T. H. White, G. P. Putnam's Sons, 1954. Used by permission.

Weldon Owen: Excerpts by Mel Sunquist and Fiona Sunquist and Blaire Van Valkenberg from *Great Cats: Majestic Creatures of the Wild*. Copyright © 1991 by Weldon Owen Pty Limited. Published by Rodale Press. Reprinted by permission.

Wendy Weil Agency: *Portraits in the Wild: Behavior Studies of East African Mammals*, by Cynthia Moss. Copyright © 1975, 1982 by Cynthia Moss. Published by the University of Chicago Press. Used by permission.

William Collins: *A Bevy of Beasts*, by Gerald Durrell. Copyright © 1973 by Gerald Durrell. Reprinted by permission.

William Morrow and Co., Inc. and Chatto & Windus [UK]: *The Heart of the Hunter*, by Laurens van der Post. Copyright © 1961 by Laurens van der Post. *The Lost World of the Kalahari*, text by Laurens van der Post, photographs by David Coulson. Copyright © 1988 by Laurens van der Post. Reprinted by permission of the publishers.

William Morrow and Co., Inc.: *Talking with the Animals: How to Communicate with Wildlife*, by Bill Thomas. Copyright © 1985 by Bill Thomas. Reprinted by permission of the publisher.

Mrs. D. M. Newton-Wood: "The Lion" by W. J. Turner, from *The Penguin Book of Animal Verse*, introduced and edited by George MacBeth. Copyright © 1965 by George MacBeth.

The Word Works: "Stalking the Florida Panther" from *Stalking the Florida Panther*, by Enid Shomer. Copyright © 1987 by Enid Shomer. Reprinted by permission of the publisher.

ILLUSTRATION CREDITS

Page 7. *Tiger*, by Edvard Munch. Lithograph, 1908–1909. The Munch Museum, Oslo/The Munch–Ellingsen-group/ARS 1996.

Page 8. *Striped Tabby*, by Théophile Steinlen (1859–1923). The British Museum.

Page 9, top. *Belt mask in leopard form*, Benin Kingdom, Nigeria, c. 16th century. Ivory and brass, 7" high, 3 ¾" wide, 1 ½" deep. Gift of Katherine White and the Boeing Company, Seattle Art Museum/Paul Macapia photo. Bottom: *Squatting Jaguar*, c. 1440–1521 A.D. Dark gray stone, 28 cm long, 12.5 cm high, 14.4 cm wide. The Brooklyn Museum, 38.45. Carll de Silva Fund.

Page 10. *Tiger*, by Ito Jakuchu, Japan (1716–1800). Hanging scroll, color on silk, 130.3 cm x 71.4 cm. Joe and Etsuko Price Collection. Museum Associates, Los Angeles County Museum of Art.

Page 16. *Lion's Head (Tête de Lion)*, by Eugène Delacroix, 1843. Watercolor on black lead with touches of white gouache, 7" x 7 ½". Musée du Louvre/RMN photo.

Page 18, center: Illustration of Miacis, by John McLoughlin from *The Canine Clan*. Bottom: Engraving of a genet. Corbis-Bettman.

Page 19. *Smilodon*, the great Pleistocene saber-toothed cat, by C. R. Knight, 1906. Trans. No. 2435(²), Courtesy Department Library Services, American Museum of Natural History, New York.

Page 21. Illustration by Robert W. Kane from *Kantchil's Lime Pit and Other Stories from Indonesia*, by Harold Courlander. By permission of Harcourt Brace, Inc.

Page 24. *The Cougar*, female and young, by John James Audubon (1785–1851). Superstock photo.

Page 33. *L'Once* (the ounce), engraving from *Histoire Naturelle, Generale et Particuliere*, by Comte de Buffon, 1776.

Page 45. *L'hiver: Chat sur un Coussin*, 1909, by Théophile Steinlen (1859–1923). Color lithograph. The British Museum.

Page 50. *Peruvian Jaguars (Deux Leopards du Perou)*, by Antoine-Louis Barye (1795–1875). Watercolor with traces of varnish, 9 ½" x 12 ½". Musee du Louvre/RMN photo.

Page 54. *Serval profile* by Todd Sherman, 1996. Conte drawing, 11" wide x 17" high. James Barker photo. Courtesy of the artist.

Page 65. *Tropical Storm with Tiger—Surprise*, by Henri ("Le Douanier") Rousseau, 1844–1910. The National Gallery, London/Superstock.

Page 70. *A Lion in a Jungle Landscape*, by William Huggins (1820–1884). Christie's London/Superstock.

Page 74. *Five tigers with a single head*, from an album of watercolors created in 1785 in Madras. Courtesy of the Board of Trustees of the Victoria & Albert Museum.

Page 84. *Cat Studies*, by Leonardo da Vinci (1452–1519). The Royal Collection © Her Majesty Queen Elizabeth II.

Page 92. *Rio Balsas*, by Alfredo Arreguin, 1990. Oil on canvas, 48" high x 72" wide. Courtesy of the artist.

Page 100. *Mountain Lion Series #2*, by Linda Lomahaftewa, 1988. Monotype, 22" high x 30" wide. Courtesy of the artist.

Page 119. *Leopards Attacking a Spotted Deer*, by Louis A. Sargent, 1909. Mary Evans Picture Library, London.

Page 120. *The Cat*, American, anonymous, c. 1850–1899. Canvas, .0407cm x .508 cm. Gift of Edgar William and Bernice Crysler Garbisch, National Gallery of Art, Washington.

Page 129. Jaguar illustration by Cal Roy from *The Serpent and the Sun: Myths of the Mexican World*. By permission of Farrar, Straus & Giroux, Inc.

Page 135. *Canadian Lynx*, artist unknown. Watercolor. Superstock photo.

Page 136. *Toho, Mountain Lion Kachina*, by Oren Poley, Jr., c. 1960s. Wood, yarn, fur, eagle feathers, horsehair and leather. Jerry Jacka photo.

Page 137. *Leopard Prestige Chair*, Cameroon, Africa. Wood, 32 ½" high x 22 ¾" diam. x 20 ½" deep. Gift of Katherine White and the Boeing Company, Seattle Art Museum.

Page 138. *Lion spearing in Tanganyika*, by W. R. Leigh, c. 1930s, from *Frontiers of Enchantment* by W. R. Leigh. Courtesy of the artist.

Page 139. *Tepeyollotl, "Heart of the Mountain" (Texcatlipoca in Jaguar Guise)*. Codex Aubin *tonalamatl*, p. 3. Screenfold manuscript, panel 24 cm x 27 cm. Probably Tlaxcala. Early Colonial. Bibliothèque Nationale, Paris.

Page 140. *Hunting tigers from the back of an elephant*, ivory miniature, Patiala State, India, c. 1892. Courtesy of the Board of Trustees of the Victoria & Albert Museum.

Page 141. *Leopard from Senegal*. Corbis-Bettman.

Page 145. *Key Marco Cat Figure*. Mississippian, c. 6 to 8 centuries ago. Catalogue No. 240915, Department of

Anthropology, Smithsonian Institution.

Page 146. *On the Prowl: Cougar*, by Todd Sherman, 1996. Conte pencil, 11" x 17". James Barker photo.

Page 148, top. Rendering of an Ice Age pictograph by Léon Pales, from *Les Gravures De La Marche, I. Félins et Ours*, Imprimeries Delmas, Bordeaux, 1969. Bottom: Lion guardian of the temple of Dagon, Mesopotamia. Bronze sculpture from early in the second millennium B.C. Musée du Louvre/RMN photo.

Page 150. *Cats and Mice*, page from a bestiary ("Workshop Bestiary"), England, before 1187. M.81, f.46v. The Pierpont Morgan Library/Art Resource.

Page 151. *Fowling in the Marshes*. Ancient Egyptian printing from the Tomb of Nabamun, Thebes, c. 1400 B.C. Courtesy of the Oriental Institute of the University of Chicago.

Page 153. *The Woman Within*, by Mira Reisberg, 1996. Acrylic on board, 24" x 36". Courtesy of the artist.

Page 154. *Young Tiger*, by Christian Pierre (American, b. 1962). Superstock photo.

Page 155. *Cat Mummy*, an Egyptian artifact, possibly from Abydos, Roman period, after 30 B.C. Catalogue No. 381569, Department of Anthropology, Smithsonian Institution.

Page 156, top. *Amulet of a Seated Goddess with Lion Head*, c. 1070–712 B.C. Faience, height 6.5 cm. Metropolitan Museum of Art, Purchase, Edward Harkness Gift, 1926 (26.7.868). Bottom: *The Great Lion Hunt: Detail*, limestone relief in the North Palace of Assurbanipal at Nineveh, 7th century B.C. The British Museum/Werner Forman.

Page 157. *Tiger rug from Tibet*, by an unknown weaver, c. early 20th century. 166 cm x 90 cm. Courtesy of Mimi Lipton and the Tibet Charitable Trust/Heini Schneebeli photo.

Page 158. *Hunting leopard in India*, antique postcard. Mary Evans Picture Library, London.

Page 159. *Constellation Leo*. Photo by John Sanford and David Parker, Science Photo Library/Photo Researchers, Inc.; drawing by Miriam Lewis.

Page 160. *Lion*, relief in molded bricks of glazed terra-cotta from the "Processional Way" in Babylon, 6th century. Staatliche Museen zu Berlin–Preussischer Kulturbesitz Vorderasiatisches Museum/J. Liepe photo.

Page 161. *Lion and Hedgehog*, from Villard de Honnecourt's *Sketchbook*, early 13th century. Bibliothèque Nationale, Paris.

Page 162. *Daniel in the Lion's Den*, by Peter Paul Rubens, 1613–1615. Oil on canvas, 88 ¼" x 130 ⅛". Ailsa Mellon Bruce Fund, National Gallery of Art, Washington/Richard Carafelli photo.

Page 163, top. *Lion of St. Mark* in the Piazza San Marco, Venice, late 15th century. Cameraphoto/Art Resource. Bottom: Peacocks and lions in a Byzantine relief at the Cattedrale di Santa Maria Assunta, Torcello, Italy. Camera Photo/Art Resource.

Page 164, bottom: *French Circus Poster*, c. 1887. The Granger Collection, New York.

Page 165. *Black Beast*, by Darrel Austin, 1941. Oil on canvas, 24" x 30". Smith College Museum of Art, Northhampton, Massachussetts.

Page 166. *Mountain Lion petroglyph*, in the Petrified Forest in Arizona. Petrified Forest Museum Association/National Park Service photo.

Page 167. *Puma*, color lithograph, c. 1870. 5 ½" x 8 ½". Mary Evans Picture Library, London.

Page 169. *Benin Leopards*, probably 19th century. Ivory and copper. The British Museum.

Page 170, top. *Transformation #4*, by George Littlechild, 1991. Acrylic on paper, 44" x 30". Courtesy of the artist. Bottom: *Incense Burner in Feline Form*, Iranian, c. 1182. Bronze, 36" high. The Metropolitan Museum of Art, Rogers Fund, 1951 (51.56). Schecter Lee photo.

Page 171. *Mola Panel*, by the Kuna Indians of Panama, 1920s. Cotton, plain weave with appliqués, 43.2 cm x 49.5 cm. Gift

of F. Louis Hoover, the Art Institute of Chicago.

Page 172. *Naked ascetic in leopard skin, seated outside a cave with a tiger lying nearby*, in the style of Dipchand, possibly painted for Win Fullerton, Murshidabad, India, c. 1760–1763. Courtesy of the Trustees of the Victoria & Albert Museum.

Page 173. "The Tyger" by William Blake (1757–1827) from his *Songs of Experience*, 1794. The British Museum.

Page 177. *Leopard Bust*, by Todd Sherman, 1996. Acrylic on paper, 23" x 23". James Barker photo.

Page 181. *The Sleeping Gypsy*, by Henri ("Le Douanier") Rousseau, 1897. Oil on canvas, 130 cm x 201 cm. Museum of Modern Art/Superstock.

Page 182. *The Beast and the Blackberry*, by Nicholas Wilton, 1995. Acrylic on wood, 12 ½" x 16".

Page 184. *Paris Through the Window*, by Marc Chagall, 1913. Oil on canvas, 53 ½" x 55 ¾". Gift of Solomon R. Guggenheim, 1937. Courtesy of the Solomon R. Guggenheim Museum/David Heald.

Map Photo Credits

Photos appearing on the map on pages 22–23 are by the following:

Mountain lion, by Jim Dutcher.
North American lynx, by Joseph Van Os/Image Bank.
Bobcat, by R. E. Barber.
Jaguar, by Frans Lanting/Minden Pictures.
Margay, by François Gohier/Photo Researchers.
Jaguarundi, by Tom & Pat Leeson.
Ocelot, by Art Wolfe.
Eurasian lynx, by Art Wolfe.
European wildcat, by Jany Sauvanet/Photo Researchers.
Scottish wildcat, by Erwin & Peggy Bauer.
Lion, by Joseph Van Os/Image Bank.
African golden cat, by Art Wolfe.
Leopard, by Benjamin Rondel/First Light.
Caracal, by Jim Brandenburg/Minden Pictures.
Tiger, by John Giustina/The Wildlife Collection.
Snow leopard, by Alan & Sandy Carey.
Indian desert cat, by Art Wolfe.
Leopard cat, by Art Wolfe.
Jungle cat, by Erwin & Peggy Bauer.
Sand cat, by Art Wolfe.

ACKNOWLEDGMENTS

We wish to express our gratitude to the many individuals and entities who helped this book into being. First and foremost, to the project staff at Walking Stick Press: especially Miriam Lewis, who set all the type and somehow made the layouts fit, and who also drew the constellation Leo; thanks for all the above and beyond. Also to Nancy Barnes, for so conscientiously keeping track of who, what and where, and for researching the list of wildlife organizations; and to Rebecca Freedman, for coordinating permissions and proofreading.

The mechandising staff of The Nature Company, especially Tracy Fortini, Georganne Papac, and Steve Manning, were the most supportive of collaborators.

William J. Dusel of the U.S. Fish and Wildlife Service provided helpful information, as did the representatives of organizations working on behalf of wild cats, listed in the appendix.

Many thanks are due to our freelance contributors: Paul Kratter, the gifted artist who created original illustrations of several rare cat species, as well as the anatomical and behavioral illustrations and the map, bringing great enthusiasm and skill to the project; Cynthia Bix, for her sterling job of research and writing for the identification section in Part I; Beatriz Coll, who photographically created the background pattern printed on some of the pages; and calligrapher Verne Lindner.

We're grateful to the photographers and photo agencies whose images are reproduced; the fine artists, museums, galleries and archives who who provided images and permission to reproduce them; and the authors, publishers, and literary agents whose texts are excerpted or who granted permission for the same.

We vastly appreciate the craft, cooperation and good will of the personnel at A. Mondadori Editore, who printed and bound this book: Dan Krebs and Peter Garlid in the New York office; and Annalisa Gambin, Luigi Sterzi, Enrico Bighin, and Enrico Battei (and the pressmen) in Verona.

Thanks, most especially, to Elizabeth Marshall Thomas for managing to deliver her wonderful introduction in the midst of other pressing deadlines, and for her contribution of the previously unpublished poem by Harold Nelson.

For their support, patience and understanding, we're grateful as always to our nearest and dearest, Greg, Wayne, and Dana.

And above all, to the wild cats, those elegants beasts who prowl the forests, plains, and peaks and are models for so much of what we find beautiful and fascinating in nature, along with their domestic cousins, who bring some of the wild into our homes.

D. L. and L. H.
Walking Stick Press

Clan of the Wild Cats

This book was designed by Linda Herman, produced at Walking Stick Press, San Francisco, and printed and bound by A. Mondadori, Verona. The text was composed in Spectrum by Miriam Lewis; titles and drop capitals were hand-lettered by Verne Lindner. Original illustrations are by Paul Kratter. The decorative texture was created by Beatriz Coll. The text paper is Gardamatte Brillante, 150 gsm. Endpapers are Marcate Nettuno, 140 gsm, printed with a matte varnish. The case cloth is Scholco Selecta. Photograph on this page: Female cheetah with cubs, Masai Mara reserve, Kenya. By Manoj Shah/Tony Stone Images.